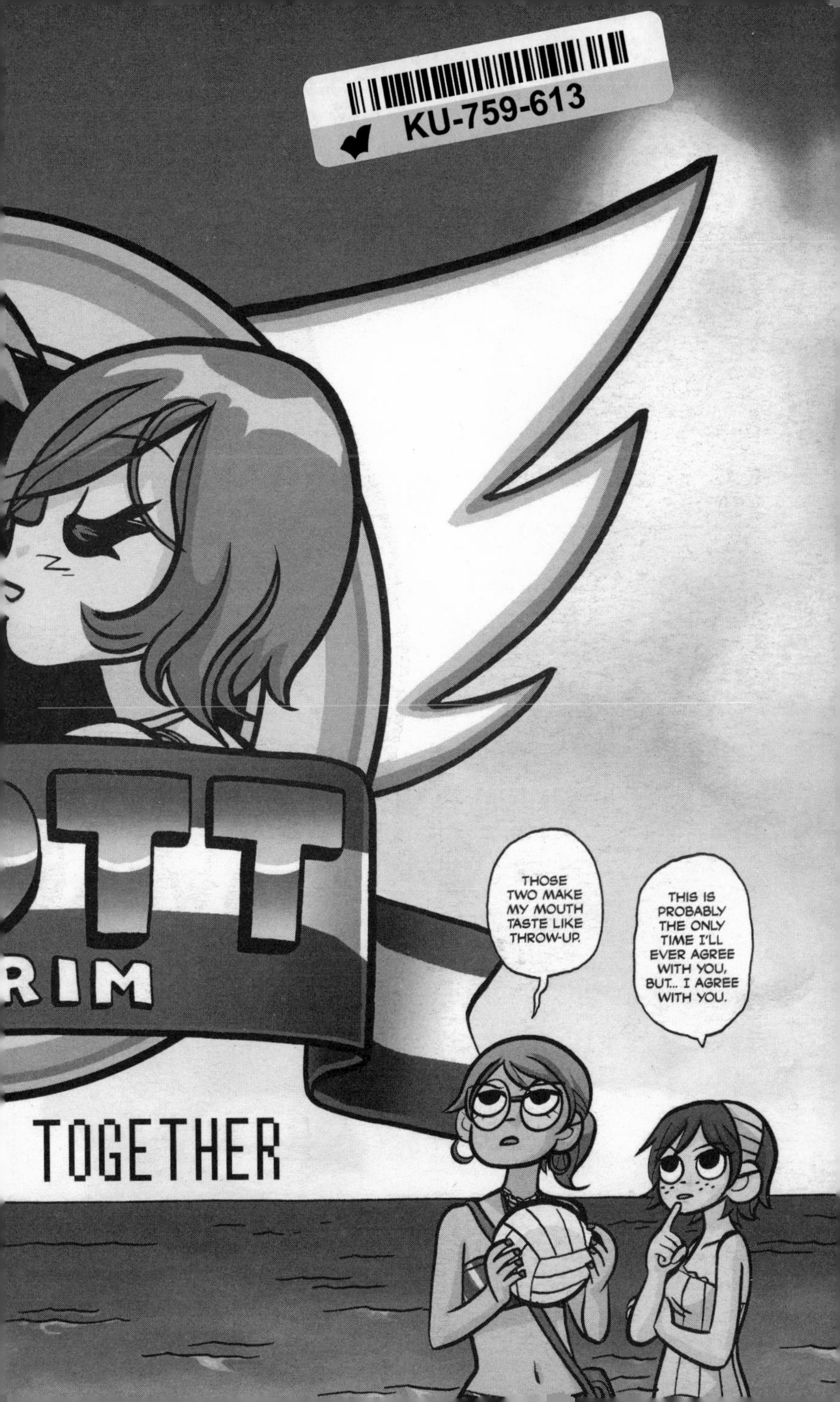

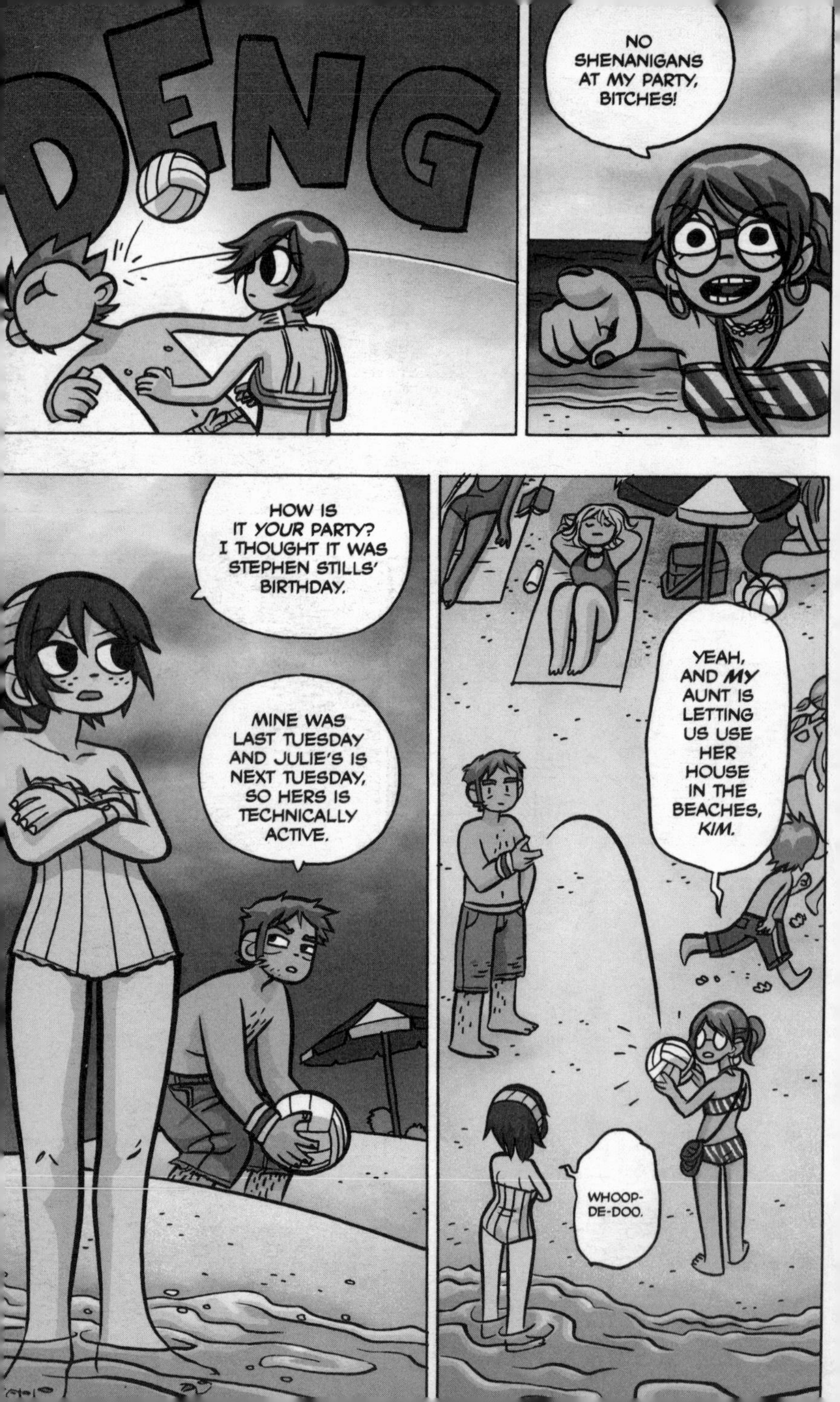
DENG
NO SHENANIGANS AT MY PARTY, BITCHES!
HOW IS IT *YOUR* PARTY? I THOUGHT IT WAS STEPHEN STILLS' BIRTHDAY.
MINE WAS LAST TUESDAY AND JULIE'S IS NEXT TUESDAY, SO HERS IS TECHNICALLY ACTIVE.
YEAH, AND *MY* AUNT IS LETTING US USE HER HOUSE IN THE BEACHES, *KIM.*
WHOOP-DE-DOO.

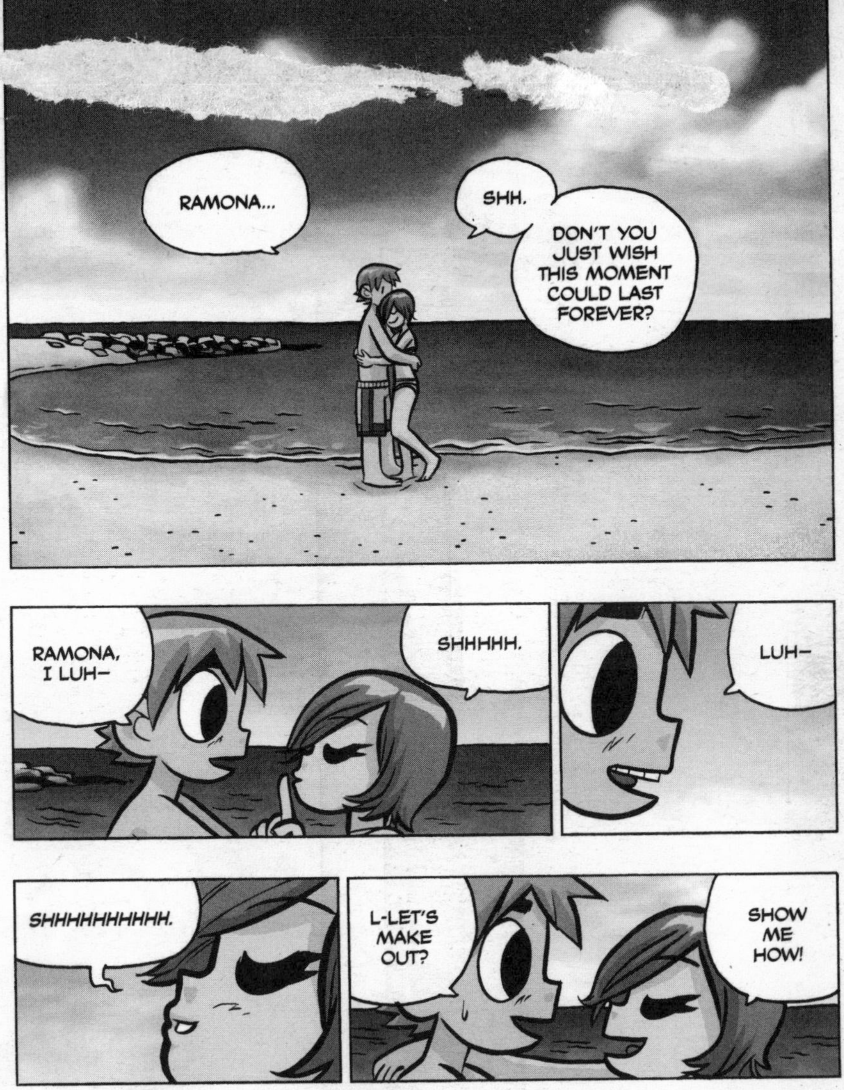

RAMONA...
SHH.
DON'T YOU JUST WISH THIS MOMENT COULD LAST FOREVER?
RAMONA, I LUH—
SHHHHH.
LUH—
SHHHHHHHHHH.
L-LET'S MAKE OUT?
SHOW ME HOW!

FOURTH ESTATE presents **BRYAN LEE O'MALLEY's**

8400000092951

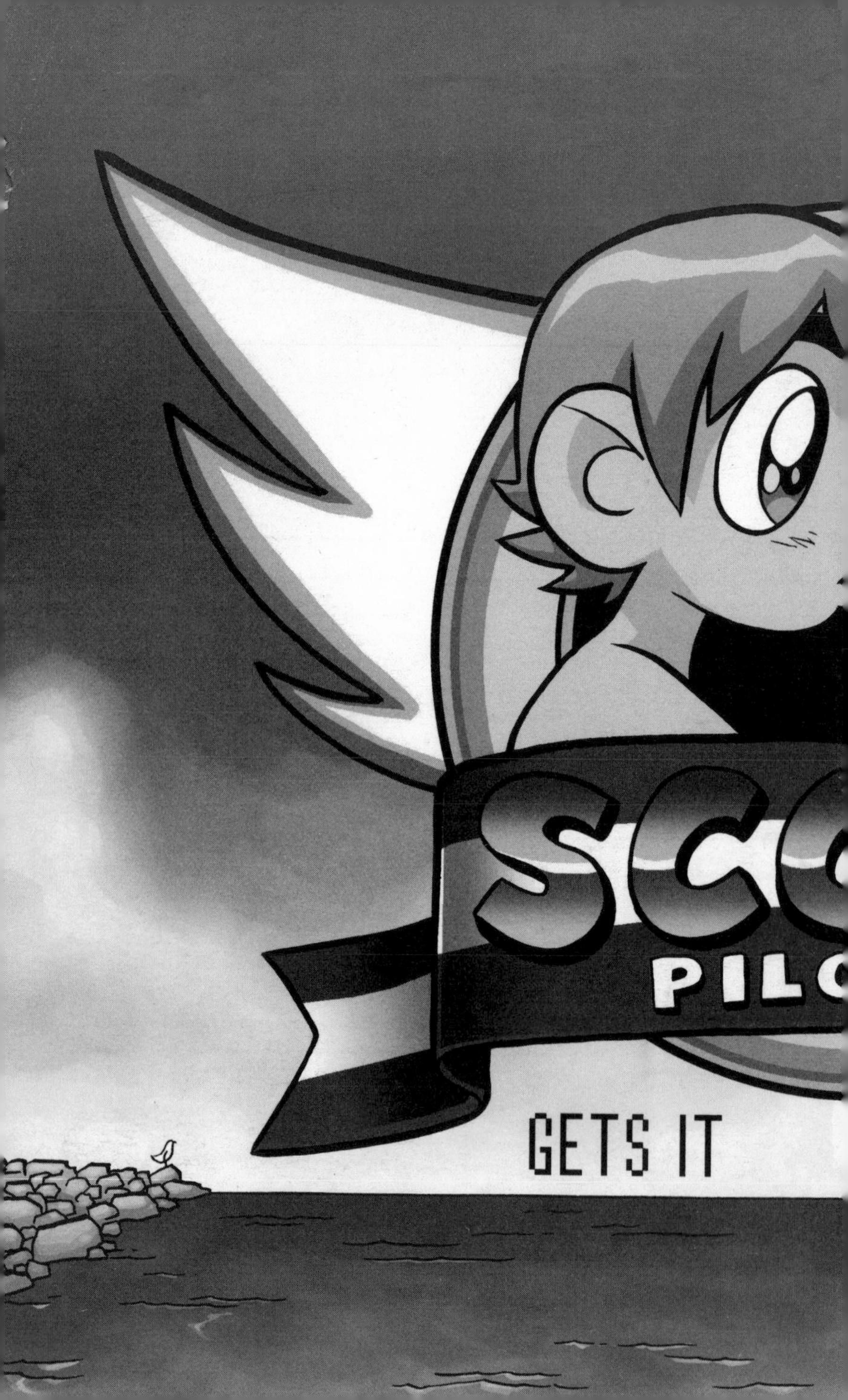
SCO
PILO
GETS IT

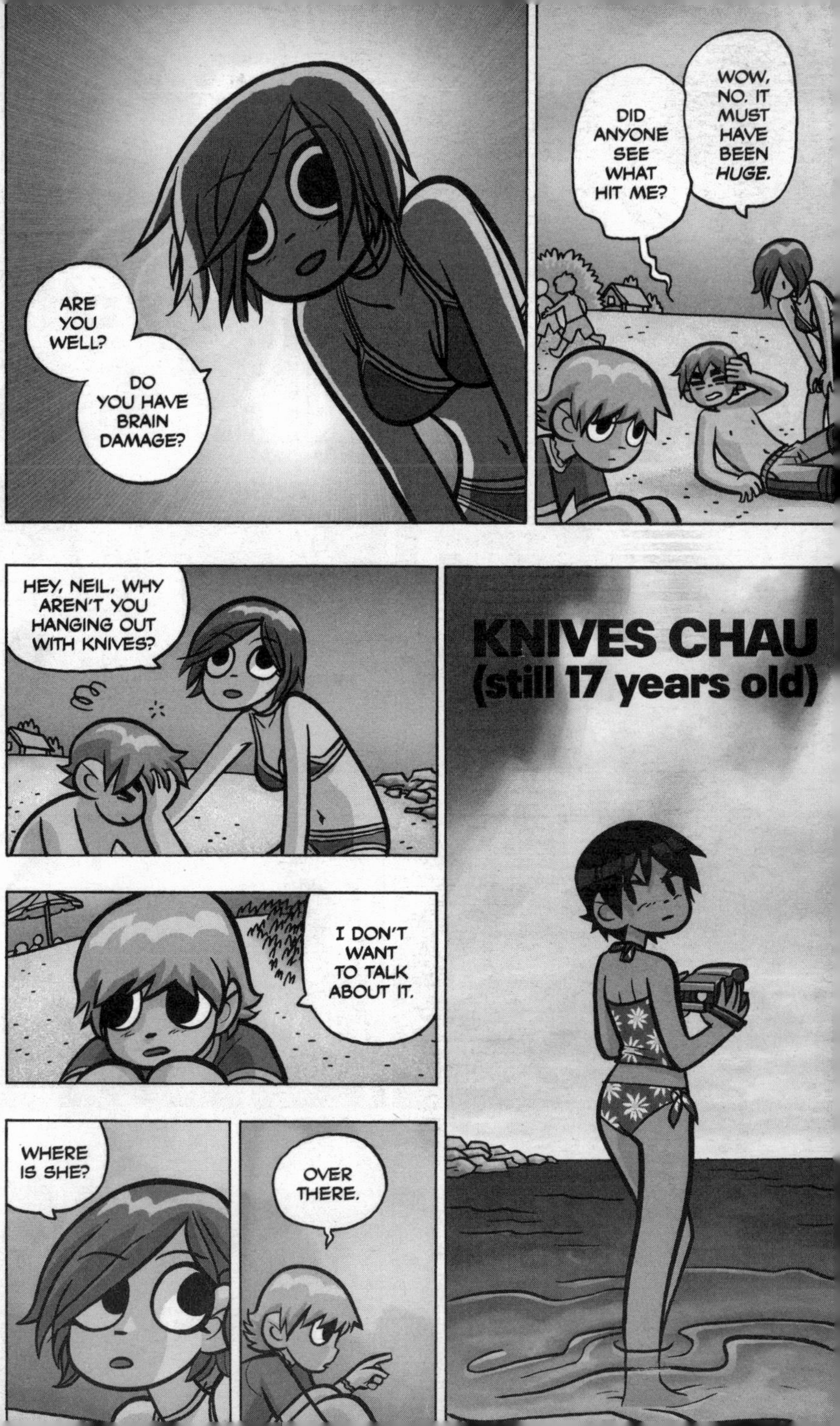
ARE YOU WELL?
DO YOU HAVE BRAIN DAMAGE?
DID ANYONE SEE WHAT HIT ME?
WOW, NO. IT MUST HAVE BEEN *HUGE.*
HEY, NEIL, WHY AREN'T YOU HANGING OUT WITH KNIVES?
I DON'T WANT TO TALK ABOUT IT.
WHERE IS SHE?
OVER THERE.
KNIVES CHAU
(still 17 years old)

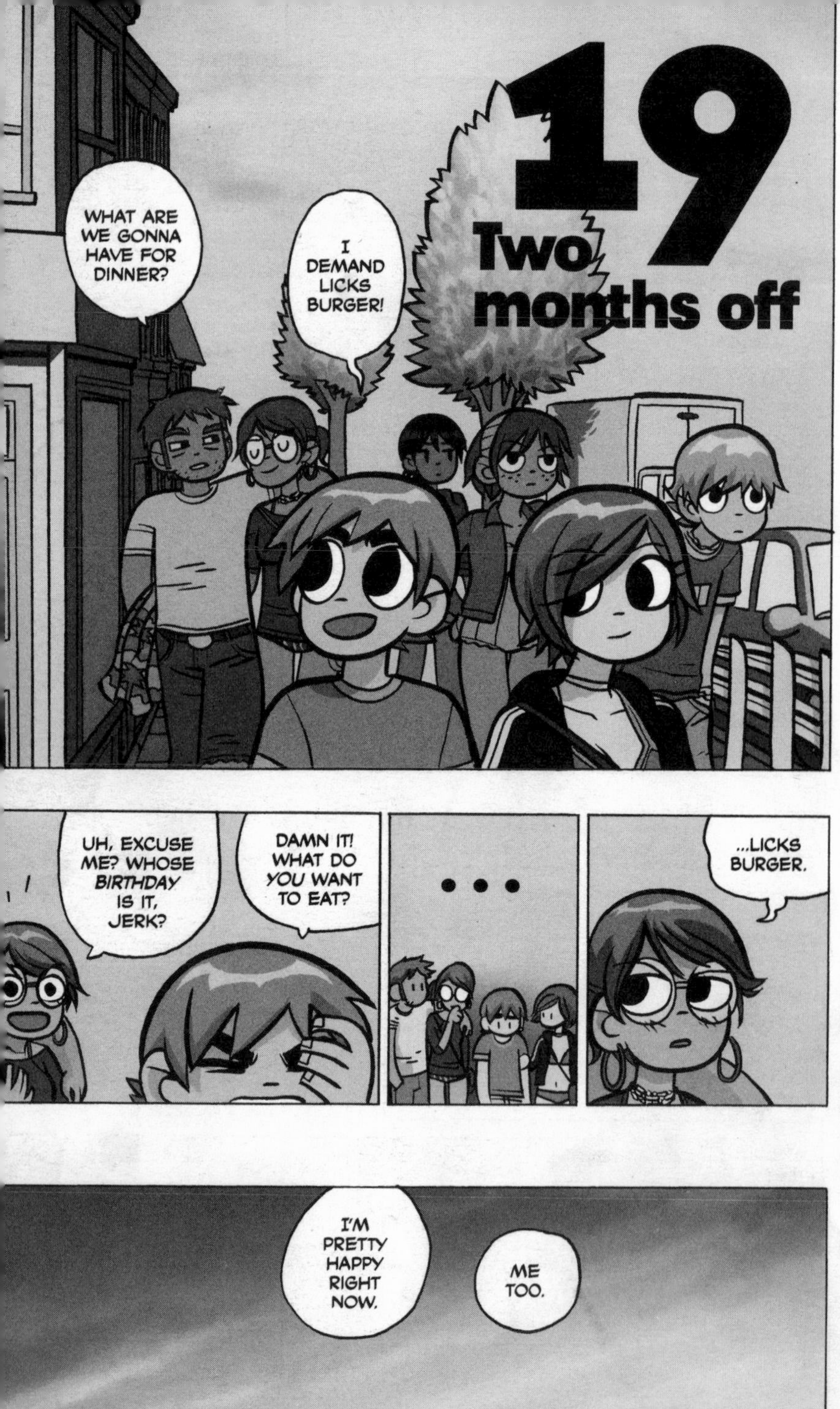
19
Two months off
WHAT ARE WE GONNA HAVE FOR DINNER?
I DEMAND LICKS BURGER!
UH, EXCUSE ME? WHOSE BIRTHDAY IS IT, JERK?
DAMN IT! WHAT DO YOU WANT TO EAT?
...
...LICKS BURGER.
I'M PRETTY HAPPY RIGHT NOW.
ME TOO.

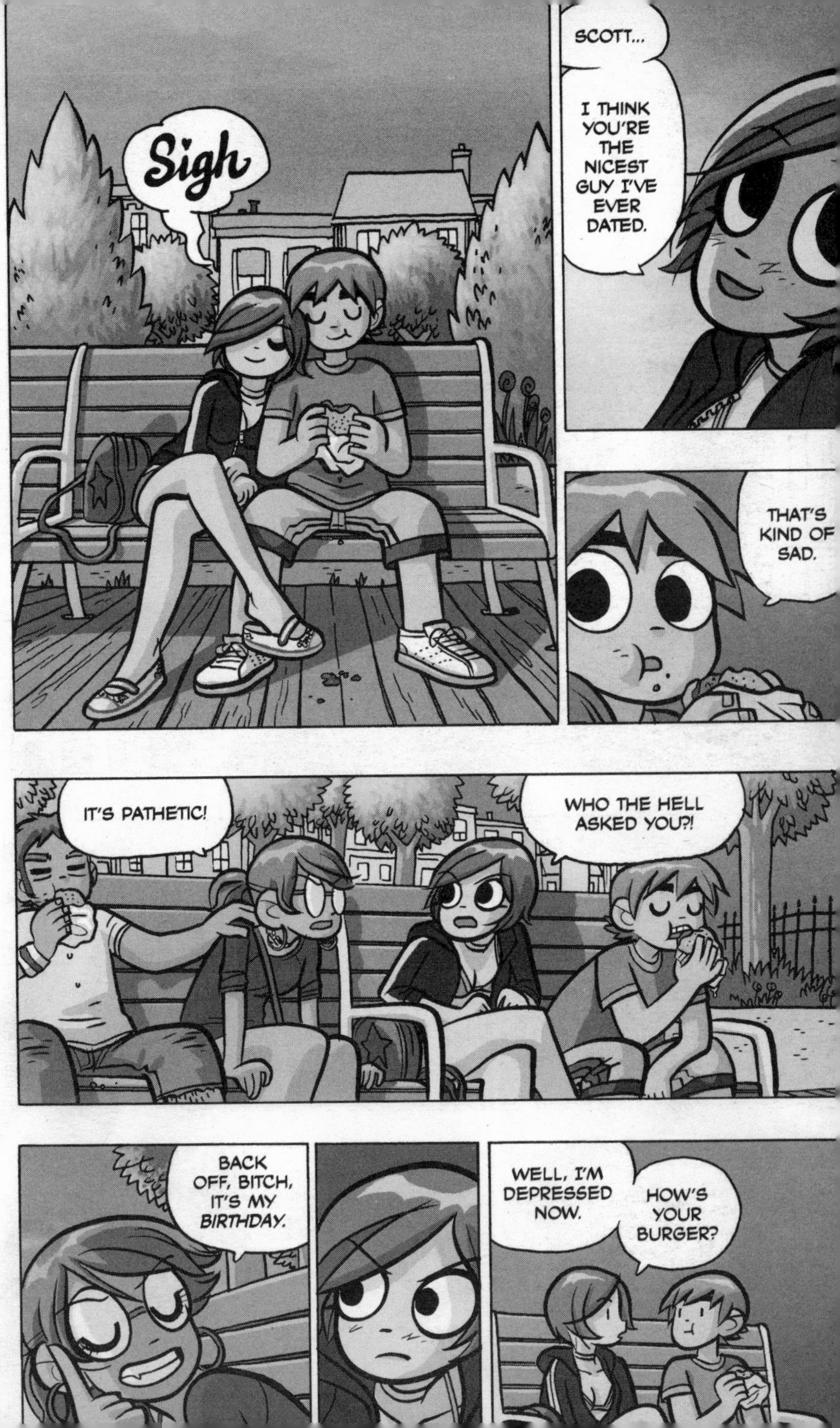
Sigh
SCOTT...
I THINK YOU'RE THE NICEST GUY I'VE EVER DATED.
THAT'S KIND OF SAD.
IT'S PATHETIC!
WHO THE HELL ASKED YOU?!
BACK OFF, BITCH, IT'S MY *BIRTHDAY.*
WELL, I'M DEPRESSED NOW.
HOW'S YOUR BURGER?

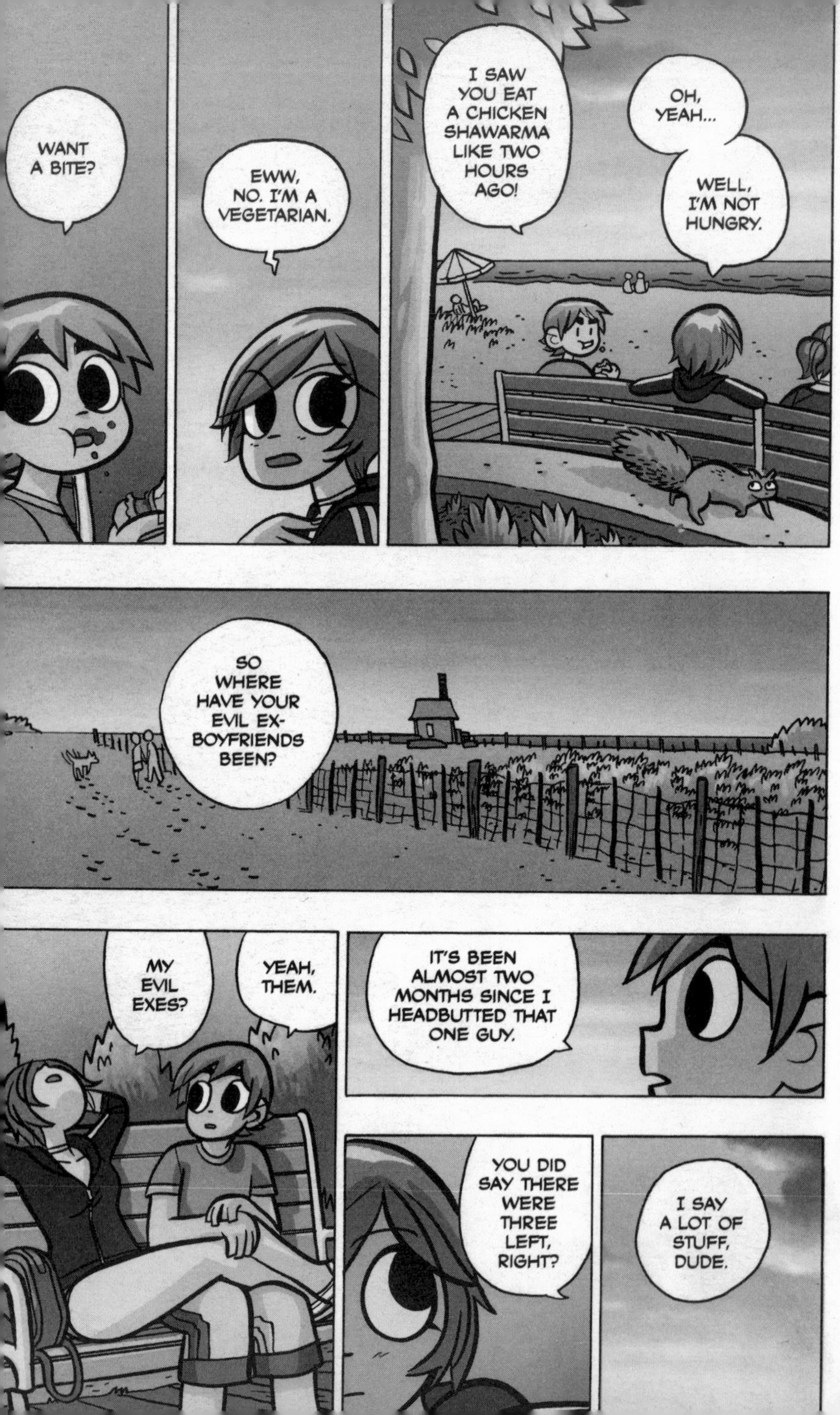
WANT A BITE?
EWW, NO. I'M A VEGETARIAN.
I SAW YOU EAT A CHICKEN SHAWARMA LIKE TWO HOURS AGO!
OH, YEAH...
WELL, I'M NOT HUNGRY.
SO WHERE HAVE YOUR EVIL EX-BOYFRIENDS BEEN?
MY EVIL EXES?
YEAH, THEM.
IT'S BEEN ALMOST TWO MONTHS SINCE I HEADBUTTED THAT ONE GUY.
YOU DID SAY THERE WERE THREE LEFT, RIGHT?
I SAY A LOT OF STUFF, DUDE.

edited by James Lucas Jones
design and layout by Bryan Lee O'Malley
production assistance from Steven Birch @ Servo

Published by Fourth Estate

4

Originally published in 2007 in the United States by Oni Press
www.onipress.com

First published in Great Britain in 2010 by
Fourth Estate
An imprint of HarperCollins*Publishers*
77–85 Fulham Palace Road
London W6 8JB
www.4thestate.co.uk

Special thanks to: Hope, the Oni boyz (DOUG!!), Gitter, E. W. Jr., Michael B., my peeps in Toronto and London, the Halifax crew and the HGPA, mom & dad, bro & sis, kitties, Kanye West, Clark and Michael . . . and YOU! Winners don't use drugs, expect Claritin this time of year.

www.scottpilgrim.com

13

ISBN: 978-0-00-734049-1

Printed in Great Britain by
Clays Ltd, St Ives plc

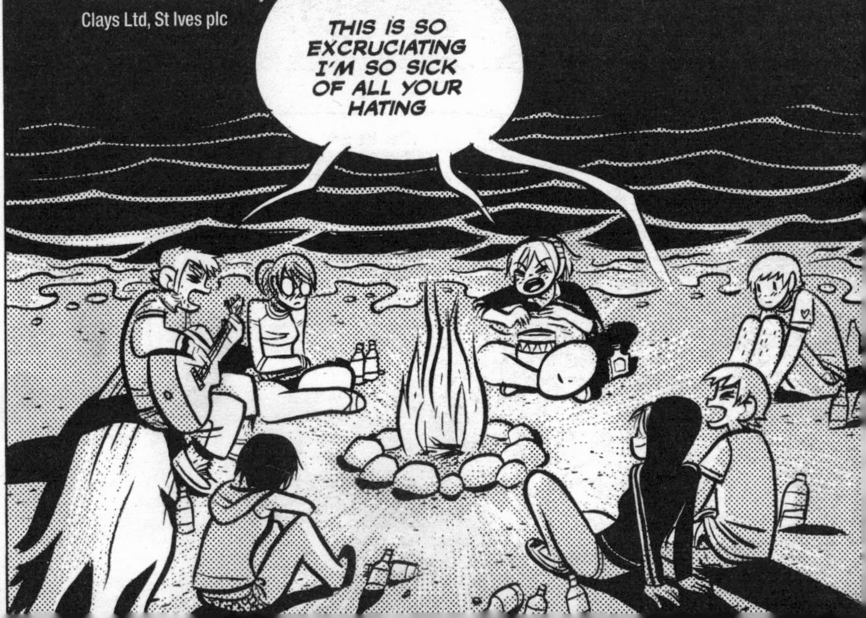
THIS IS SO EXCRUCIATING I'M SO SICK OF ALL YOUR HATING

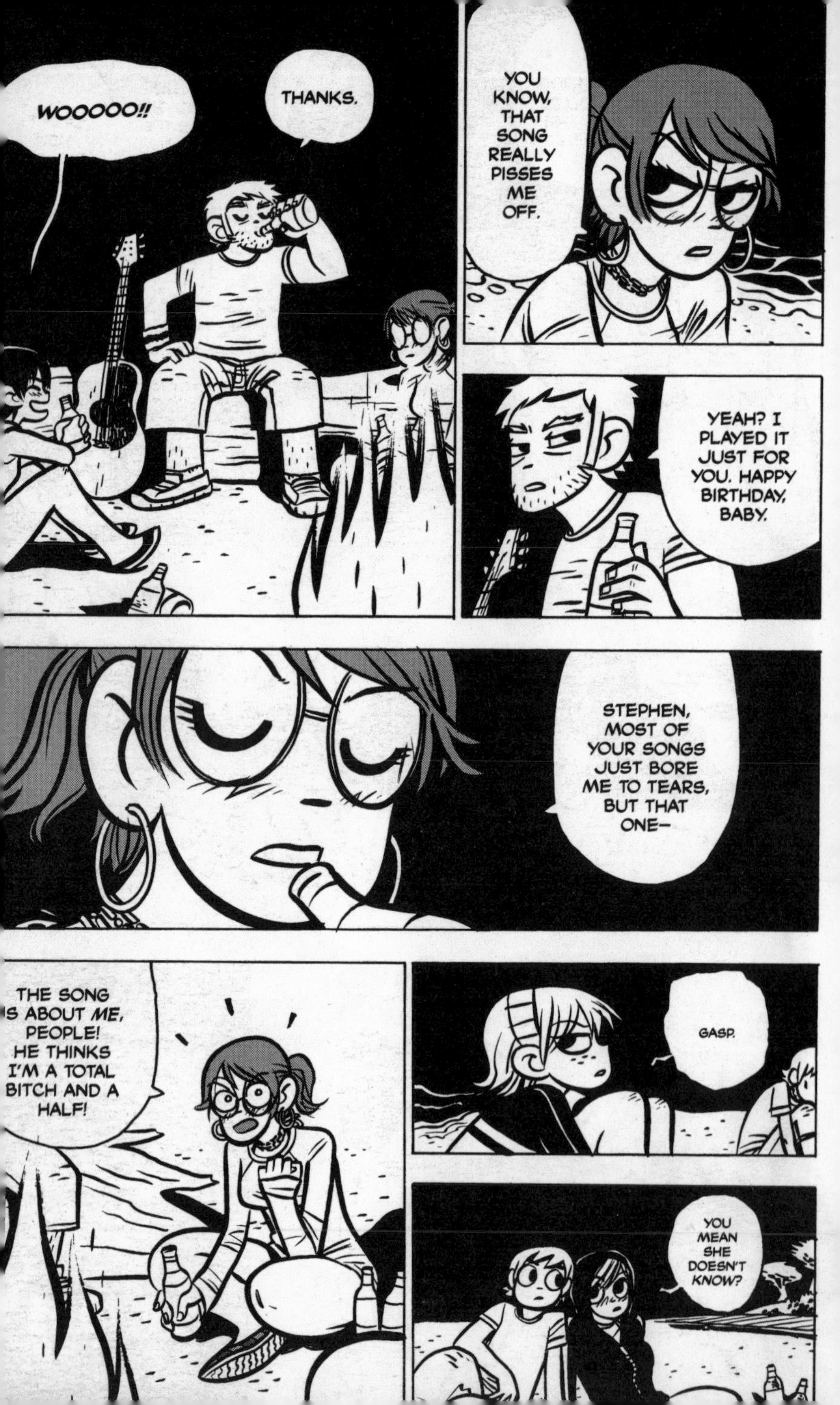
WOOOOO!!
THANKS.
YOU KNOW, THAT SONG REALLY PISSES ME OFF.
YEAH? I PLAYED IT JUST FOR YOU. HAPPY BIRTHDAY, BABY.
STEPHEN, MOST OF YOUR SONGS JUST BORE ME TO TEARS, BUT THAT ONE–
THE SONG IS ABOUT *ME*, PEOPLE! HE THINKS I'M A TOTAL BITCH AND A HALF!
GASP.
YOU MEAN SHE DOESN'T KNOW?

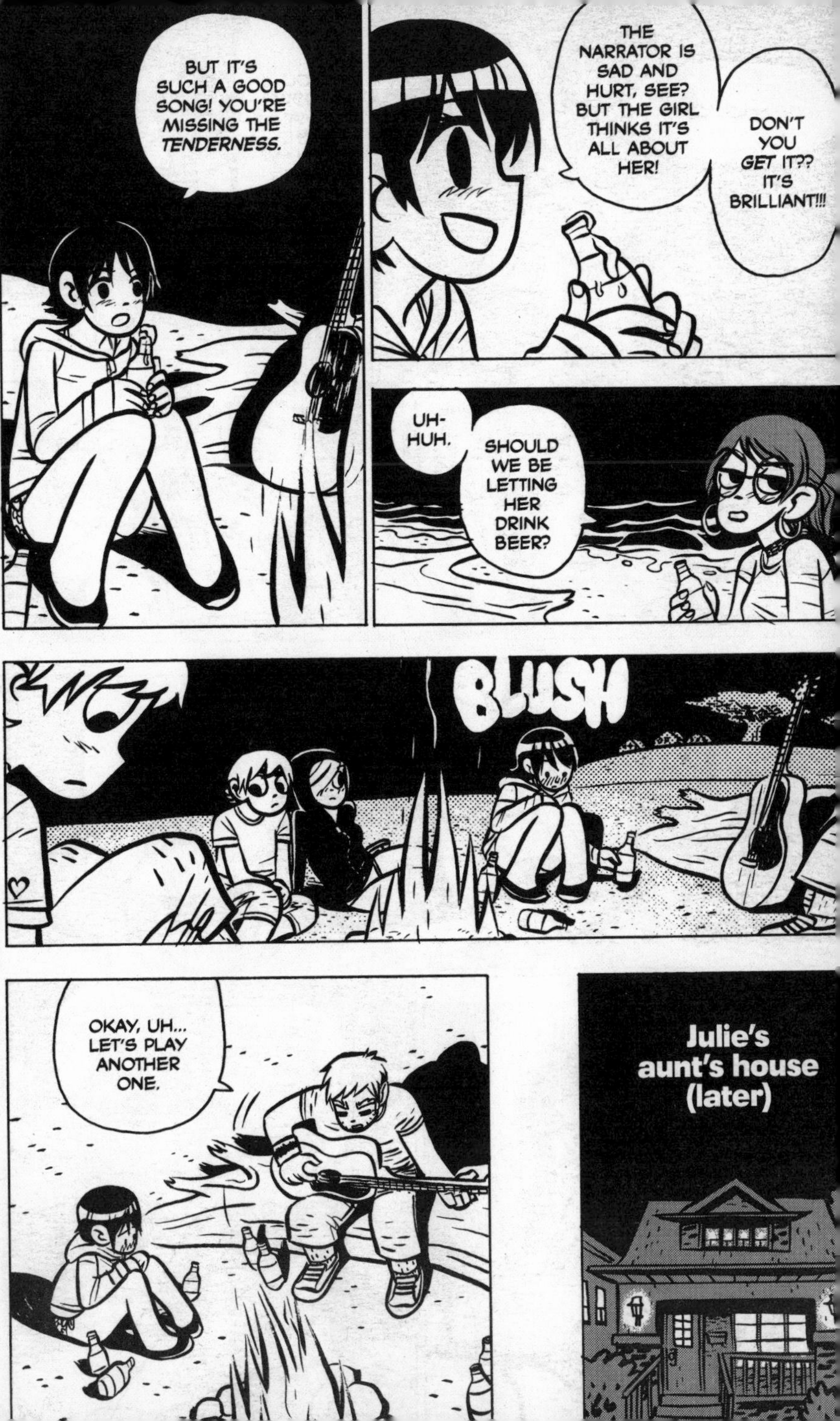
BUT IT'S SUCH A GOOD SONG! YOU'RE MISSING THE *TENDERNESS.*
THE NARRATOR IS SAD AND HURT, SEE? BUT THE GIRL THINKS IT'S ALL ABOUT HER!
DON'T YOU *GET* IT?? IT'S BRILLIANT!!!
UH-HUH.
SHOULD WE BE LETTING HER DRINK BEER?
BLUSH
OKAY, UH... LET'S PLAY ANOTHER ONE.
Julie's aunt's house (later)

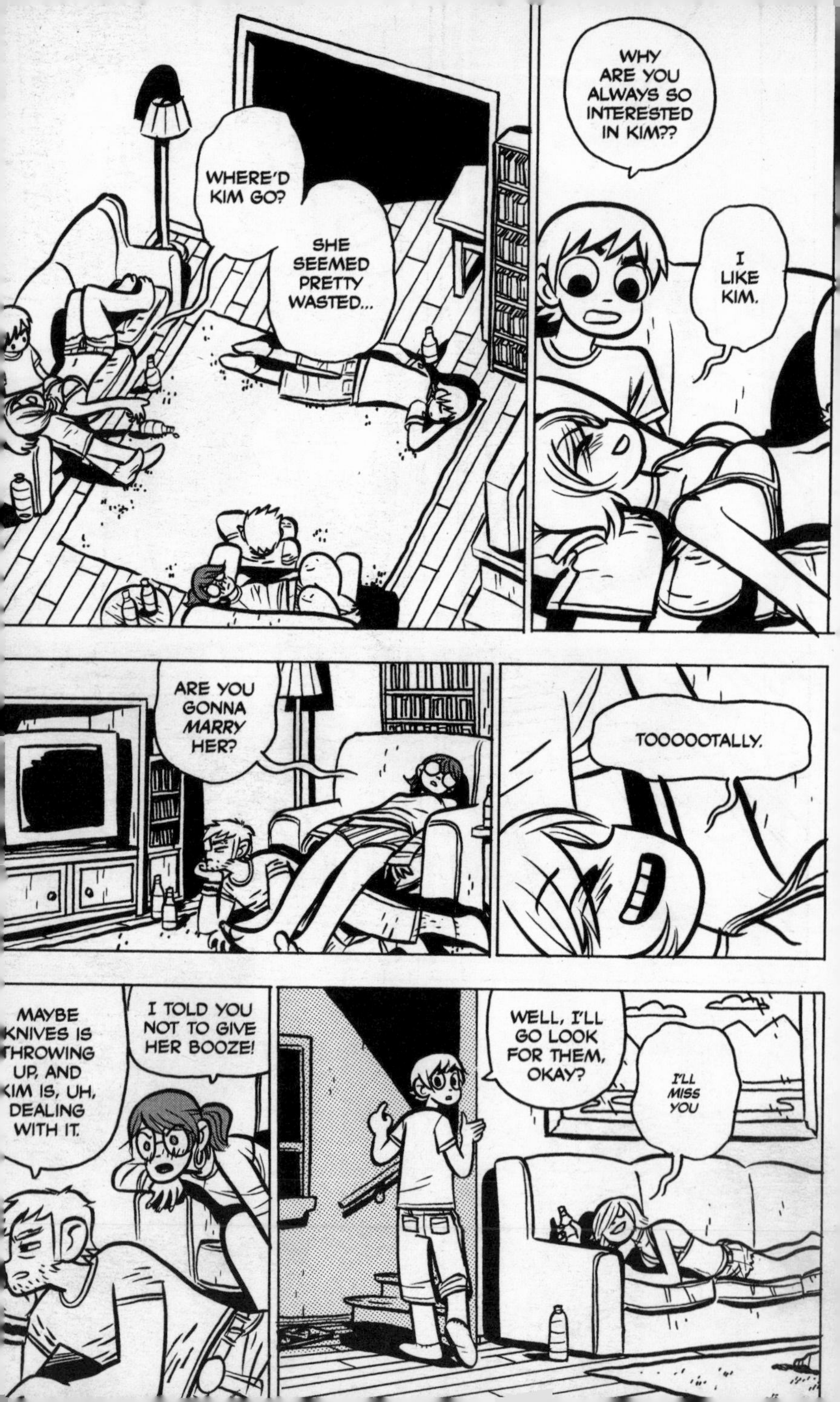
WHERE'D KIM GO?
SHE SEEMED PRETTY WASTED...
WHY ARE YOU ALWAYS SO INTERESTED IN KIM??
I LIKE KIM.
ARE YOU GONNA *MARRY* HER?
TOOOOOTALLY.
MAYBE KNIVES IS THROWING UP, AND KIM IS, UH, DEALING WITH IT.
I TOLD YOU NOT TO GIVE HER BOOZE!
WELL, I'LL GO LOOK FOR THEM, OKAY?
I'LL MISS YOU

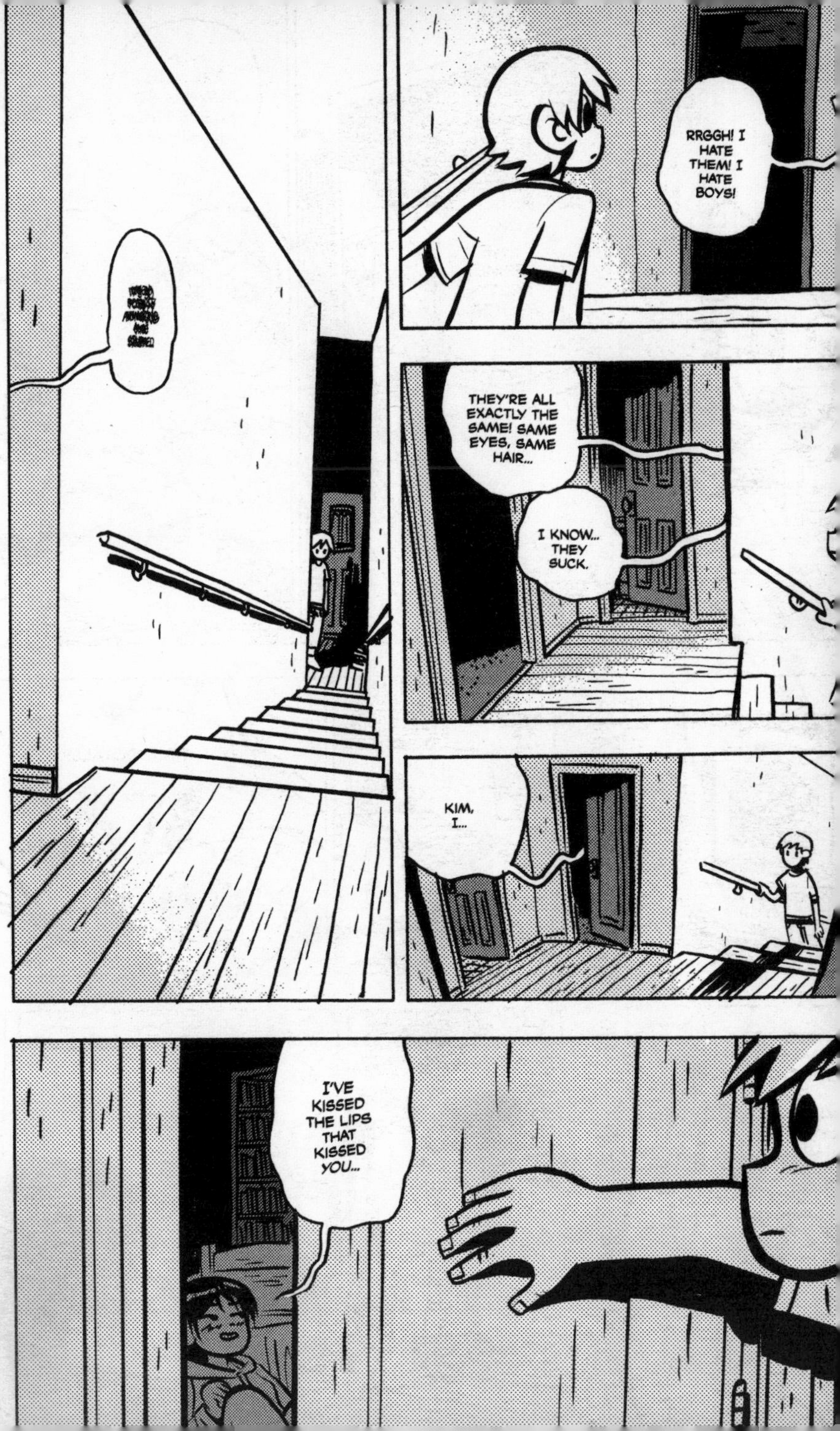
RRGGH! I HATE THEM! I HATE BOYS!
THEY'RE ALL EXACTLY THE SAME! SAME EYES, SAME HAIR...
I KNOW... THEY SUCK.
KIM, I...
I'VE KISSED THE LIPS THAT KISSED YOU...

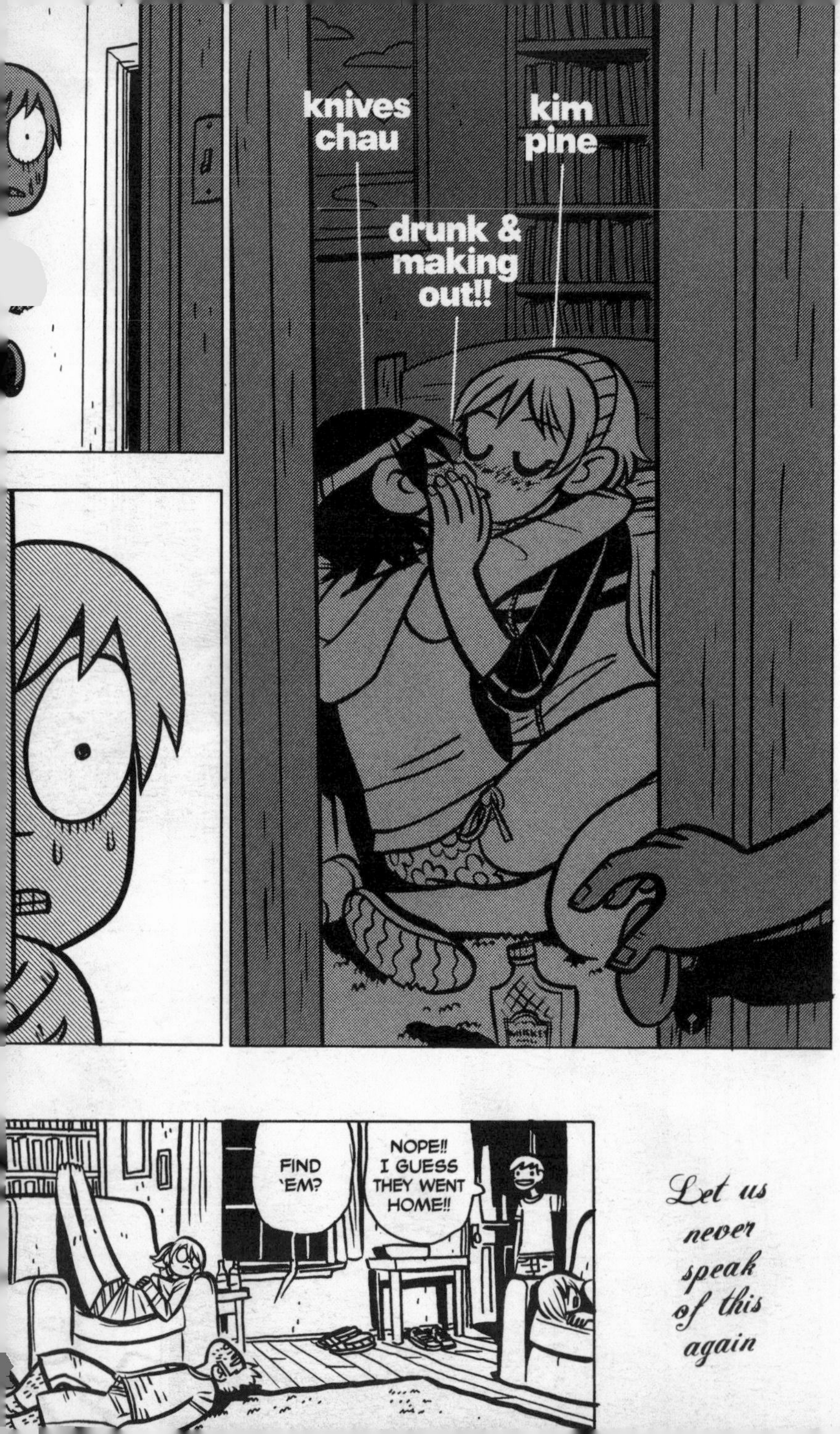
knives chau
kim pine
drunk & making out!!
FIND 'EM?
NOPE!! I GUESS THEY WENT HOME!!

Let us never speak of this again

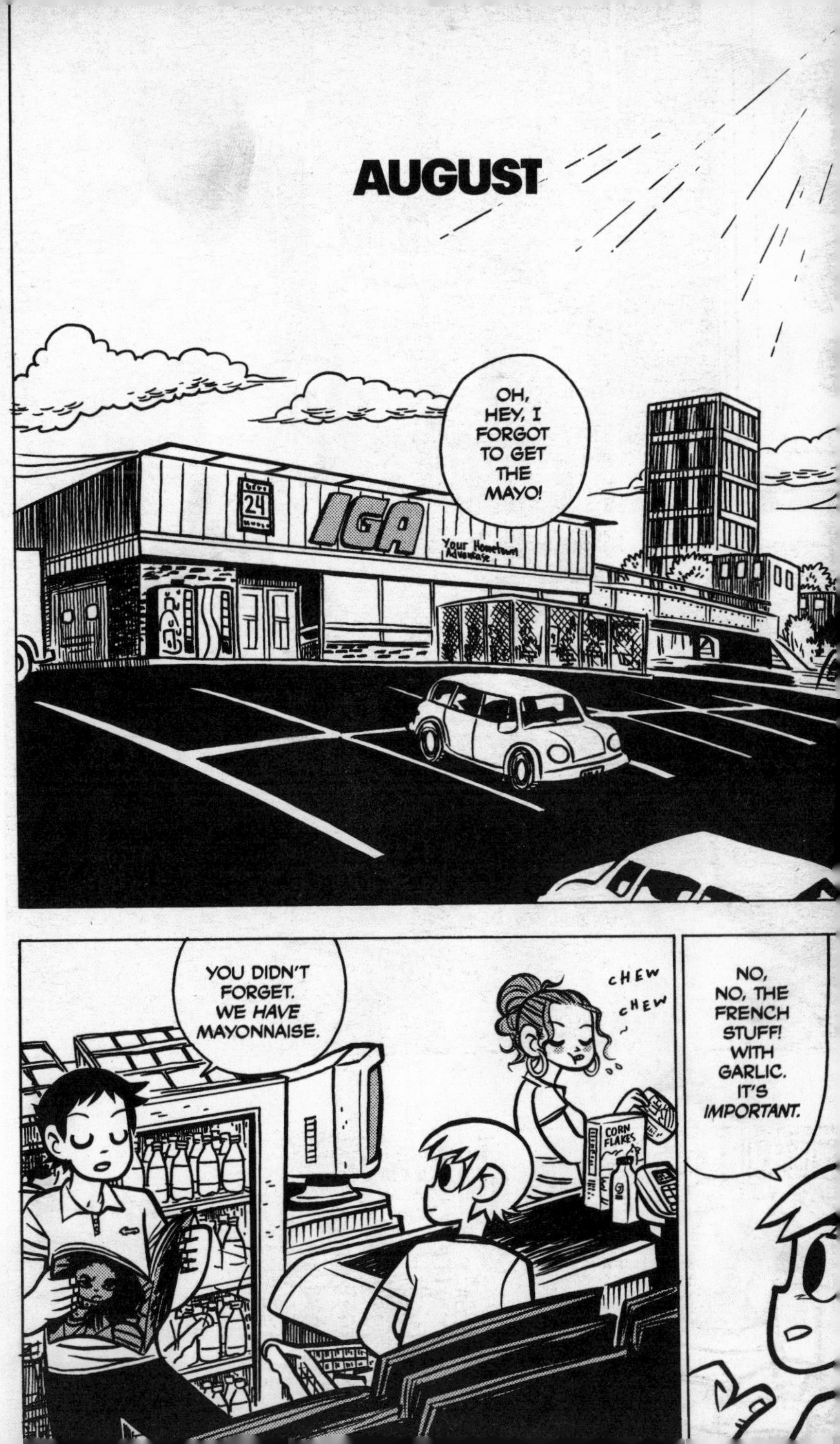
AUGUST
OH, HEY, I FORGOT TO GET THE MAYO!
24
IGA
Your Hometown Advantage
YOU DIDN'T FORGET. WE *HAVE* MAYONNAISE.
CHEW CHEW
CORN FLAKES
NO, NO, THE FRENCH STUFF! WITH GARLIC. IT'S *IMPORTANT.*

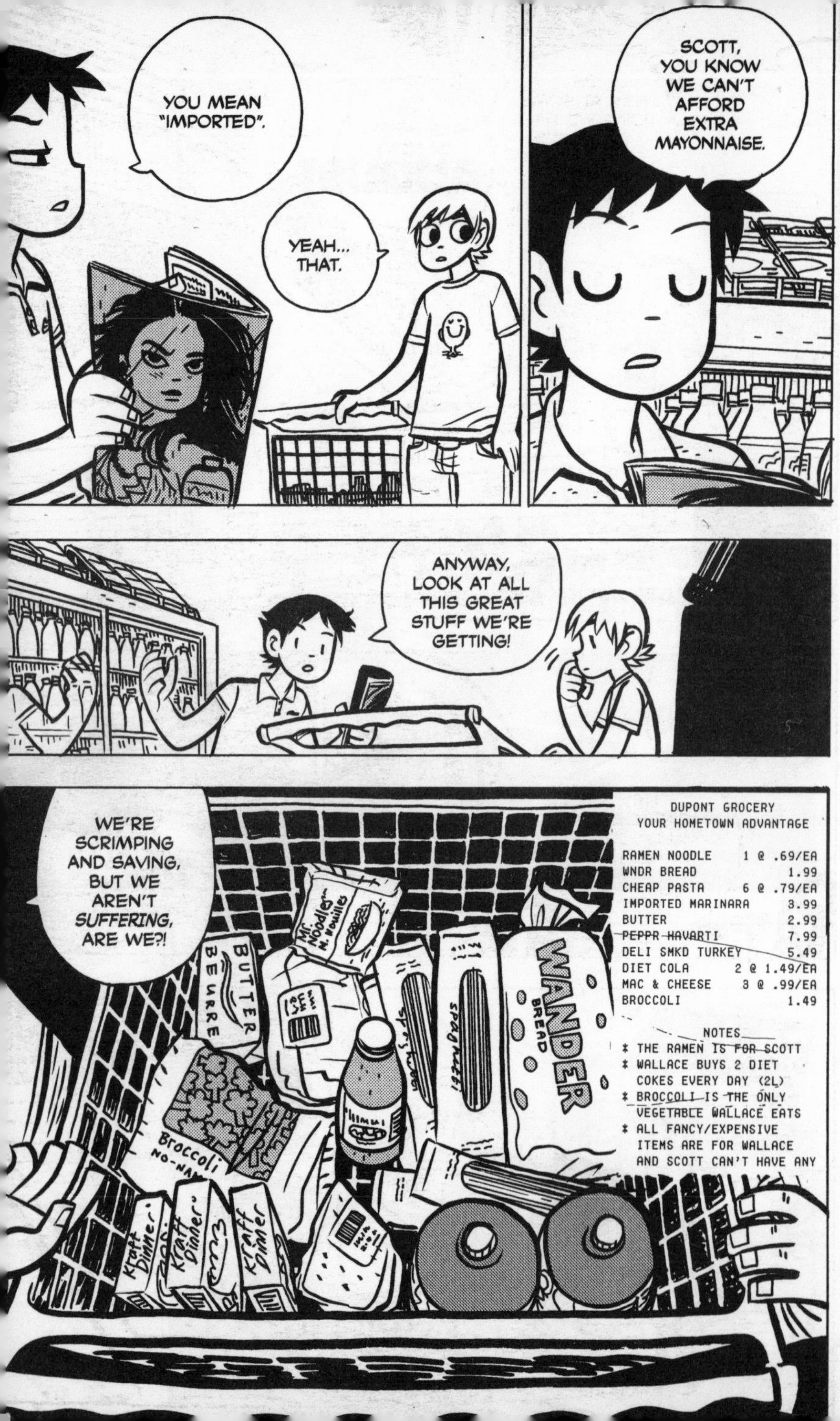
YOU MEAN "IMPORTED".
YEAH... THAT.
SCOTT, YOU KNOW WE CAN'T AFFORD EXTRA MAYONNAISE.
ANYWAY, LOOK AT ALL THIS GREAT STUFF WE'RE GETTING!
WE'RE SCRIMPING AND SAVING, BUT WE AREN'T SUFFERING, ARE WE?!
DUPONT GROCERY
YOUR HOMETOWN ADVANTAGE
RAMEN NOODLE 1 @ .69/EA
WNDR BREAD 1.99
CHEAP PASTA 6 @ .79/EA
IMPORTED MARINARA 3.99
BUTTER 2.99
PEPPR HAVARTI 7.99
DELI SMKD TURKEY 5.49
DIET COLA 2 @ 1.49/EA
MAC & CHEESE 3 @ .99/EA
BROCCOLI 1.49
NOTES
* THE RAMEN IS FOR SCOTT
* WALLACE BUYS 2 DIET COKES EVERY DAY (2L)
* BROCCOLI IS THE ONLY VEGETABLE WALLACE EATS
* ALL FANCY/EXPENSIVE ITEMS ARE FOR WALLACE AND SCOTT CAN'T HAVE ANY
BUTTER BEURRE
Mr. Noodles M. Nouilles
spaghetti
WANDER BREAD
Broccoli
Kraft Dinner
Kraft Dinner
Kraft Dinner

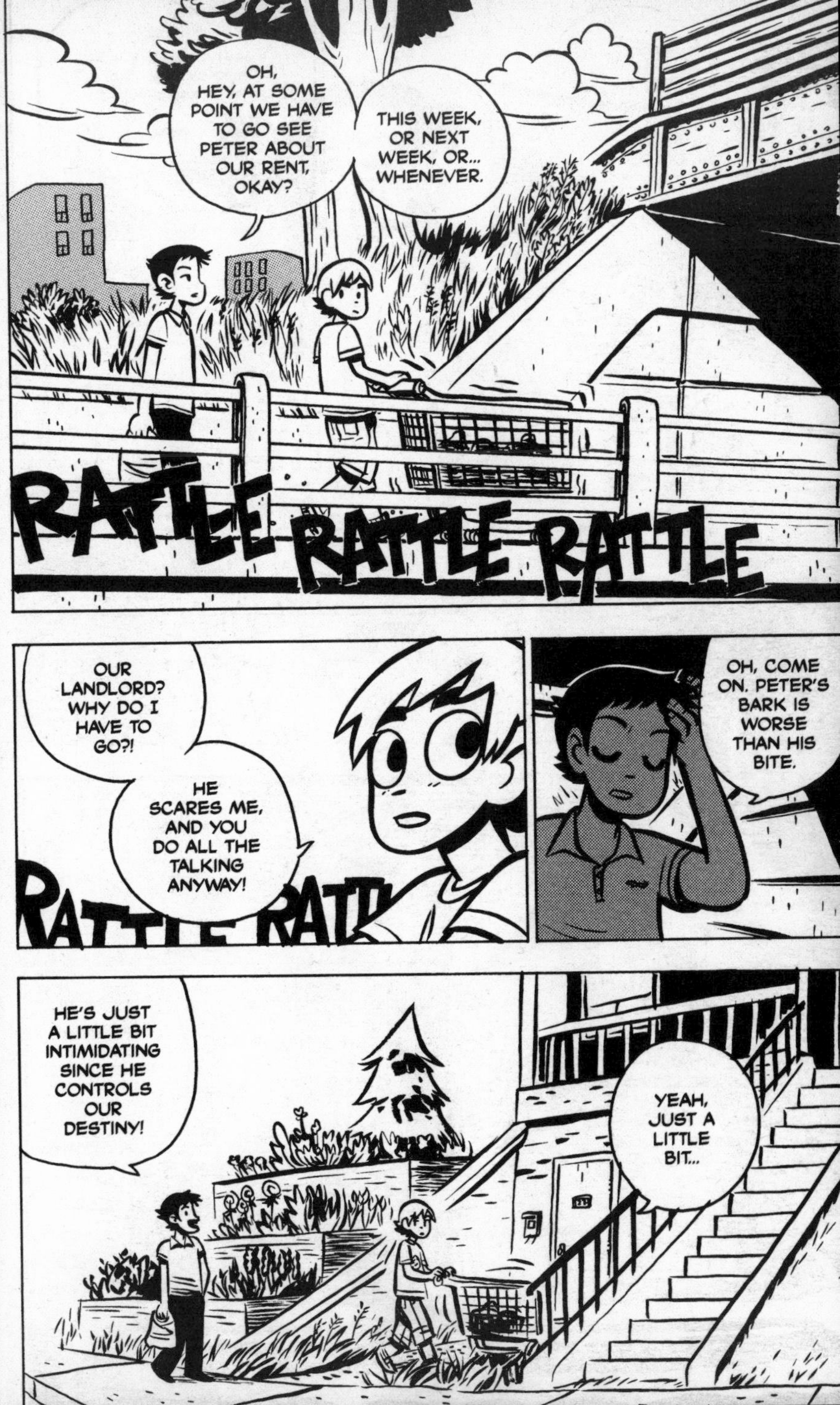
OH, HEY, AT SOME POINT WE HAVE TO GO SEE PETER ABOUT OUR RENT, OKAY?
THIS WEEK, OR NEXT WEEK, OR... WHENEVER.
RATTLE RATTLE RATTLE
OUR LANDLORD? WHY DO I HAVE TO GO?!
HE SCARES ME, AND YOU DO ALL THE TALKING ANYWAY!
OH, COME ON. PETER'S BARK IS WORSE THAN HIS BITE.
HE'S JUST A LITTLE BIT INTIMIDATING SINCE HE CONTROLS OUR DESTINY!
YEAH, JUST A LITTLE BIT...

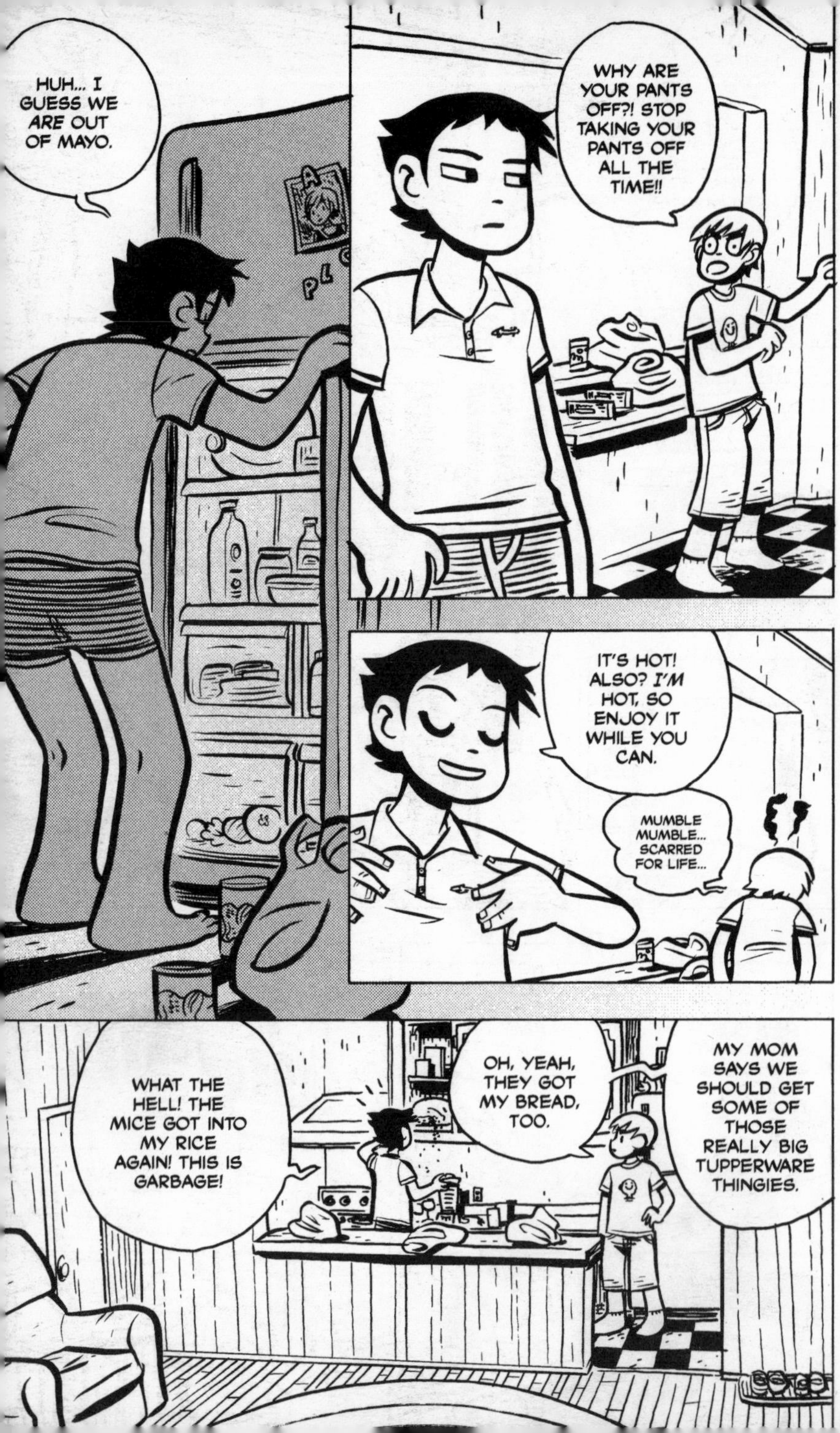
HUH... I GUESS WE ARE OUT OF MAYO.
WHY ARE YOUR PANTS OFF?! STOP TAKING YOUR PANTS OFF ALL THE TIME!!
IT'S HOT! ALSO? I'M HOT, SO ENJOY IT WHILE YOU CAN.
MUMBLE MUMBLE... SCARRED FOR LIFE...
WHAT THE HELL! THE MICE GOT INTO MY RICE AGAIN! THIS IS GARBAGE!
OH, YEAH, THEY GOT MY BREAD, TOO.
MY MOM SAYS WE SHOULD GET SOME OF THOSE REALLY BIG TUPPERWARE THINGIES.

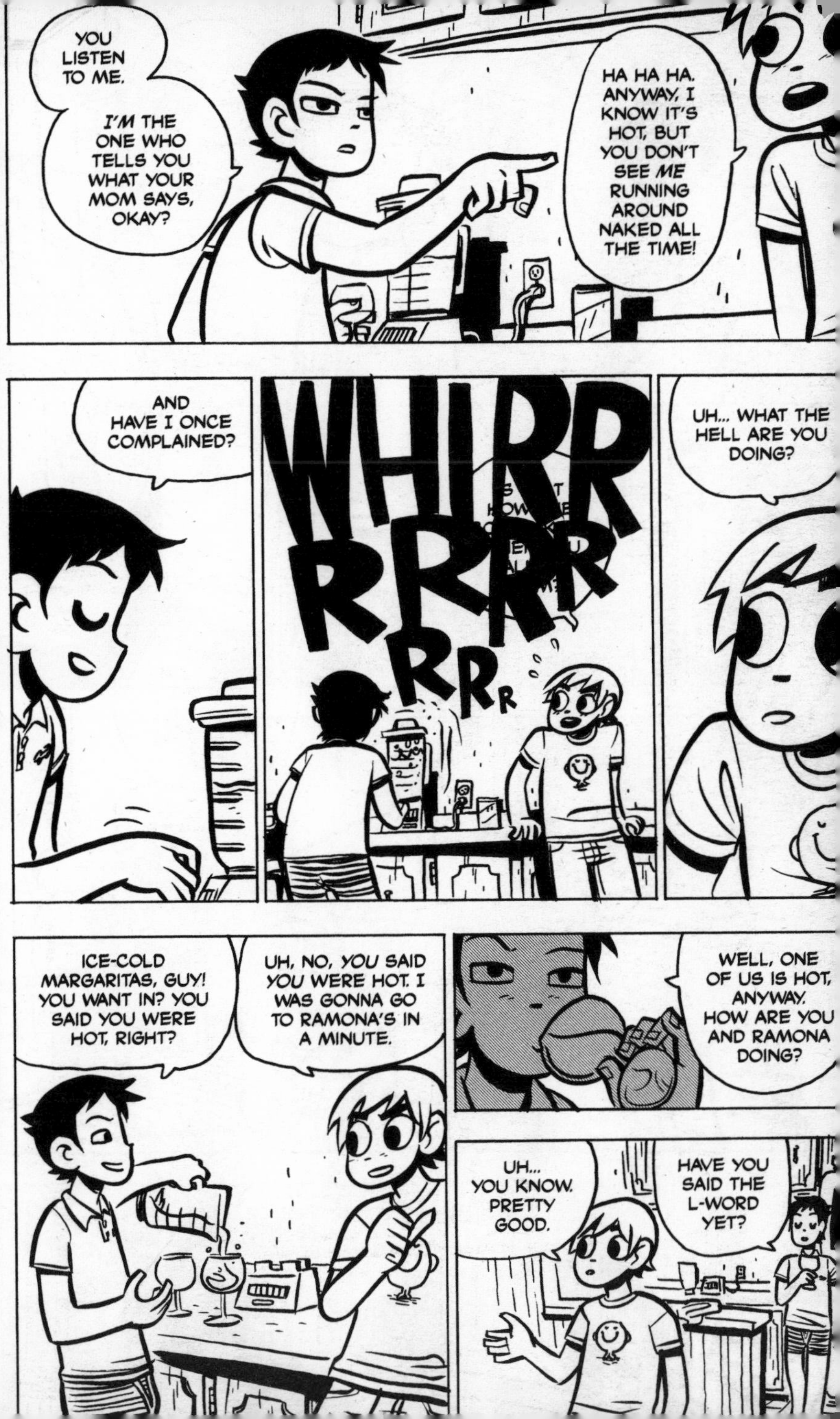

YOU LISTEN TO ME.
I'M THE ONE WHO TELLS YOU WHAT YOUR MOM SAYS, OKAY?
HA HA HA. ANYWAY, I KNOW IT'S HOT, BUT YOU DON'T SEE ME RUNNING AROUND NAKED ALL THE TIME!
AND HAVE I ONCE COMPLAINED?
WHIRR RRRR RRr
UH... WHAT THE HELL ARE YOU DOING?
ICE-COLD MARGARITAS, GUY! YOU WANT IN? YOU SAID YOU WERE HOT, RIGHT?
UH, NO, YOU SAID YOU WERE HOT. I WAS GONNA GO TO RAMONA'S IN A MINUTE.
WELL, ONE OF US IS HOT, ANYWAY. HOW ARE YOU AND RAMONA DOING?
UH... YOU KNOW. PRETTY GOOD.
HAVE YOU SAID THE L-WORD YET?

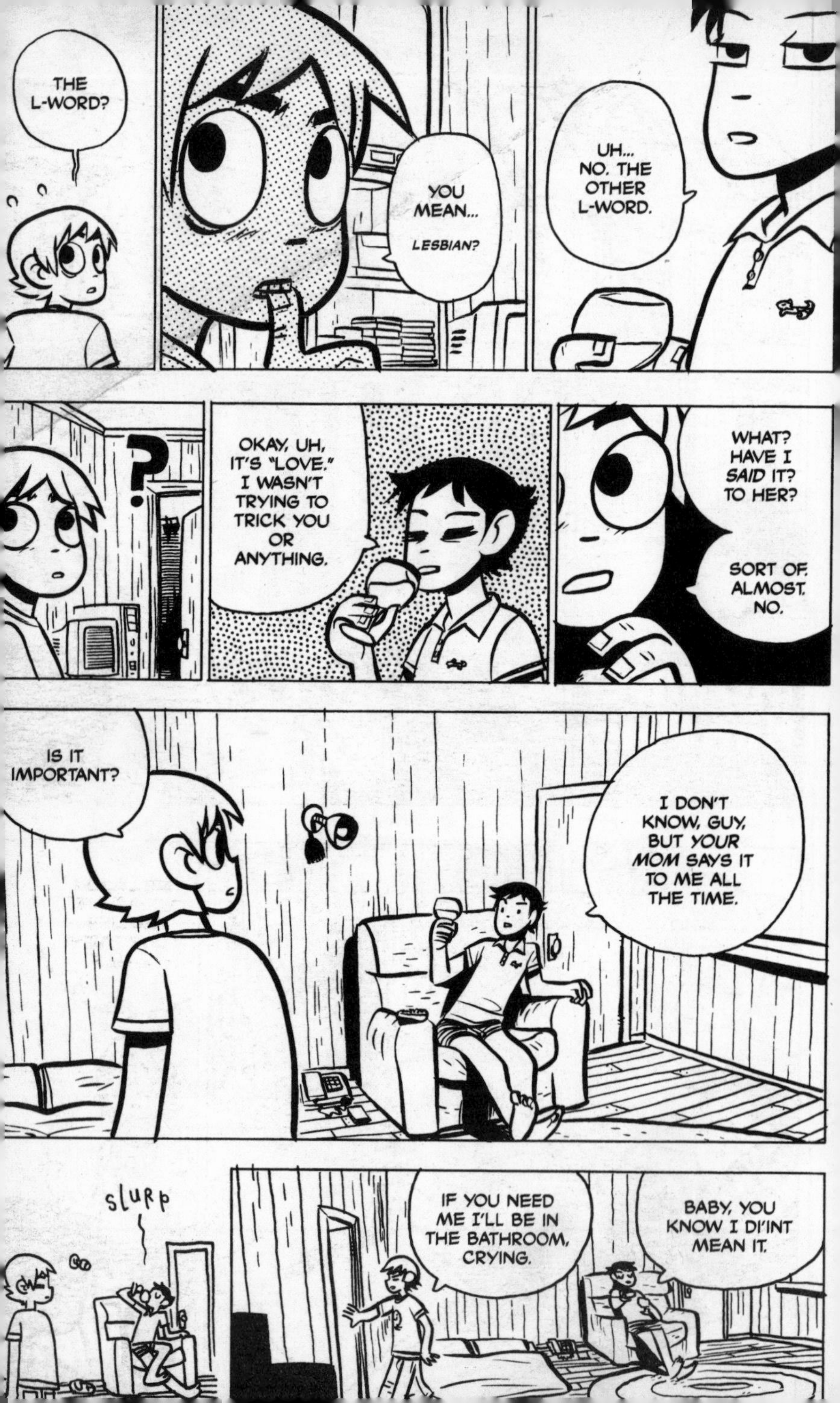
THE L-WORD?
YOU MEAN... LESBIAN?
UH... NO. THE OTHER L-WORD.
?
OKAY, UH, IT'S "LOVE." I WASN'T TRYING TO TRICK YOU OR ANYTHING.
WHAT? HAVE I *SAID* IT? TO HER?
SORT OF. ALMOST. NO.
IS IT IMPORTANT?
I DON'T KNOW, GUY, BUT *YOUR MOM* SAYS IT TO ME ALL THE TIME.
SLURP
IF YOU NEED ME I'LL BE IN THE BATHROOM, CRYING.
BABY, YOU KNOW I DI'INT MEAN IT.

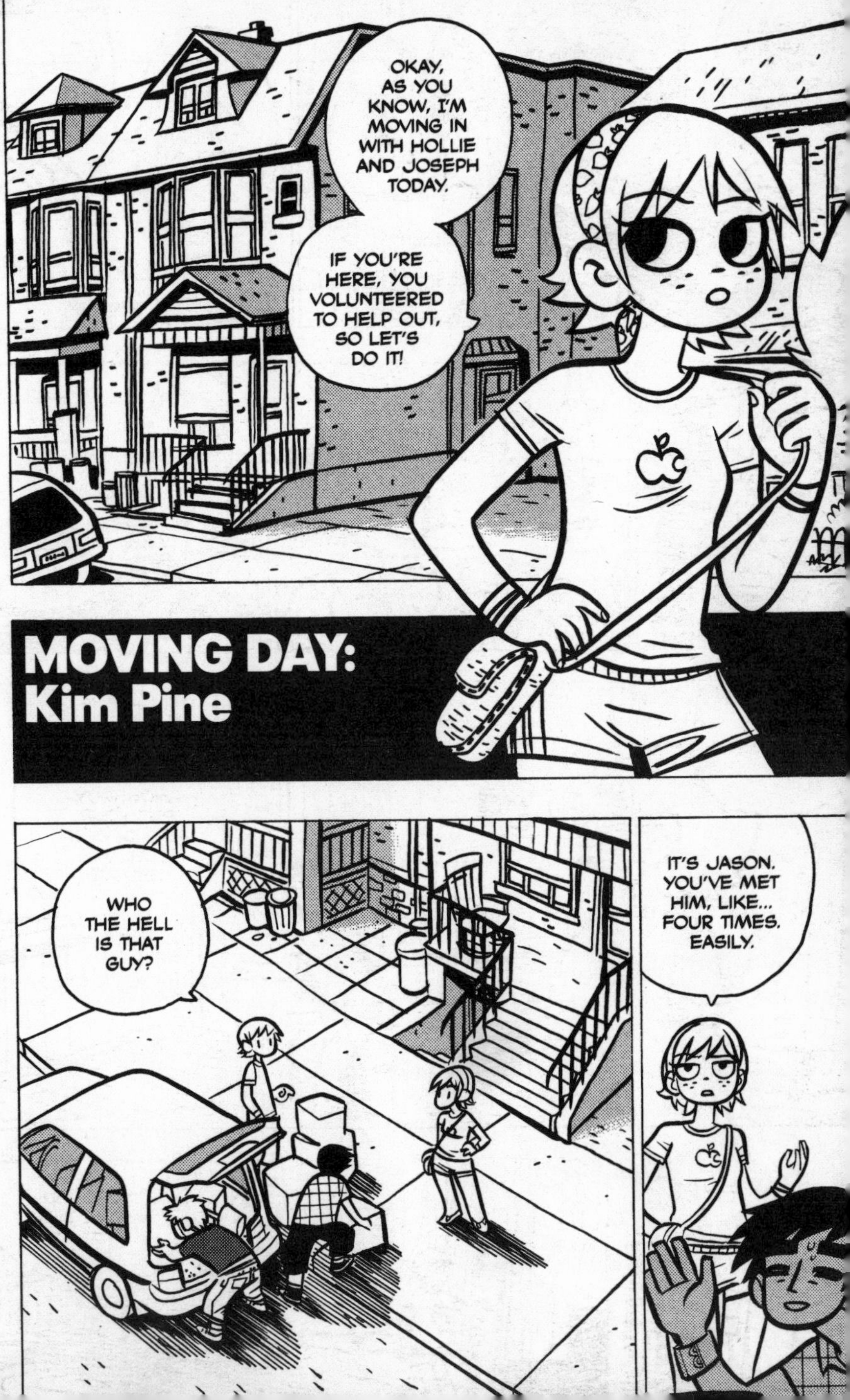
OKAY, AS YOU KNOW, I'M MOVING IN WITH HOLLIE AND JOSEPH TODAY.
IF YOU'RE HERE, YOU VOLUNTEERED TO HELP OUT, SO LET'S DO IT!
MOVING DAY:
Kim Pine
WHO THE HELL IS THAT GUY?
IT'S JASON. YOU'VE MET HIM, LIKE... FOUR TIMES. EASILY.

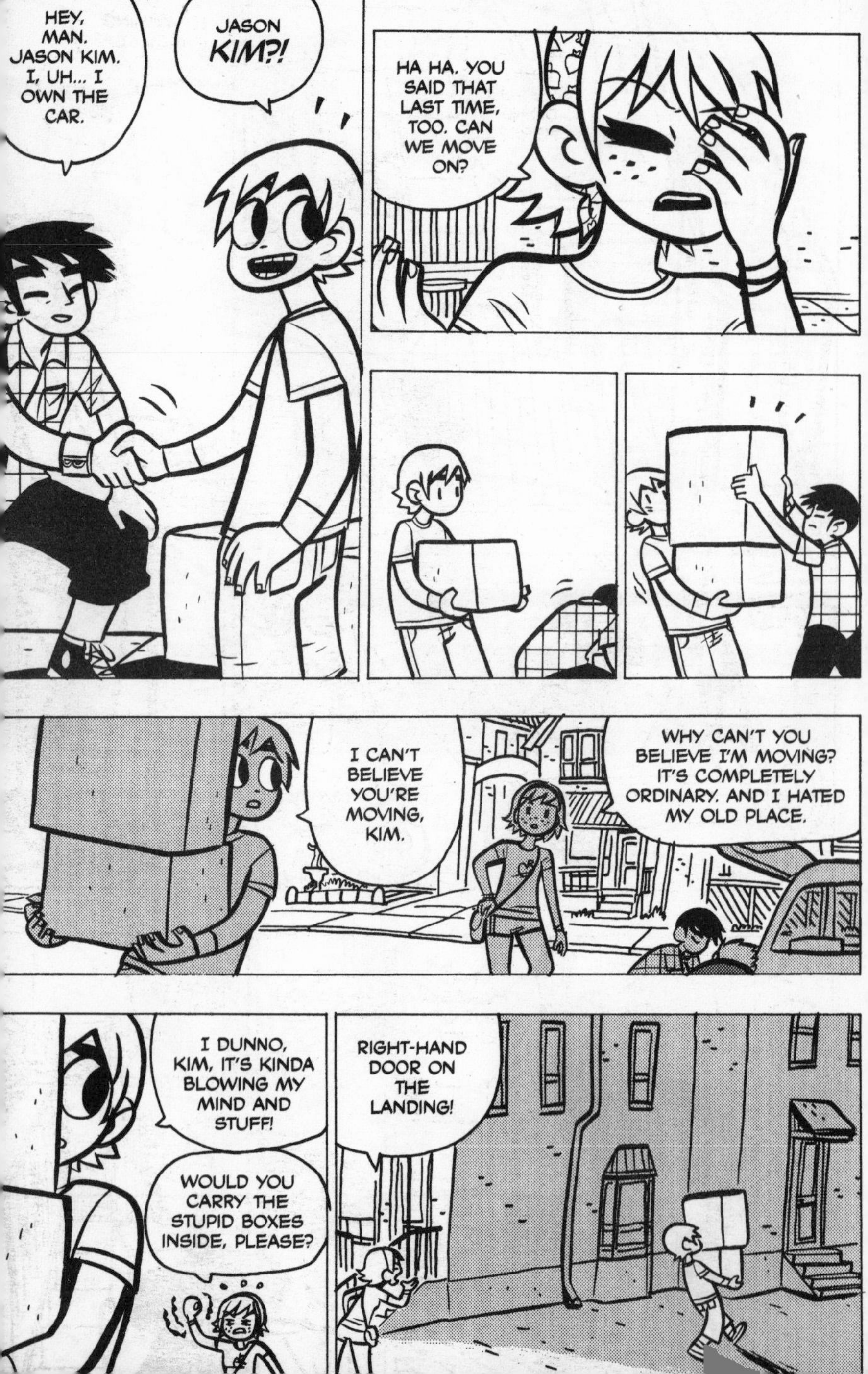
HEY, MAN. JASON KIM. I, UH... I OWN THE CAR.
JASON KIM?!
HA HA. YOU SAID THAT LAST TIME, TOO. CAN WE MOVE ON?
I CAN'T BELIEVE YOU'RE MOVING, KIM.
WHY CAN'T YOU BELIEVE I'M MOVING? IT'S COMPLETELY ORDINARY. AND I HATED MY OLD PLACE.
I DUNNO, KIM, IT'S KINDA BLOWING MY MIND AND STUFF!
WOULD YOU CARRY THE STUPID BOXES INSIDE, PLEASE?
RIGHT-HAND DOOR ON THE LANDING!

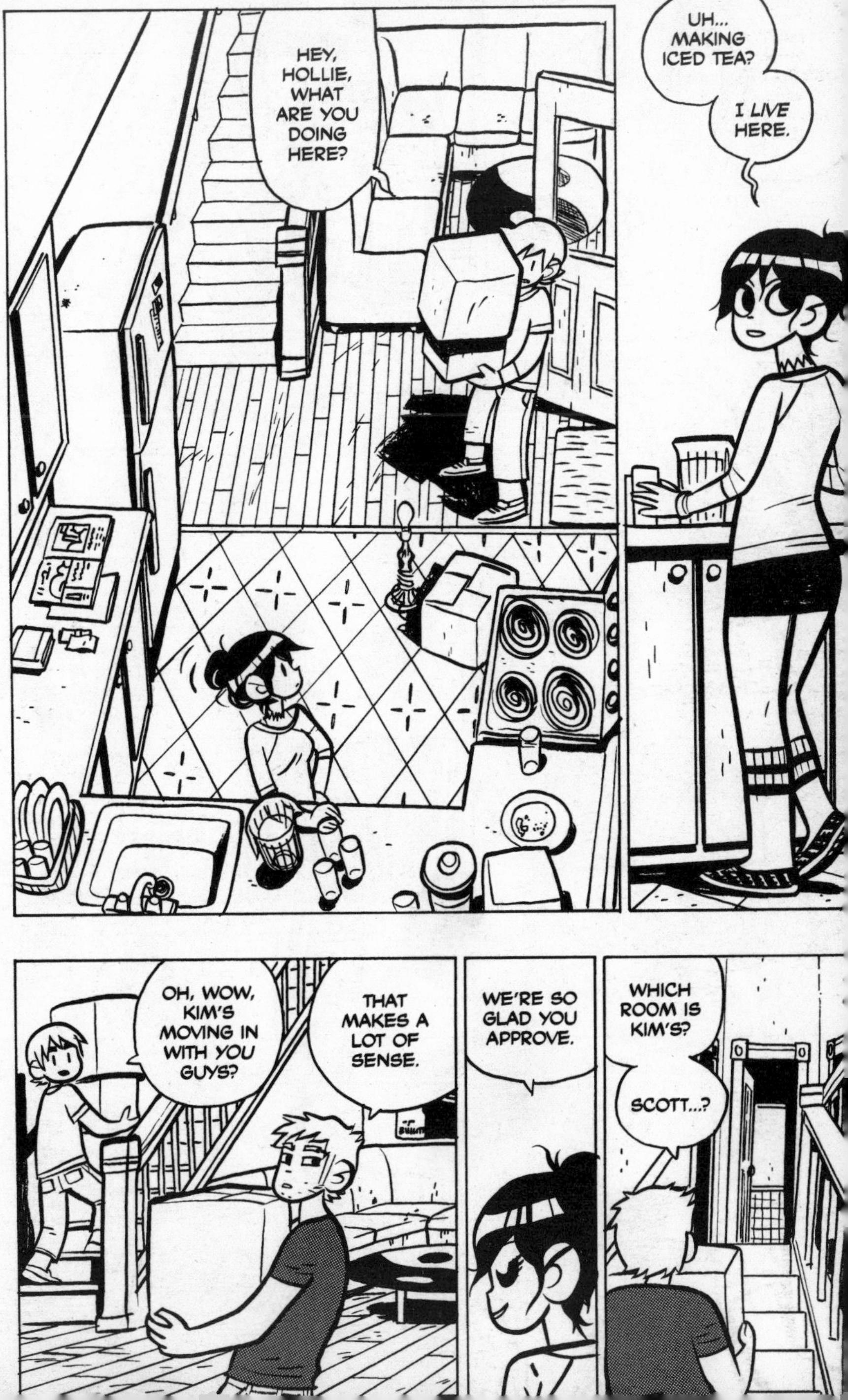
HEY, HOLLIE, WHAT ARE YOU DOING HERE?
UH... MAKING ICED TEA?
I *LIVE* HERE.
OH, WOW, KIM'S MOVING IN WITH *YOU* GUYS?
THAT MAKES A LOT OF SENSE.
WE'RE SO GLAD YOU APPROVE.
WHICH ROOM IS KIM'S?
SCOTT...?

HEY...

ARE... ARE YOU RECORDING MUSIC?

YOU HAVE A HOME STUDIO?! OH MY GOD.

DO YOU *WANT* SOMETHING? CAN I *HELP* YOU?

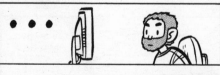

JOSEPH!!!! CAN YOU RECORD OUR ALBUM? SEX BOB-OMB NEEDS TO RECORD AN ALBUM! WE NEED TO TAKE IT TO THE NEXT LEVEL! YOU SAW US PLAY IN VOLUME 3, RIGHT? *WE AREN'T ALL THAT SUCKY, RIGHT???*

• • •

OKAY, I'LL DO IT. BUT ONLY BECAUSE I FIND YOU *ATTRACTIVE.*

I CAN LIVE WITH THAT!!!

24

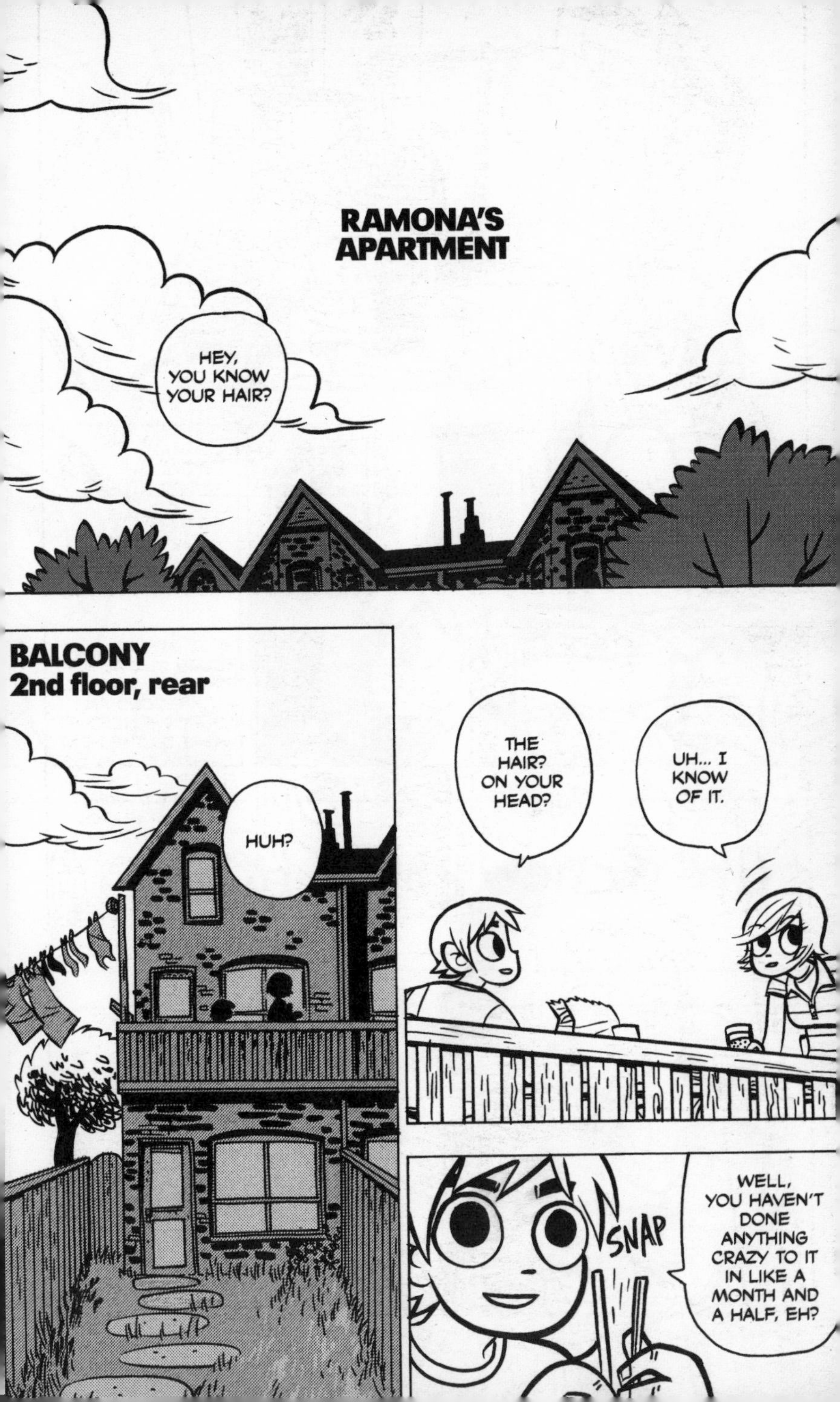
RAMONA'S
APARTMENT
HEY, YOU KNOW YOUR HAIR?
BALCONY
2nd floor, rear
HUH?
THE HAIR? ON YOUR HEAD?
UH... I KNOW OF IT.
SNAP
WELL, YOU HAVEN'T DONE ANYTHING CRAZY TO IT IN LIKE A MONTH AND A HALF, EH?

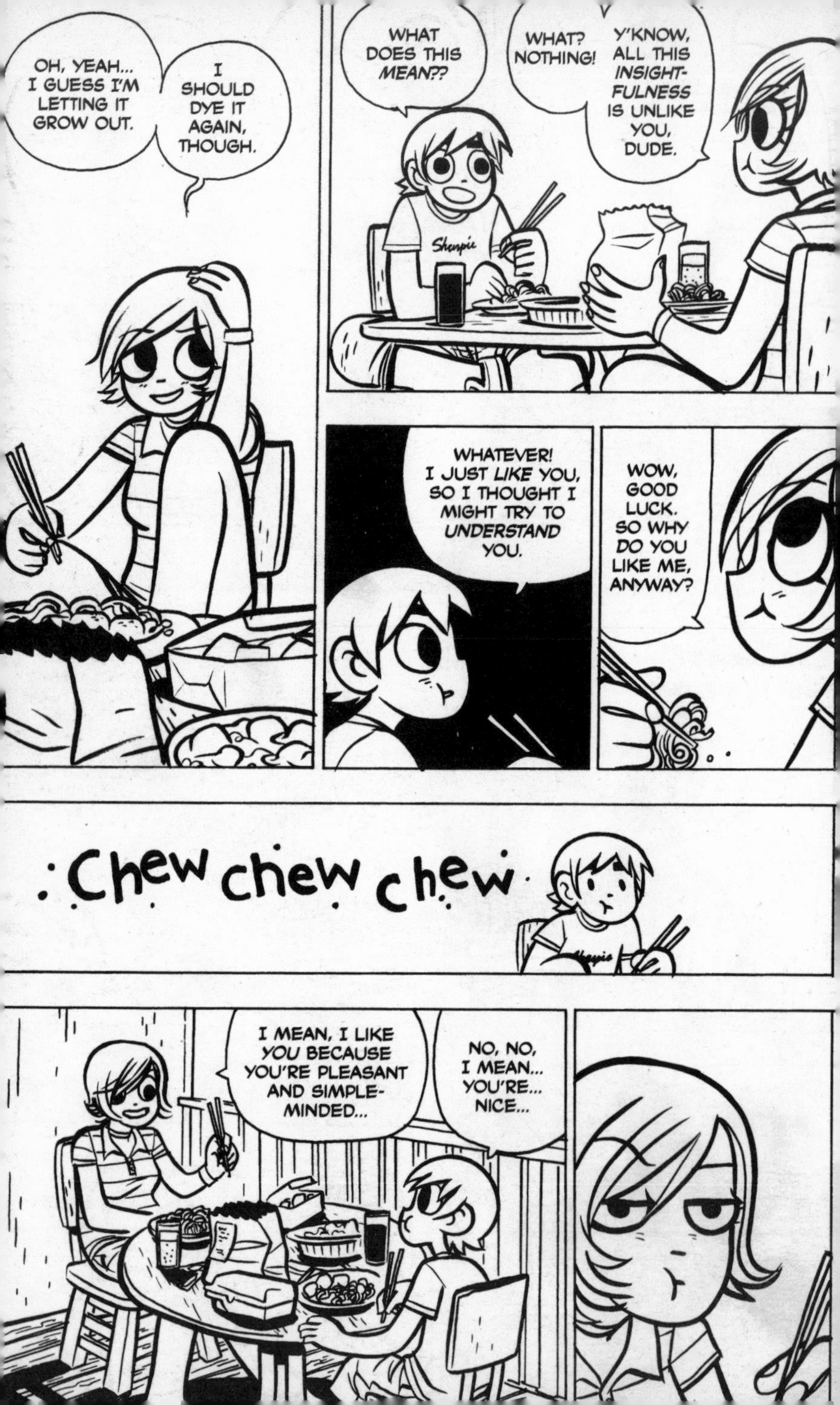
OH, YEAH... I GUESS I'M LETTING IT GROW OUT.
I SHOULD DYE IT AGAIN, THOUGH.
WHAT DOES THIS MEAN??
WHAT? NOTHING!
Y'KNOW, ALL THIS INSIGHT-FULNESS IS UNLIKE YOU, DUDE.
Shenpie
WHATEVER! I JUST LIKE YOU, SO I THOUGHT I MIGHT TRY TO UNDERSTAND YOU.
WOW, GOOD LUCK. SO WHY DO YOU LIKE ME, ANYWAY?
Chew chew chew
I MEAN, I LIKE YOU BECAUSE YOU'RE PLEASANT AND SIMPLE-MINDED...
NO, NO, I MEAN... YOU'RE... NICE...

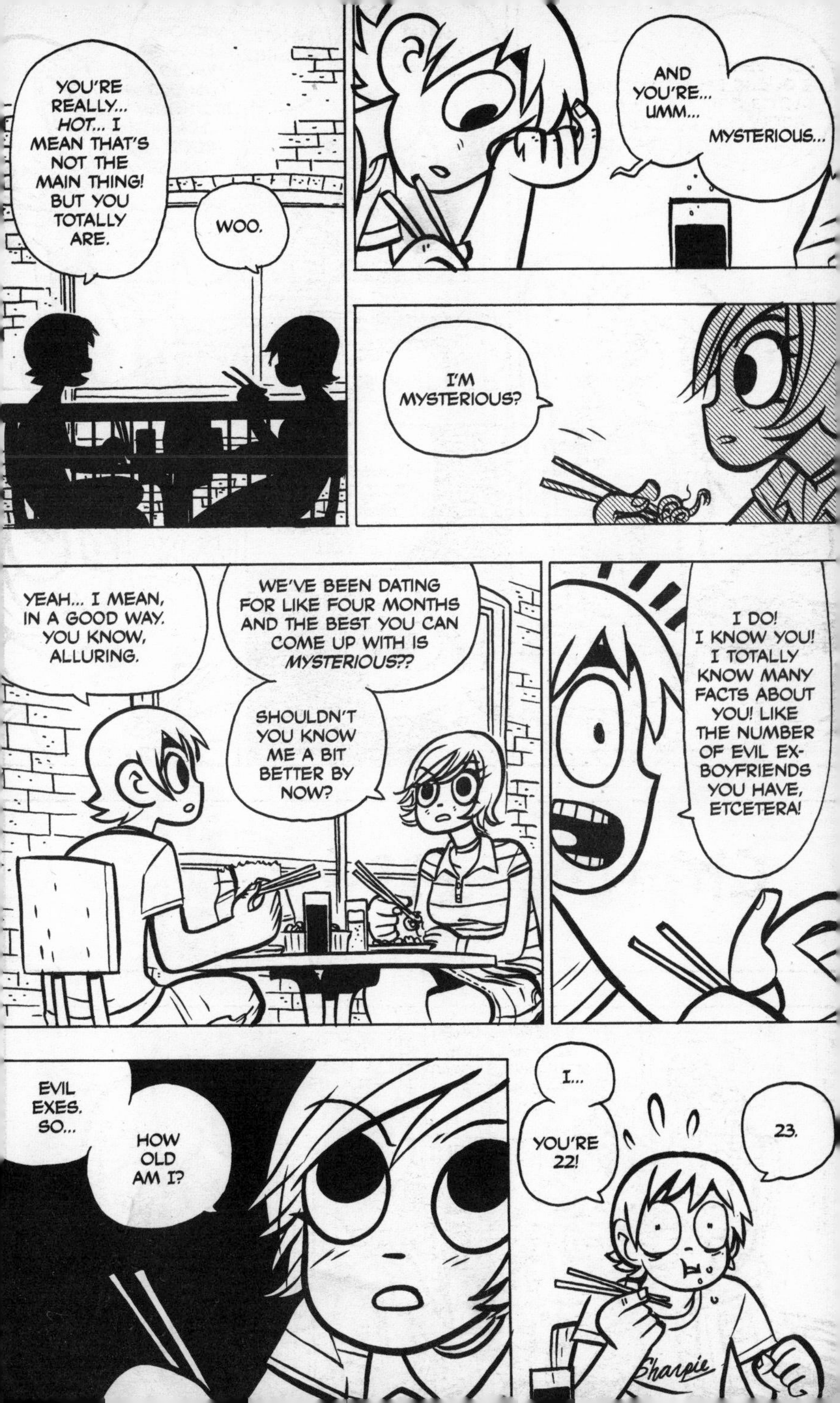
YOU'RE REALLY... HOT... I MEAN THAT'S NOT THE MAIN THING! BUT YOU TOTALLY ARE.
WOO.
AND YOU'RE... UMM...
MYSTERIOUS...
I'M MYSTERIOUS?
YEAH... I MEAN, IN A GOOD WAY. YOU KNOW, ALLURING.
WE'VE BEEN DATING FOR LIKE FOUR MONTHS AND THE BEST YOU CAN COME UP WITH IS MYSTERIOUS??
SHOULDN'T YOU KNOW ME A BIT BETTER BY NOW?
I DO! I KNOW YOU! I TOTALLY KNOW MANY FACTS ABOUT YOU! LIKE THE NUMBER OF EVIL EX-BOYFRIENDS YOU HAVE, ETCETERA!
EVIL EXES. SO...
HOW OLD AM I?
I...
YOU'RE 22!
23.
Sharpie

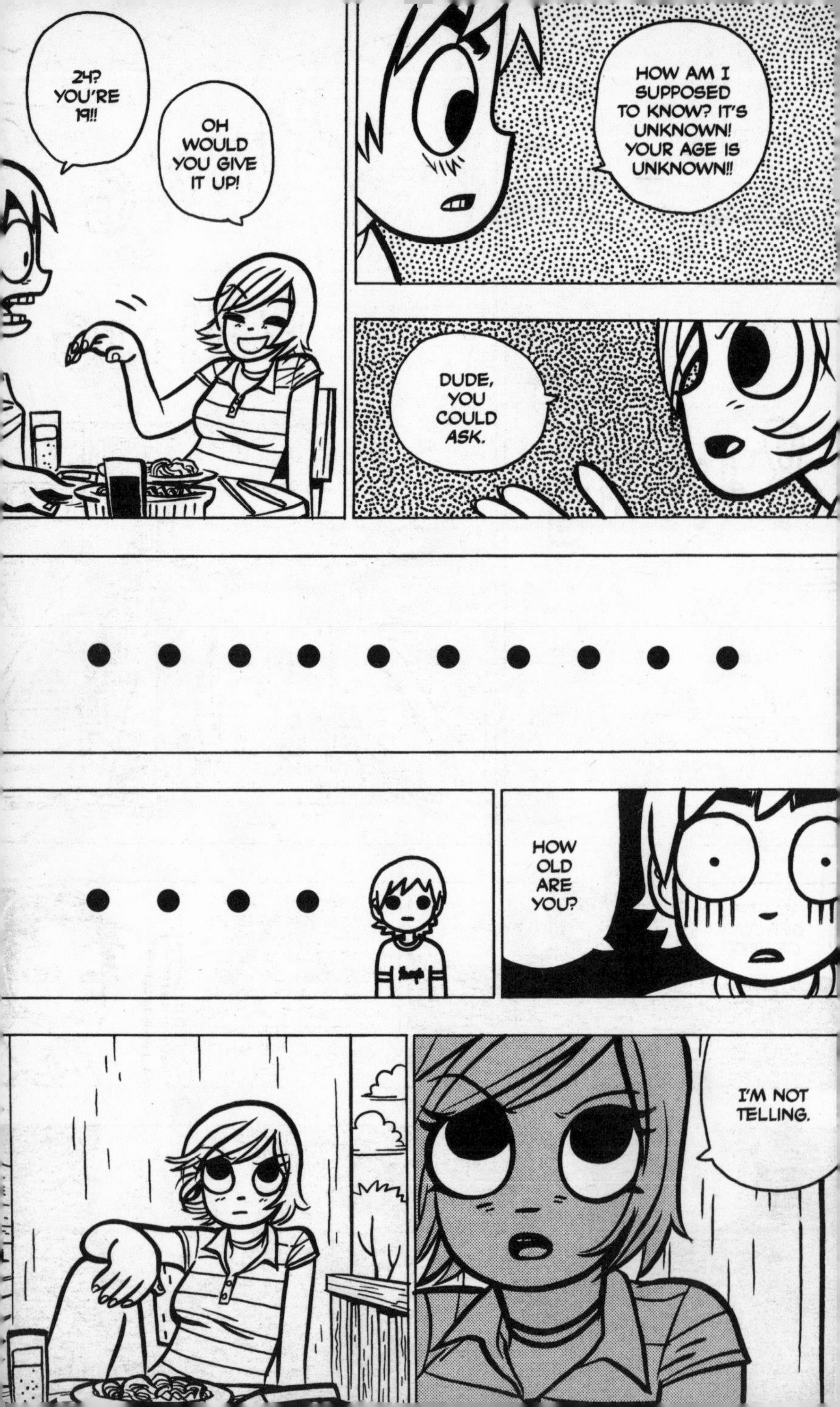
24? YOU'RE 19!!
OH WOULD YOU GIVE IT UP!
HOW AM I SUPPOSED TO KNOW? IT'S UNKNOWN! YOUR AGE IS UNKNOWN!!
DUDE, YOU COULD ASK.
HOW OLD ARE YOU?
I'M NOT TELLING.

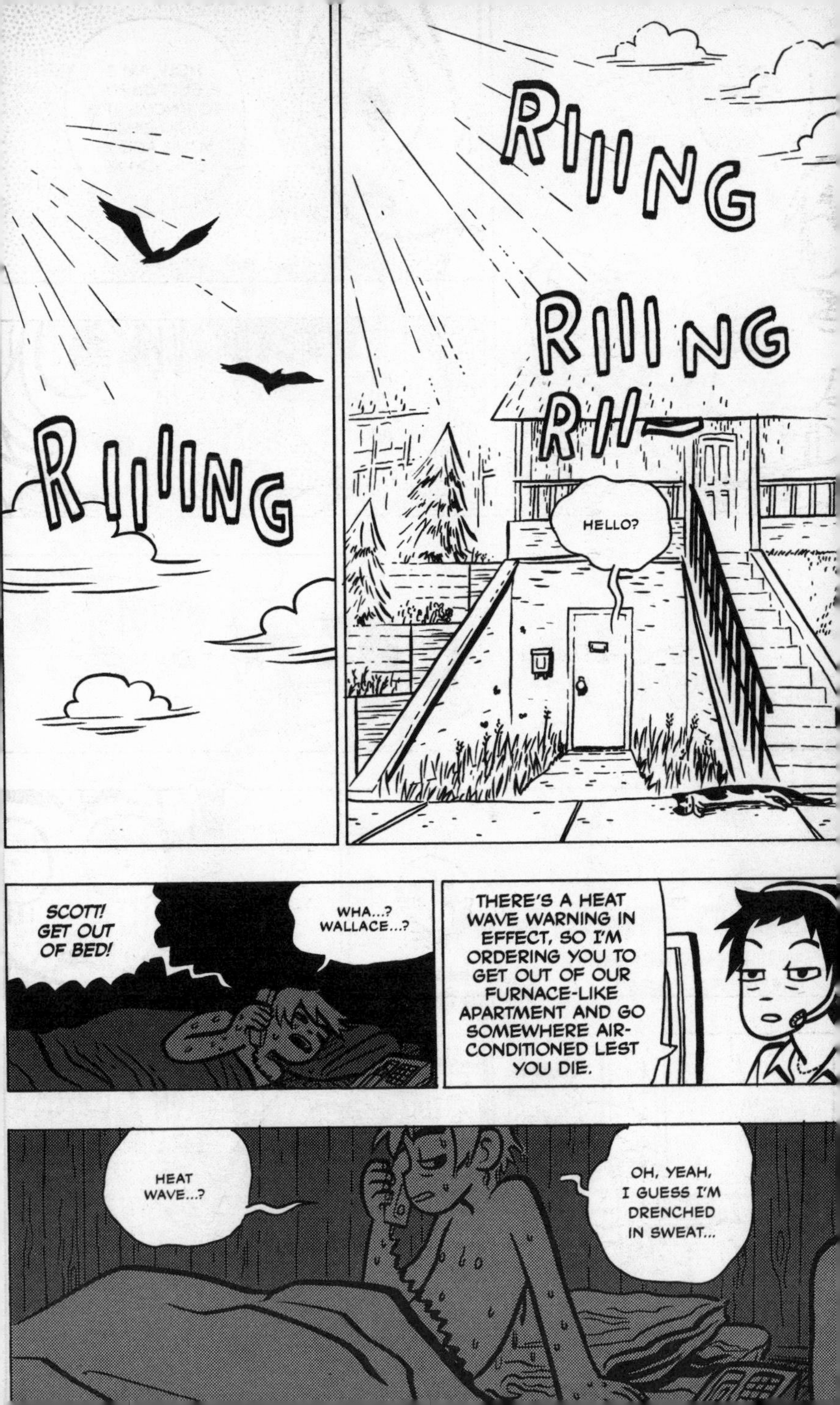
RIIING
RIIING
RIIING
RII—
HELLO?
SCOTT! GET OUT OF BED!
WHA...? WALLACE...?
THERE'S A HEAT WAVE WARNING IN EFFECT, SO I'M ORDERING YOU TO GET OUT OF OUR FURNACE-LIKE APARTMENT AND GO SOMEWHERE AIR-CONDITIONED LEST YOU DIE.
HEAT WAVE...?
OH, YEAH, I GUESS I'M DRENCHED IN SWEAT...

20 The new hotness

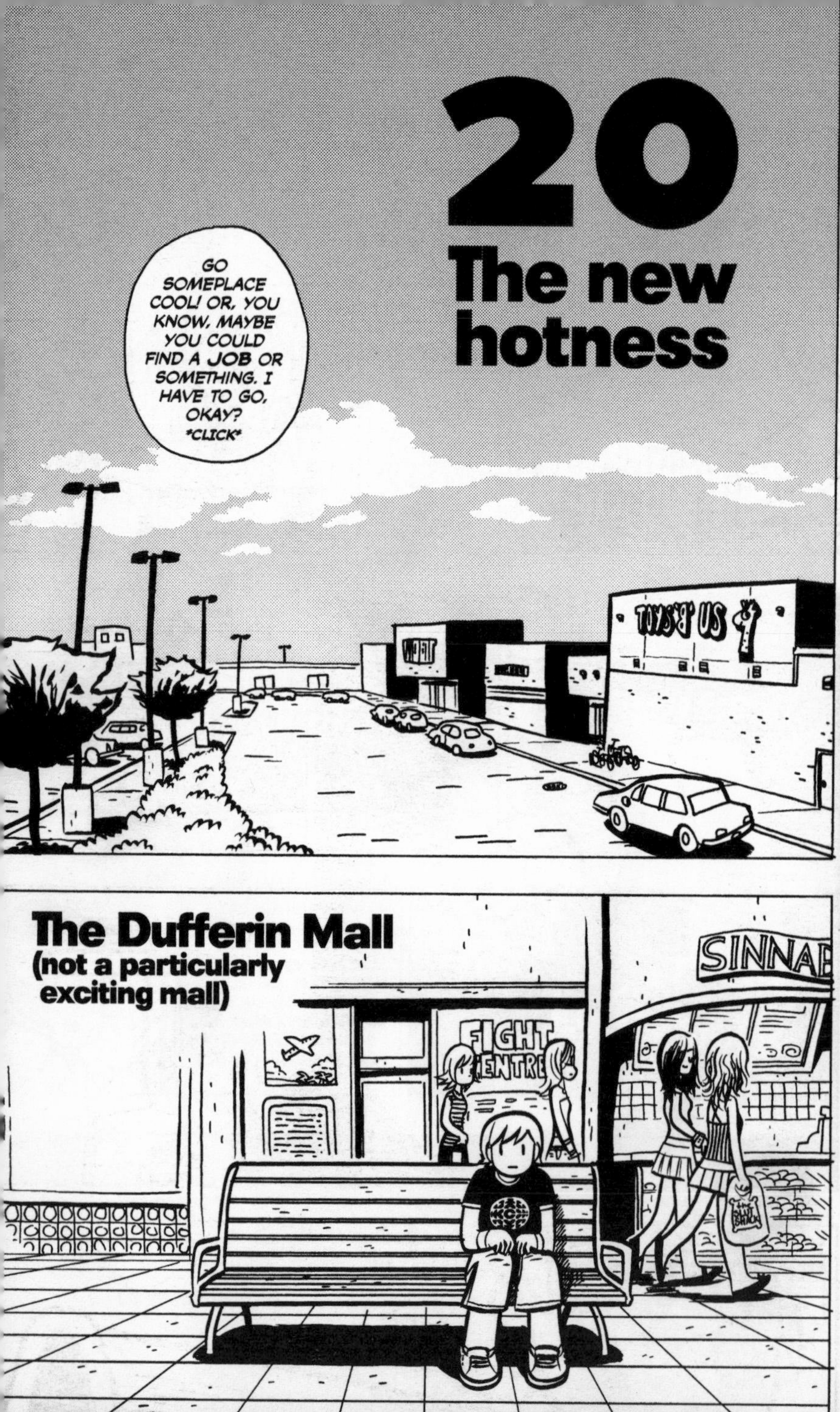
GO SOMEPLACE COOL! OR, YOU KNOW, MAYBE YOU COULD FIND A JOB OR SOMETHING. I HAVE TO GO, OKAY? *CLICK*
The Dufferin Mall (not a particularly exciting mall)
FIGHT
ENTRE
SINNAB

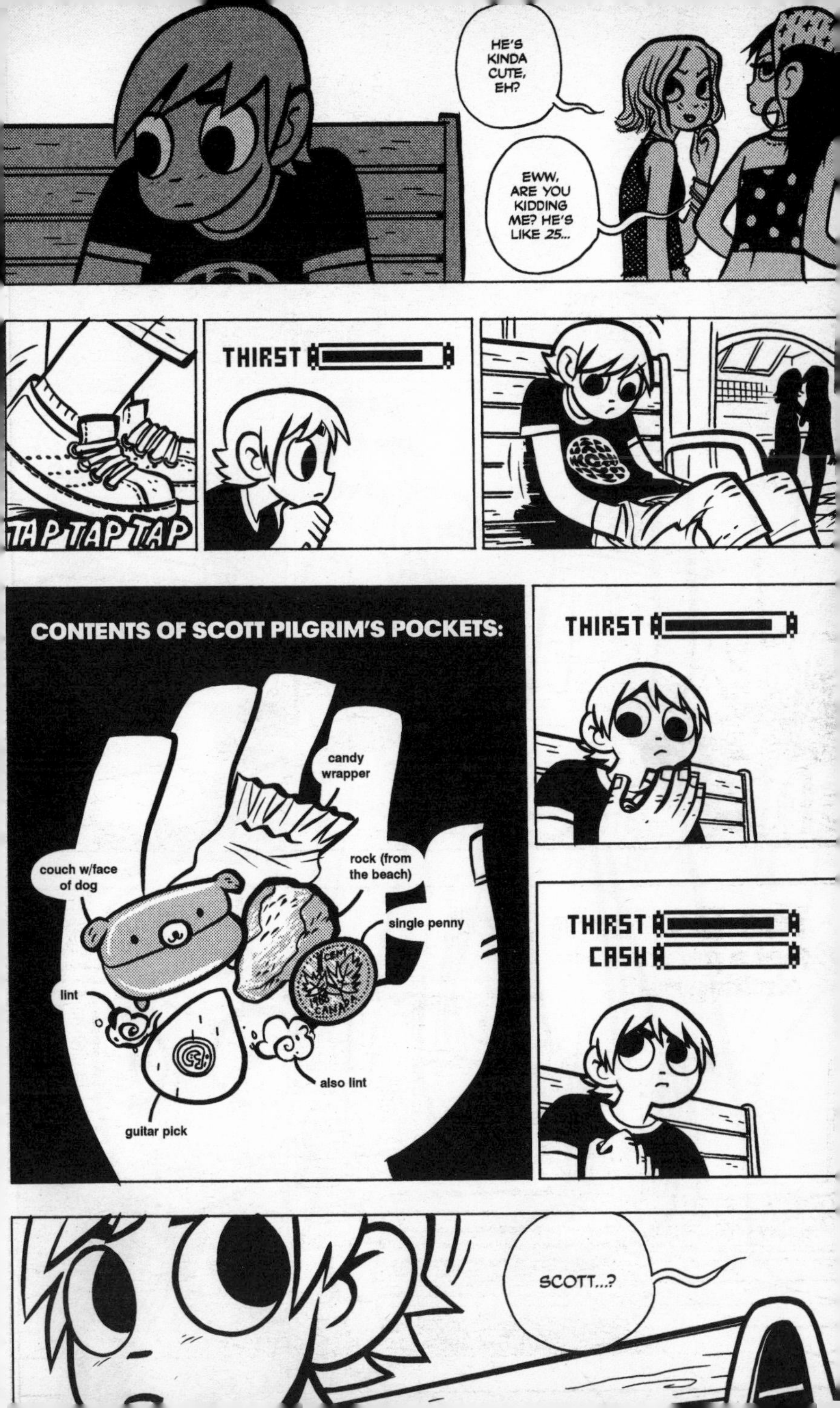
HE'S KINDA CUTE, EH?
EWW, ARE YOU KIDDING ME? HE'S LIKE *25*...
TAP TAP TAP
THIRST
CONTENTS OF SCOTT PILGRIM'S POCKETS:
candy wrapper
couch w/face of dog
rock (from the beach)
single penny
lint
also lint
guitar pick
THIRST
THIRST
CASH
SCOTT...?

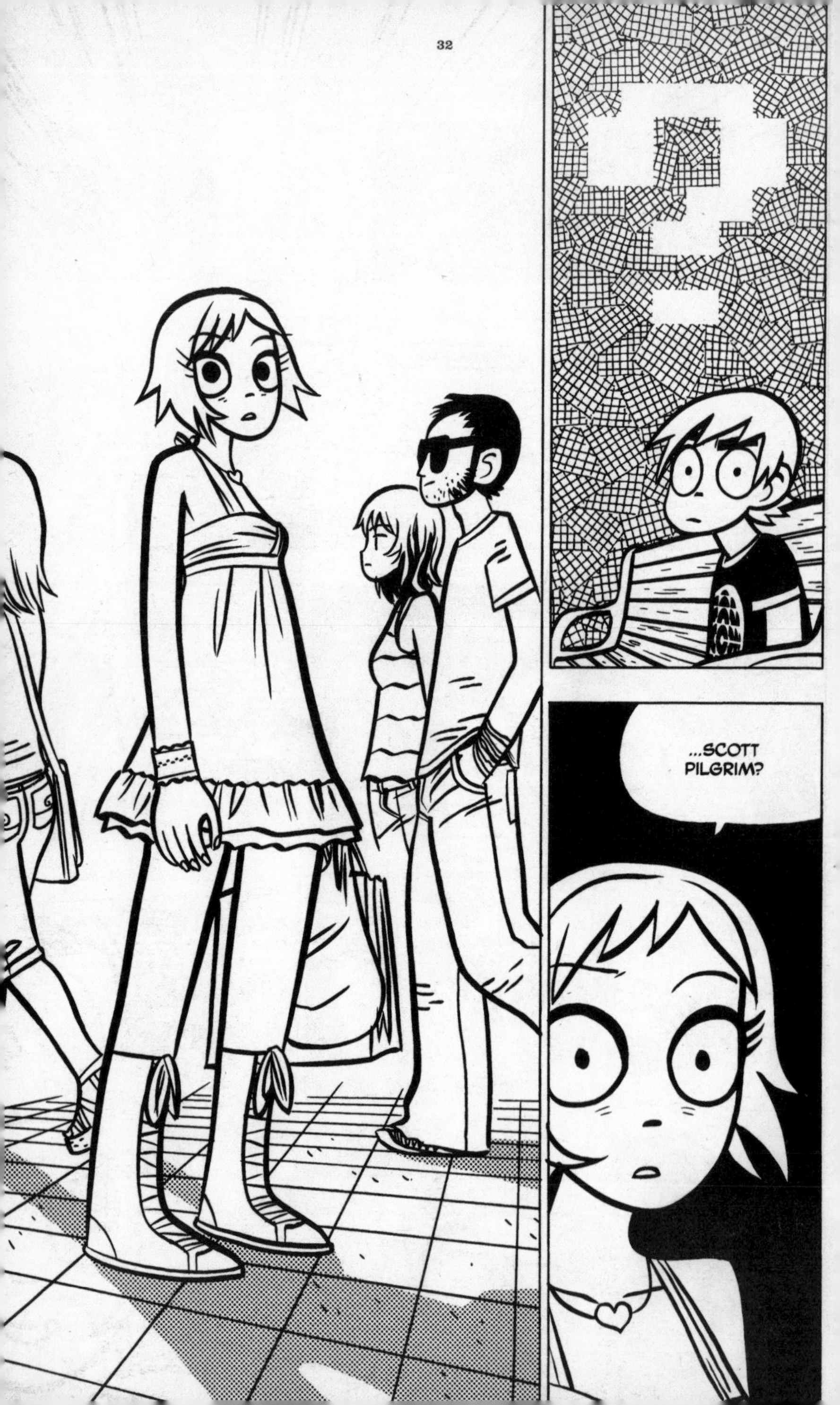
...SCOTT
PILGRIM?

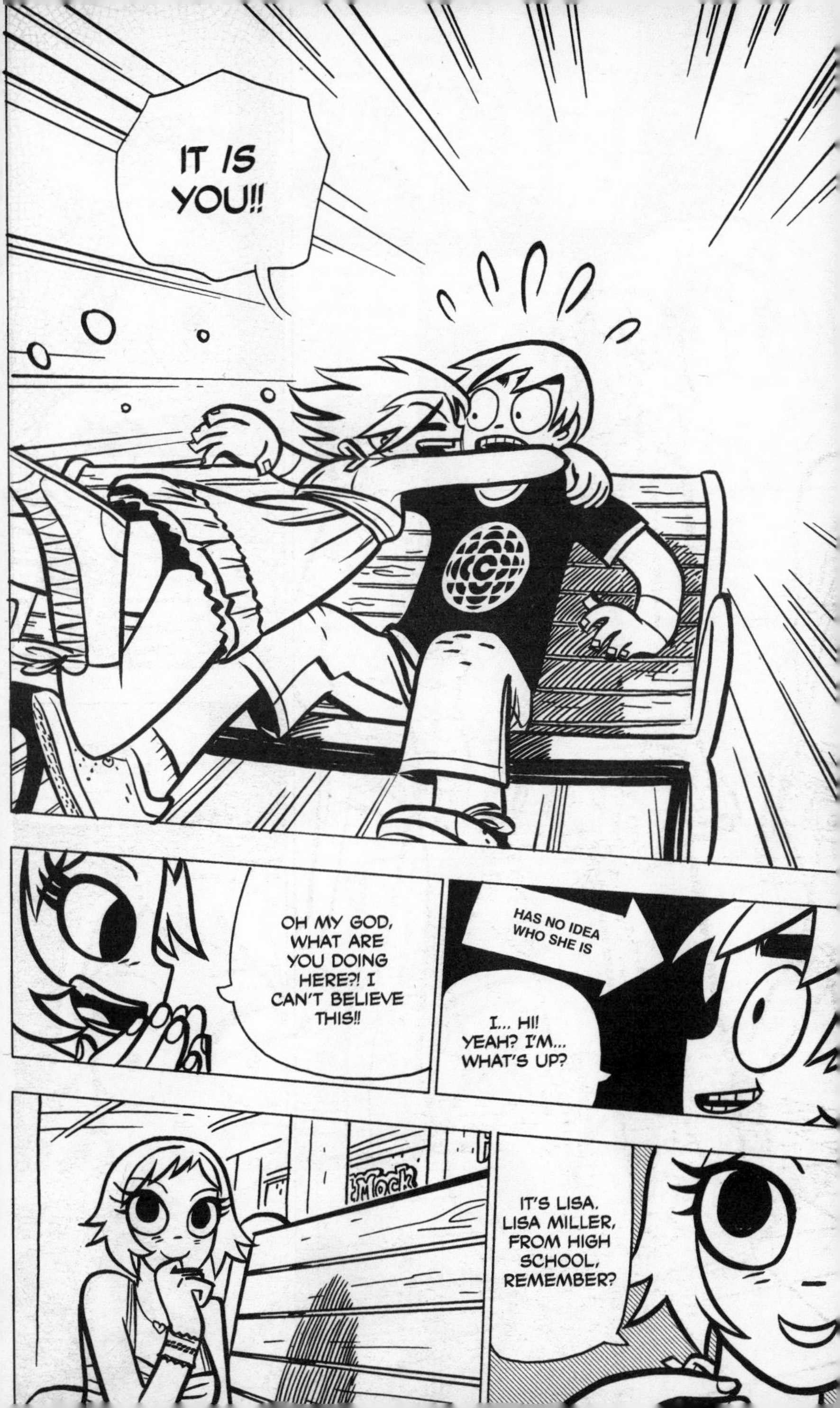
IT IS YOU!!
OH MY GOD, WHAT ARE YOU DOING HERE?! I CAN'T BELIEVE THIS!!
HAS NO IDEA WHO SHE IS
I... HI! YEAH? I'M... WHAT'S UP?
IT'S LISA. LISA MILLER, FROM HIGH SCHOOL, REMEMBER?

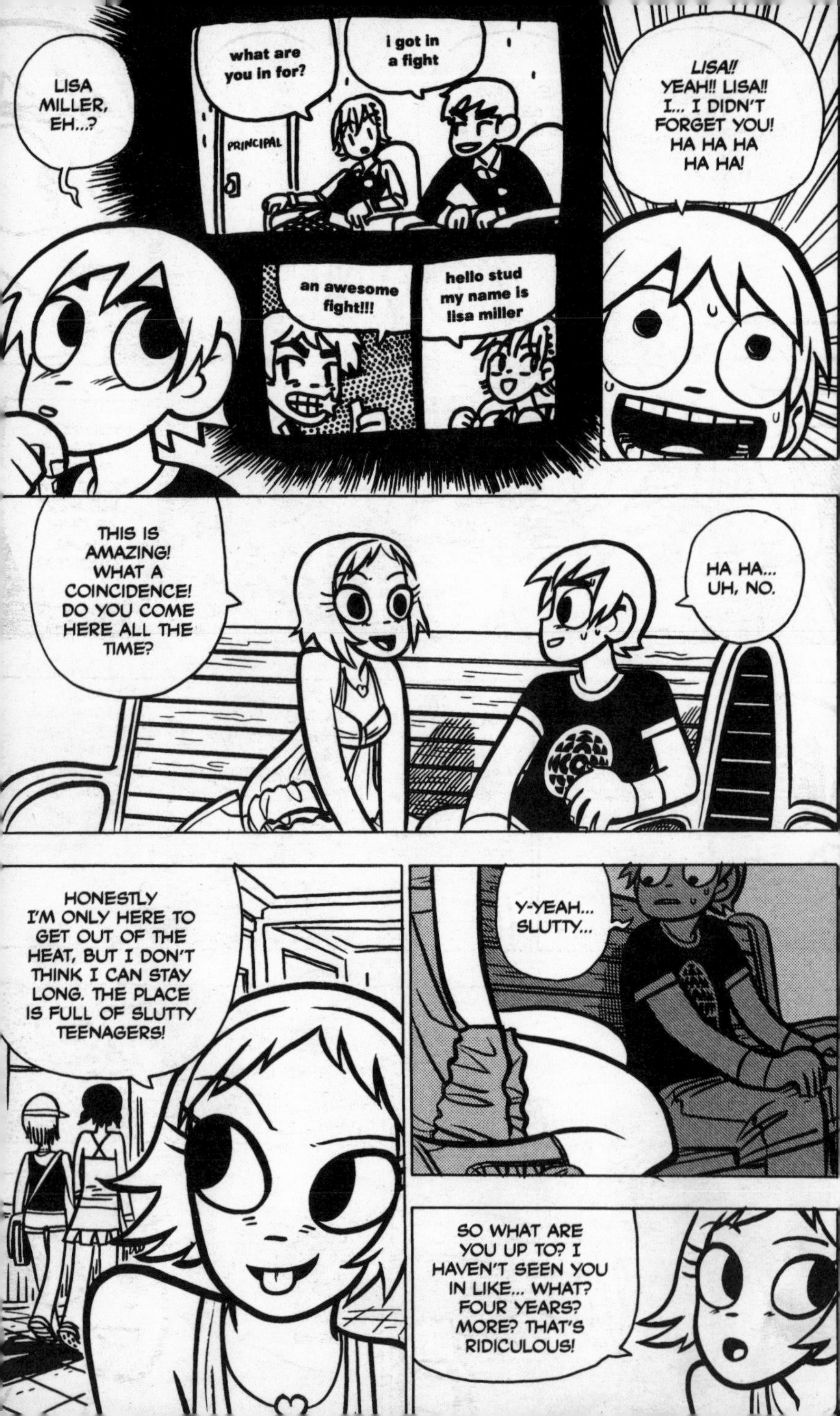
LISA MILLER, EH...?
what are you in for?
i got in a fight
PRINCIPAL
an awesome fight!!!
hello stud my name is lisa miller
LISA!! YEAH!! LISA!! I... I DIDN'T FORGET YOU! HA HA HA HA HA!
THIS IS AMAZING! WHAT A COINCIDENCE! DO YOU COME HERE ALL THE TIME?
HA HA... UH, NO.
HONESTLY I'M ONLY HERE TO GET OUT OF THE HEAT, BUT I DON'T THINK I CAN STAY LONG. THE PLACE IS FULL OF SLUTTY TEENAGERS!
Y-YEAH... SLUTTY...
SO WHAT ARE YOU UP TO? I HAVEN'T SEEN YOU IN LIKE... WHAT? FOUR YEARS? MORE? THAT'S RIDICULOUS!

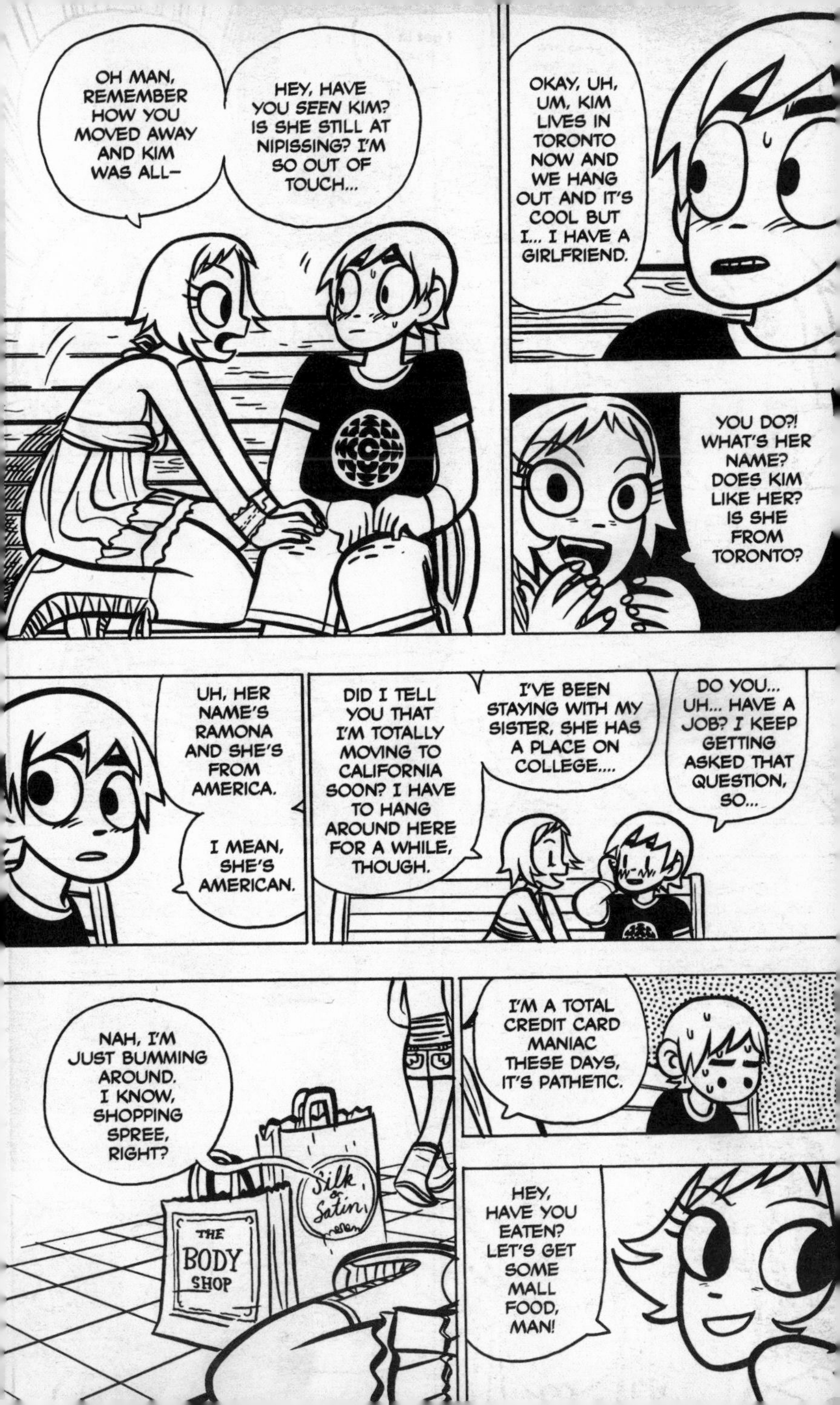

OH MAN, REMEMBER HOW YOU MOVED AWAY AND KIM WAS ALL—
HEY, HAVE YOU SEEN KIM? IS SHE STILL AT NIPISSING? I'M SO OUT OF TOUCH...
OKAY, UH, UM, KIM LIVES IN TORONTO NOW AND WE HANG OUT AND IT'S COOL BUT I... I HAVE A GIRLFRIEND.
YOU DO?! WHAT'S HER NAME? DOES KIM LIKE HER? IS SHE FROM TORONTO?
UH, HER NAME'S RAMONA AND SHE'S FROM AMERICA.
I MEAN, SHE'S AMERICAN.
DID I TELL YOU THAT I'M TOTALLY MOVING TO CALIFORNIA SOON? I HAVE TO HANG AROUND HERE FOR A WHILE, THOUGH.
I'VE BEEN STAYING WITH MY SISTER, SHE HAS A PLACE ON COLLEGE....
DO YOU... UH... HAVE A JOB? I KEEP GETTING ASKED THAT QUESTION, SO...
NAH, I'M JUST BUMMING AROUND. I KNOW, SHOPPING SPREE, RIGHT?
Silk & Satin
THE BODY SHOP
I'M A TOTAL CREDIT CARD MANIAC THESE DAYS, IT'S PATHETIC.
HEY, HAVE YOU EATEN? LET'S GET SOME MALL FOOD, MAN!

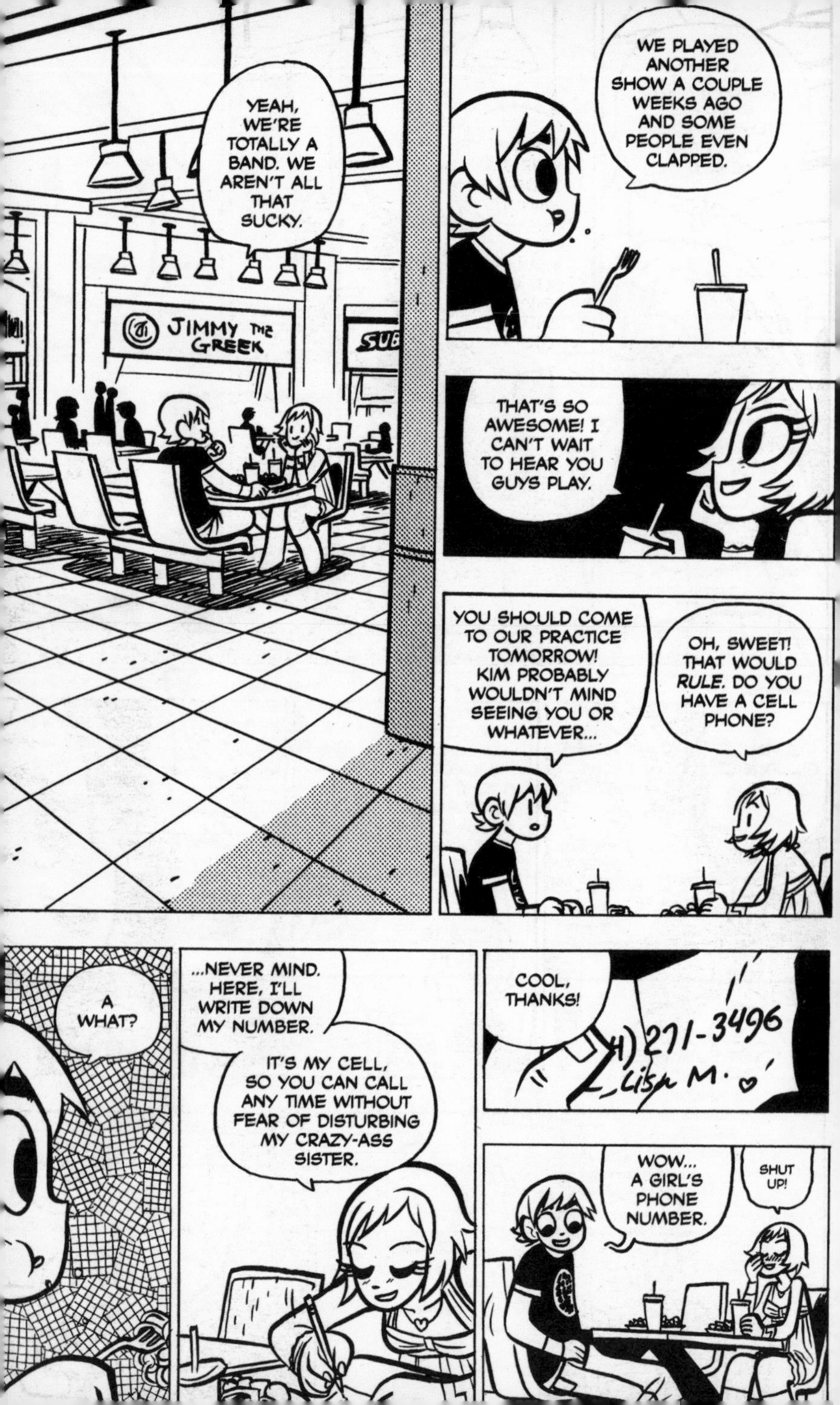
YEAH, WE'RE TOTALLY A BAND. WE AREN'T ALL THAT SUCKY.
JIMMY THE GREEK
SUB
WE PLAYED ANOTHER SHOW A COUPLE WEEKS AGO AND SOME PEOPLE EVEN CLAPPED.
THAT'S SO AWESOME! I CAN'T WAIT TO HEAR YOU GUYS PLAY.
YOU SHOULD COME TO OUR PRACTICE TOMORROW! KIM PROBABLY WOULDN'T MIND SEEING YOU OR WHATEVER...
OH, SWEET! THAT WOULD *RULE*. DO YOU HAVE A CELL PHONE?
A WHAT?
...NEVER MIND. HERE, I'LL WRITE DOWN MY NUMBER.
IT'S MY CELL, SO YOU CAN CALL ANY TIME WITHOUT FEAR OF DISTURBING MY CRAZY-ASS SISTER.
COOL, THANKS!
4) 271-3496
Lisa M.
WOW... A GIRL'S PHONE NUMBER.
SHUT UP!

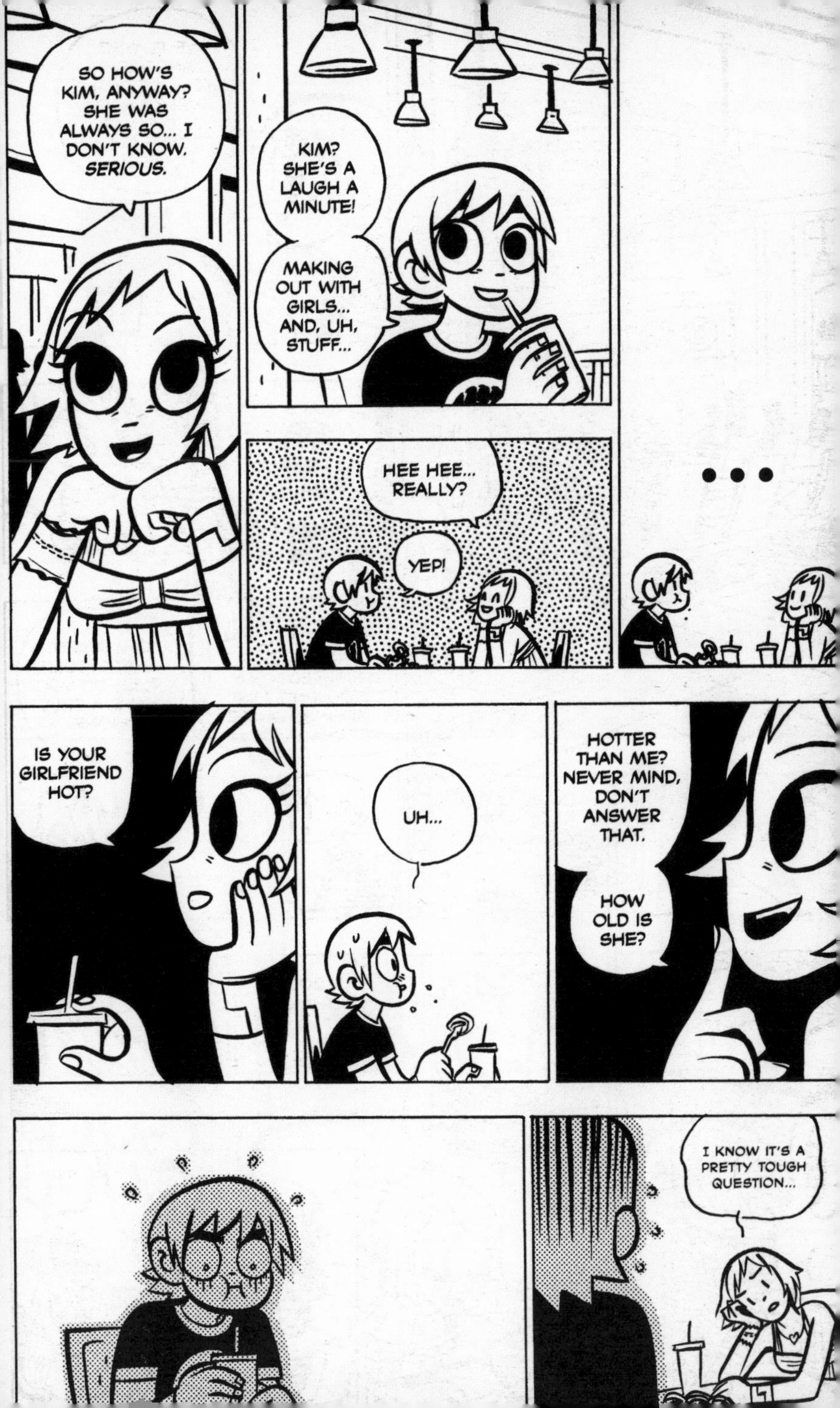
SO HOW'S KIM, ANYWAY? SHE WAS ALWAYS SO... I DON'T KNOW. *SERIOUS.*
KIM? SHE'S A LAUGH A MINUTE!
MAKING OUT WITH GIRLS... AND, UH, STUFF...
HEE HEE... REALLY?
YEP!
...
IS YOUR GIRLFRIEND HOT?
UH...
HOTTER THAN ME? NEVER MIND, DON'T ANSWER THAT.
HOW OLD IS SHE?
I KNOW IT'S A PRETTY TOUGH QUESTION...

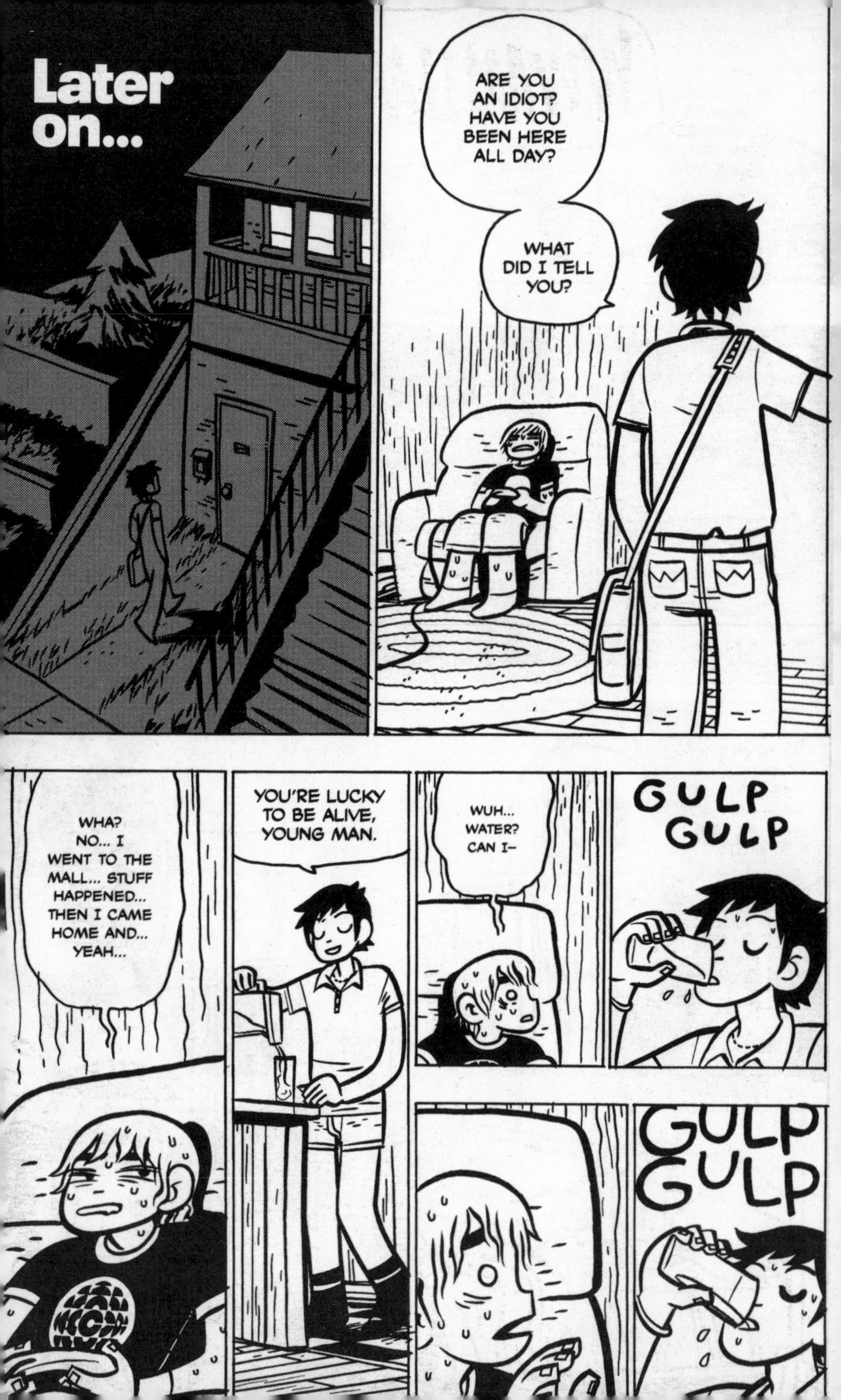

Later on...
ARE YOU AN IDIOT? HAVE YOU BEEN HERE ALL DAY?
WHAT DID I TELL YOU?
WHA? NO... I WENT TO THE MALL... STUFF HAPPENED... THEN I CAME HOME AND... YEAH...
YOU'RE LUCKY TO BE ALIVE, YOUNG MAN.
WUH... WATER? CAN I—
GULP GULP
GULP GULP

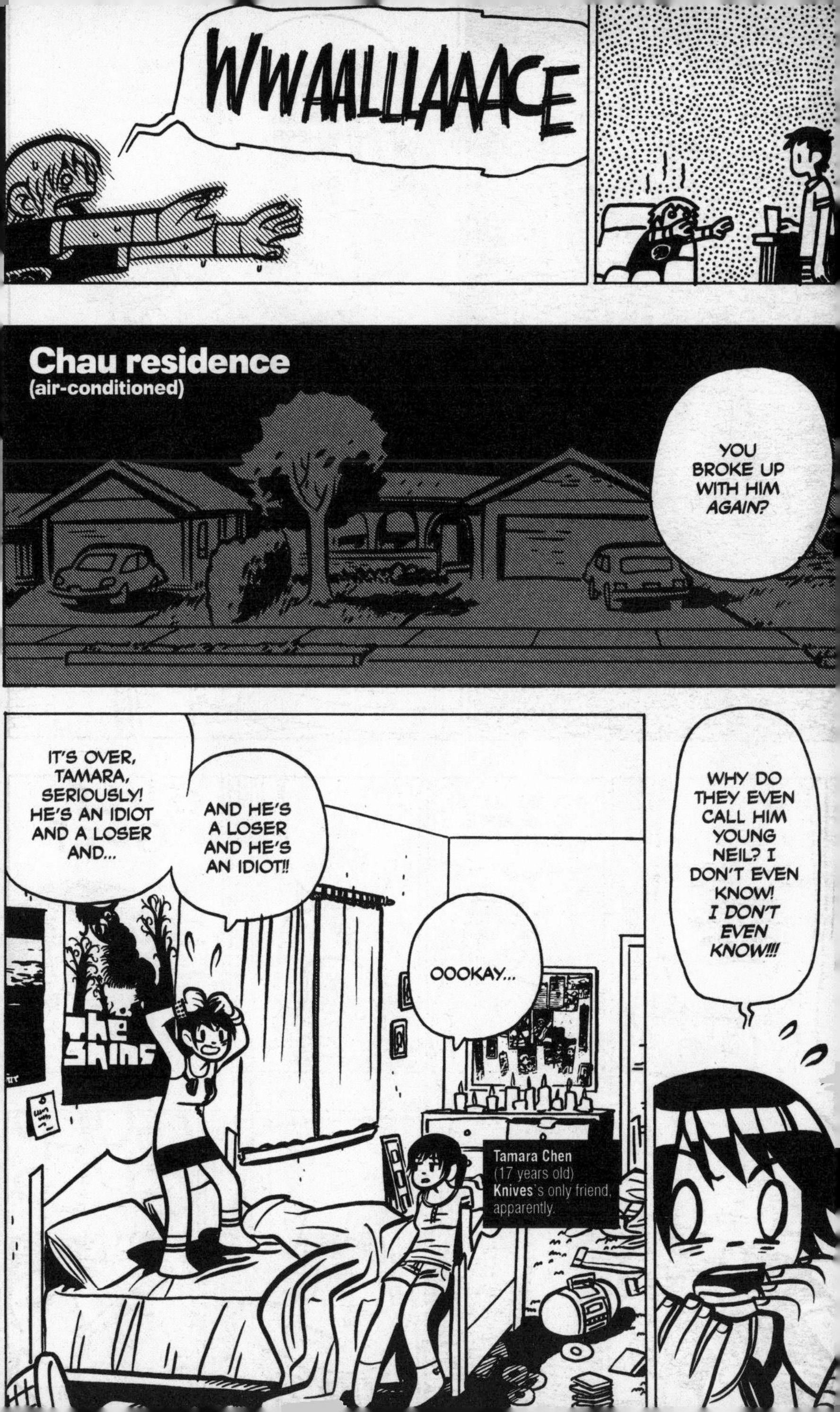
WWAALLLAAACE
Chau residence
(air-conditioned)
YOU BROKE UP WITH HIM *AGAIN?*
IT'S OVER, TAMARA, SERIOUSLY! HE'S AN IDIOT AND A LOSER AND...
AND HE'S A LOSER AND HE'S AN IDIOT!!
THE SHINS
OOOKAY...
Tamara Chen
(17 years old)
Knives's only friend, apparently.
WHY DO THEY EVEN CALL HIM YOUNG NEIL? I DON'T EVEN KNOW! *I DON'T EVEN KNOW!!!*

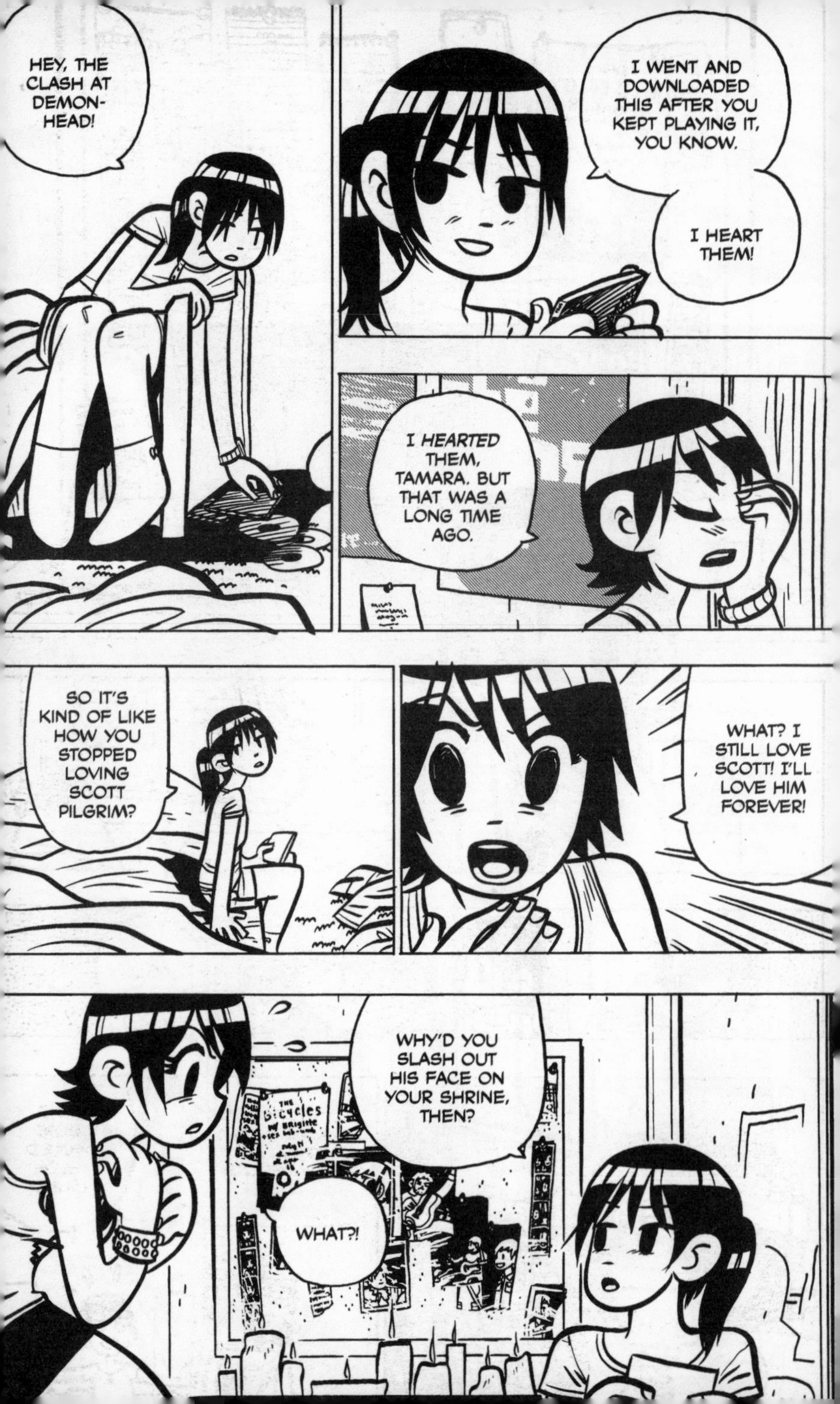
HEY, THE CLASH AT DEMON-HEAD!
I WENT AND DOWNLOADED THIS AFTER YOU KEPT PLAYING IT, YOU KNOW.
I HEART THEM!
I *HEARTED* THEM, TAMARA. BUT THAT WAS A LONG TIME AGO.
SO IT'S KIND OF LIKE HOW YOU STOPPED LOVING SCOTT PILGRIM?
WHAT? I STILL LOVE SCOTT! I'LL LOVE HIM FOREVER!
WHY'D YOU SLASH OUT HIS FACE ON YOUR SHRINE, THEN?
WHAT?!

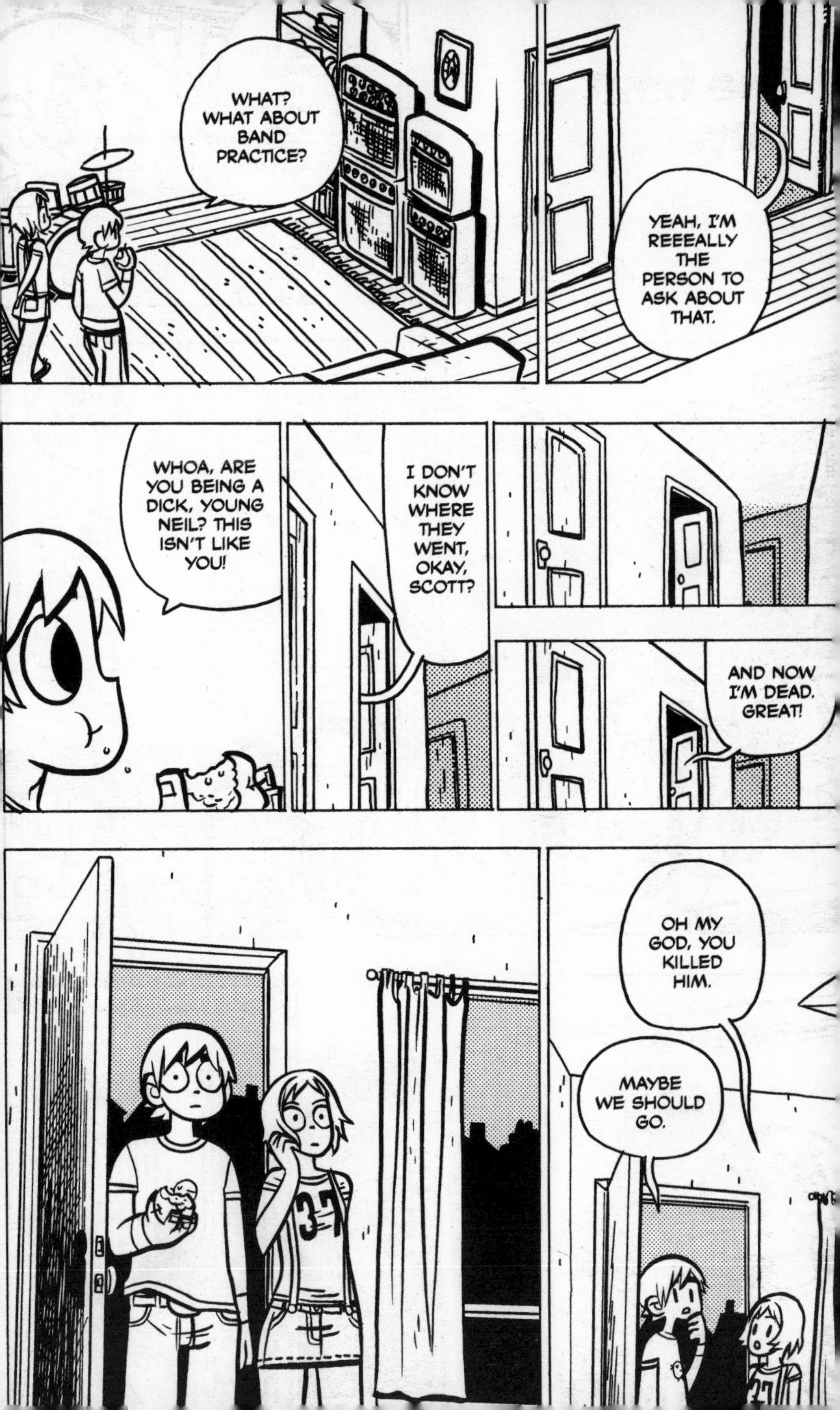
WHAT? WHAT ABOUT BAND PRACTICE?
YEAH, I'M REEEALLY THE PERSON TO ASK ABOUT THAT.
WHOA, ARE YOU BEING A DICK, YOUNG NEIL? THIS ISN'T LIKE YOU!
I DON'T KNOW WHERE THEY WENT, OKAY, SCOTT?
AND NOW I'M DEAD. GREAT!
OH MY GOD, YOU KILLED HIM.
MAYBE WE SHOULD GO.

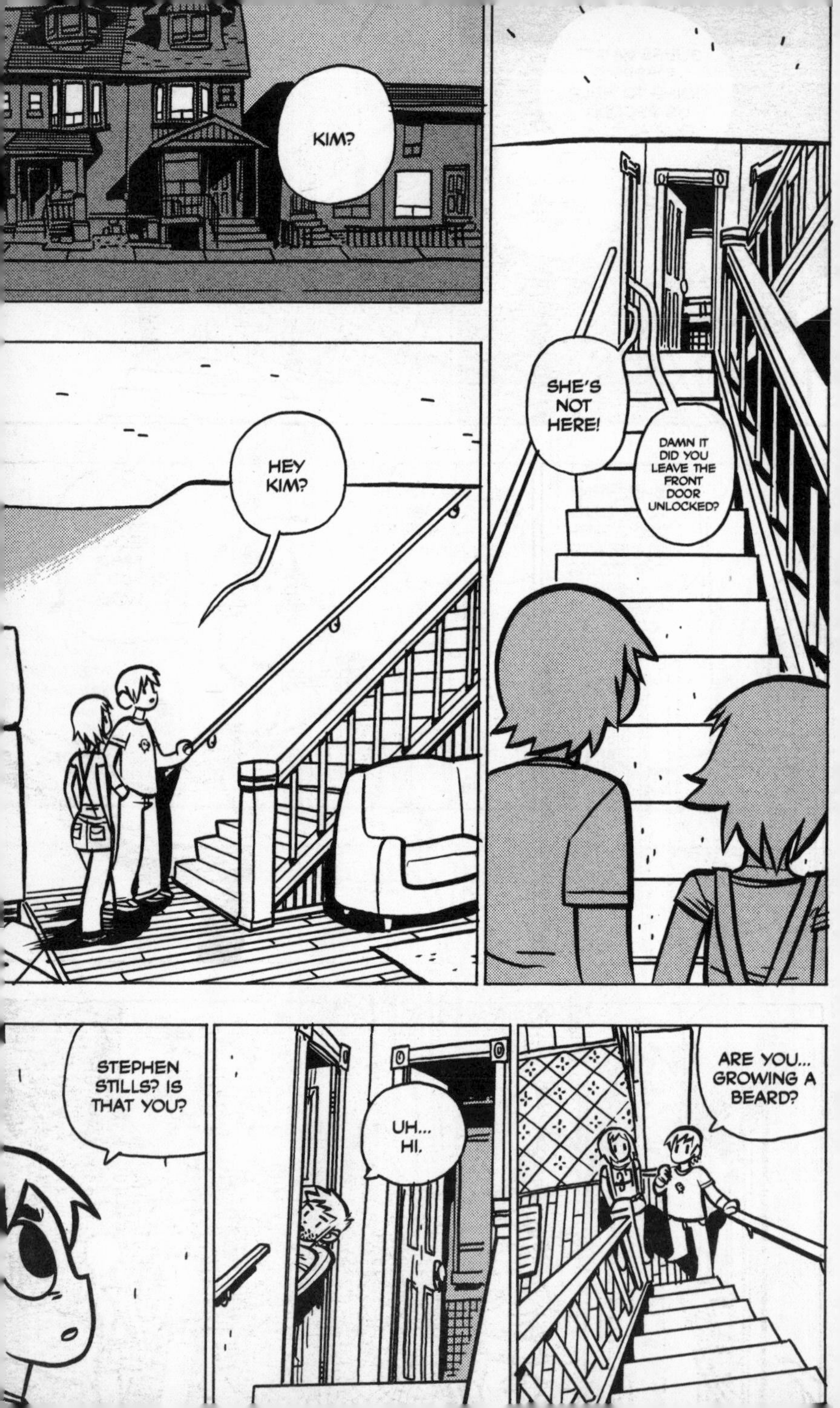
KIM?
HEY KIM?
SHE'S NOT HERE!
DAMN IT DID YOU LEAVE THE FRONT DOOR UNLOCKED?
STEPHEN STILLS? IS THAT YOU?
UH... HI.
ARE YOU... GROWING A BEARD?

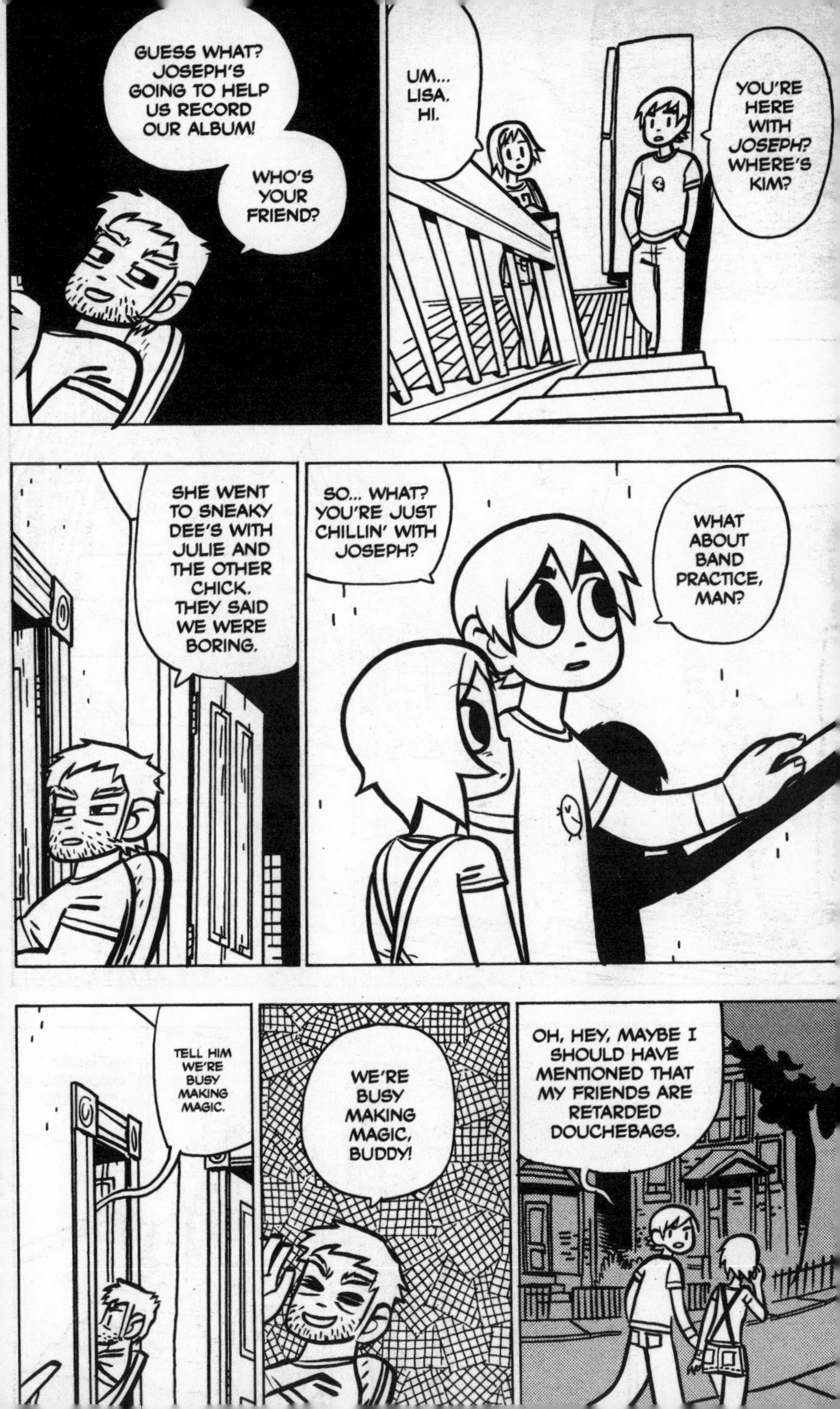
GUESS WHAT? JOSEPH'S GOING TO HELP US RECORD OUR ALBUM!
WHO'S YOUR FRIEND?
UM... LISA. HI.
YOU'RE HERE WITH JOSEPH? WHERE'S KIM?
SHE WENT TO SNEAKY DEE'S WITH JULIE AND THE OTHER CHICK. THEY SAID WE WERE BORING.
SO... WHAT? YOU'RE JUST CHILLIN' WITH JOSEPH?
WHAT ABOUT BAND PRACTICE, MAN?
TELL HIM WE'RE BUSY MAKING MAGIC.
WE'RE BUSY MAKING MAGIC, BUDDY!
OH, HEY, MAYBE I SHOULD HAVE MENTIONED THAT MY FRIENDS ARE RETARDED DOUCHEBAGS.

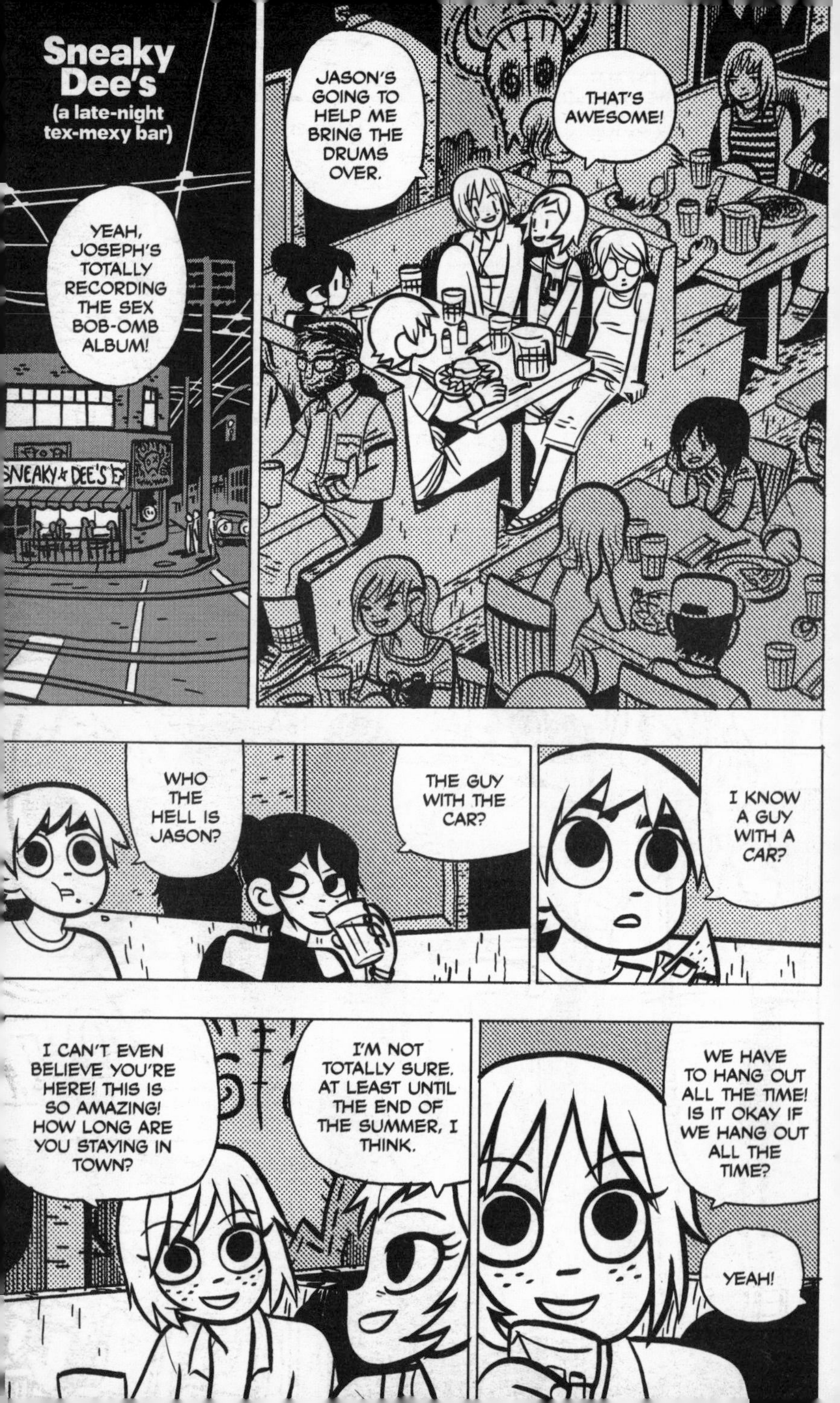
Sneaky Dee's
(a late-night tex-mexy bar)
YEAH, JOSEPH'S TOTALLY RECORDING THE SEX BOB-OMB ALBUM!
SNEAKY DEE'S
JASON'S GOING TO HELP ME BRING THE DRUMS OVER.
THAT'S AWESOME!
WHO THE HELL IS JASON?
THE GUY WITH THE CAR?
I KNOW A GUY WITH A CAR?
I CAN'T EVEN BELIEVE YOU'RE HERE! THIS IS SO AMAZING! HOW LONG ARE YOU STAYING IN TOWN?
I'M NOT TOTALLY SURE. AT LEAST UNTIL THE END OF THE SUMMER, I THINK.
WE HAVE TO HANG OUT ALL THE TIME! IS IT OKAY IF WE HANG OUT ALL THE TIME?
YEAH!

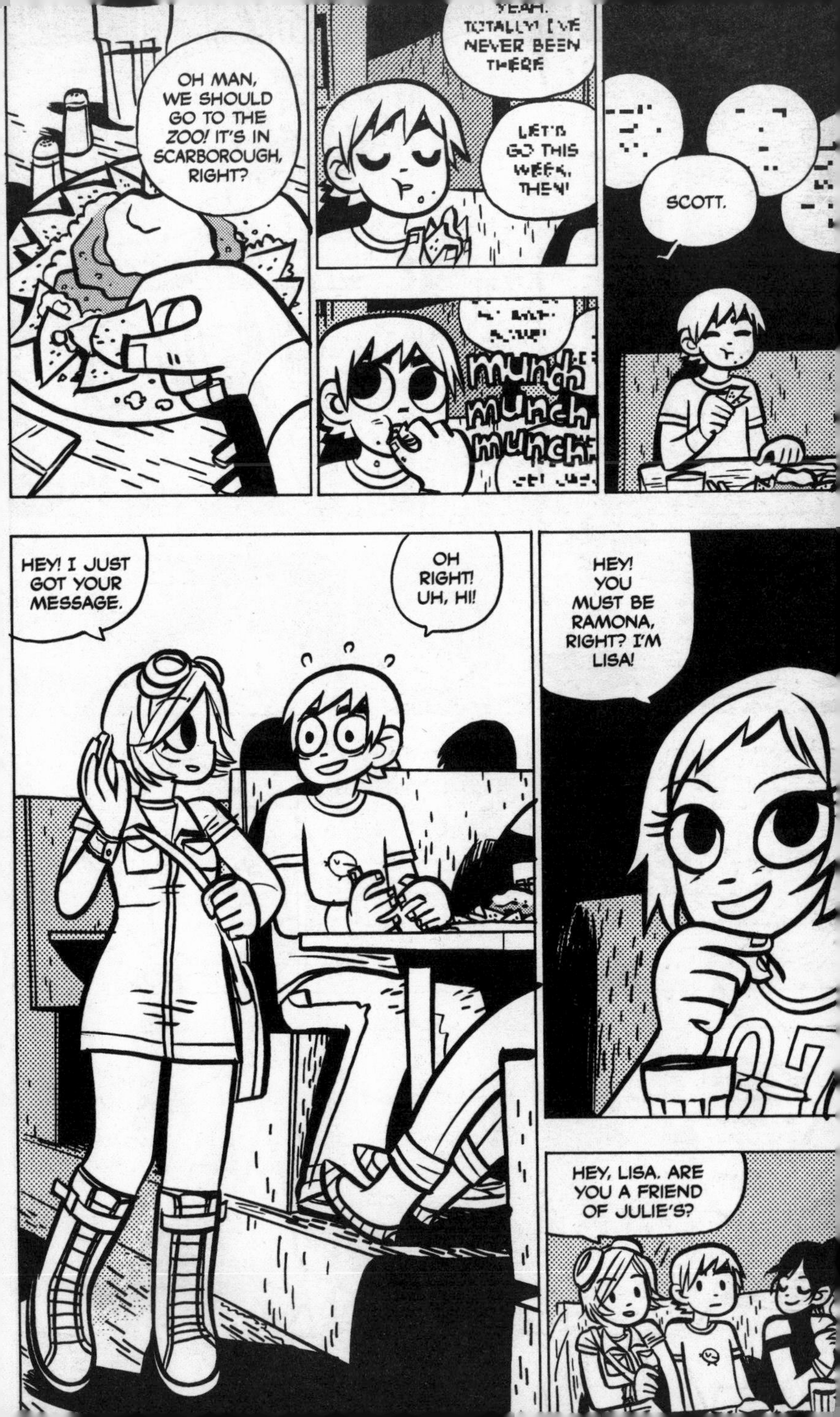
OH MAN, WE SHOULD GO TO THE ZOO! IT'S IN SCARBOROUGH, RIGHT?
YEAH. TOTALLY! I'VE NEVER BEEN THERE
LET'S GO THIS WEEK, THEN!
munch munch munch
SCOTT.
HEY! I JUST GOT YOUR MESSAGE.
OH RIGHT! UH, HI!
HEY! YOU MUST BE RAMONA, RIGHT? I'M LISA!
HEY, LISA. ARE YOU A FRIEND OF JULIE'S?

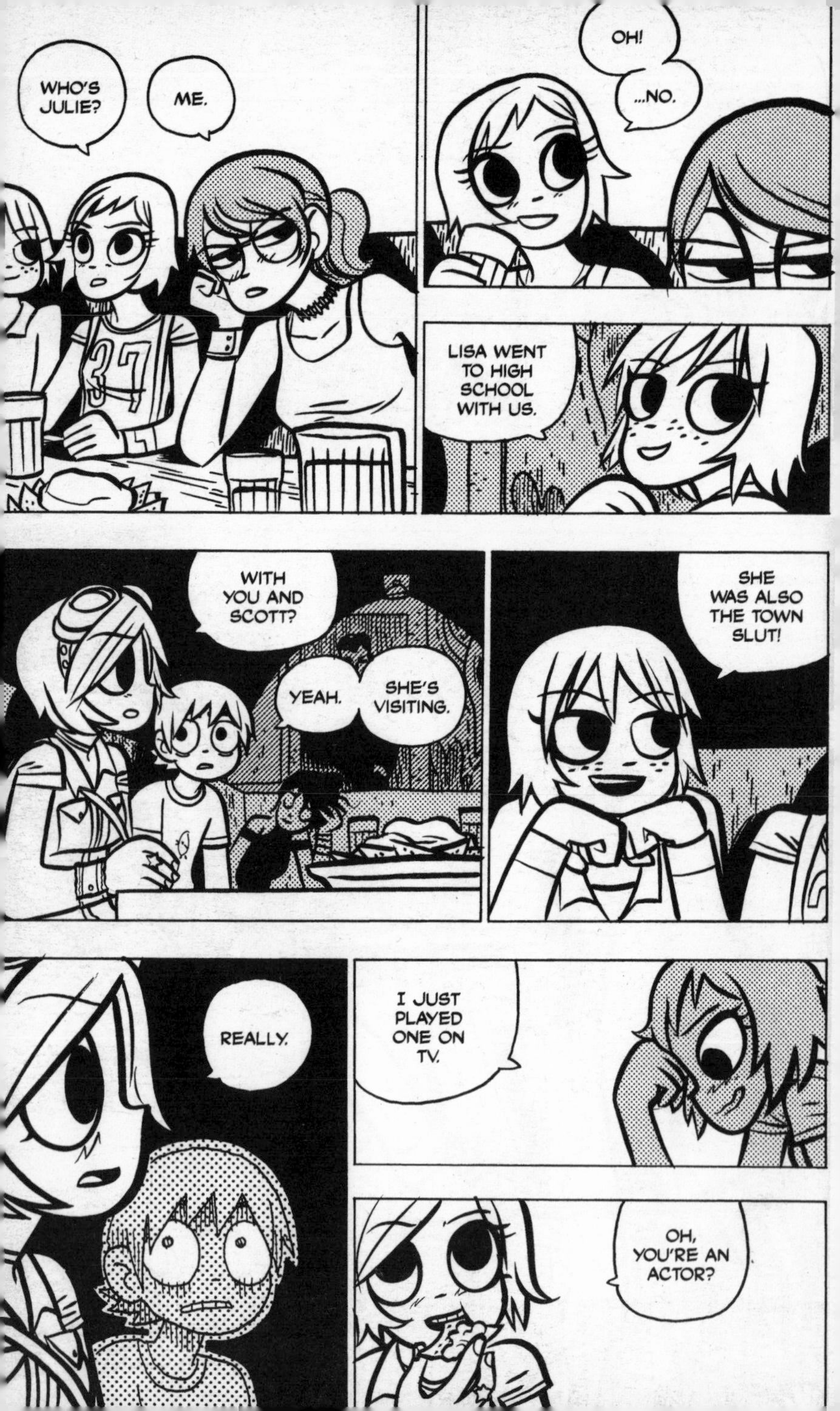
WHO'S JULIE?
ME.
OH!
...NO.
LISA WENT TO HIGH SCHOOL WITH US.
WITH YOU AND SCOTT?
YEAH.
SHE'S VISITING.
SHE WAS ALSO THE TOWN SLUT!
REALLY.
I JUST PLAYED ONE ON TV.
OH, YOU'RE AN ACTOR?

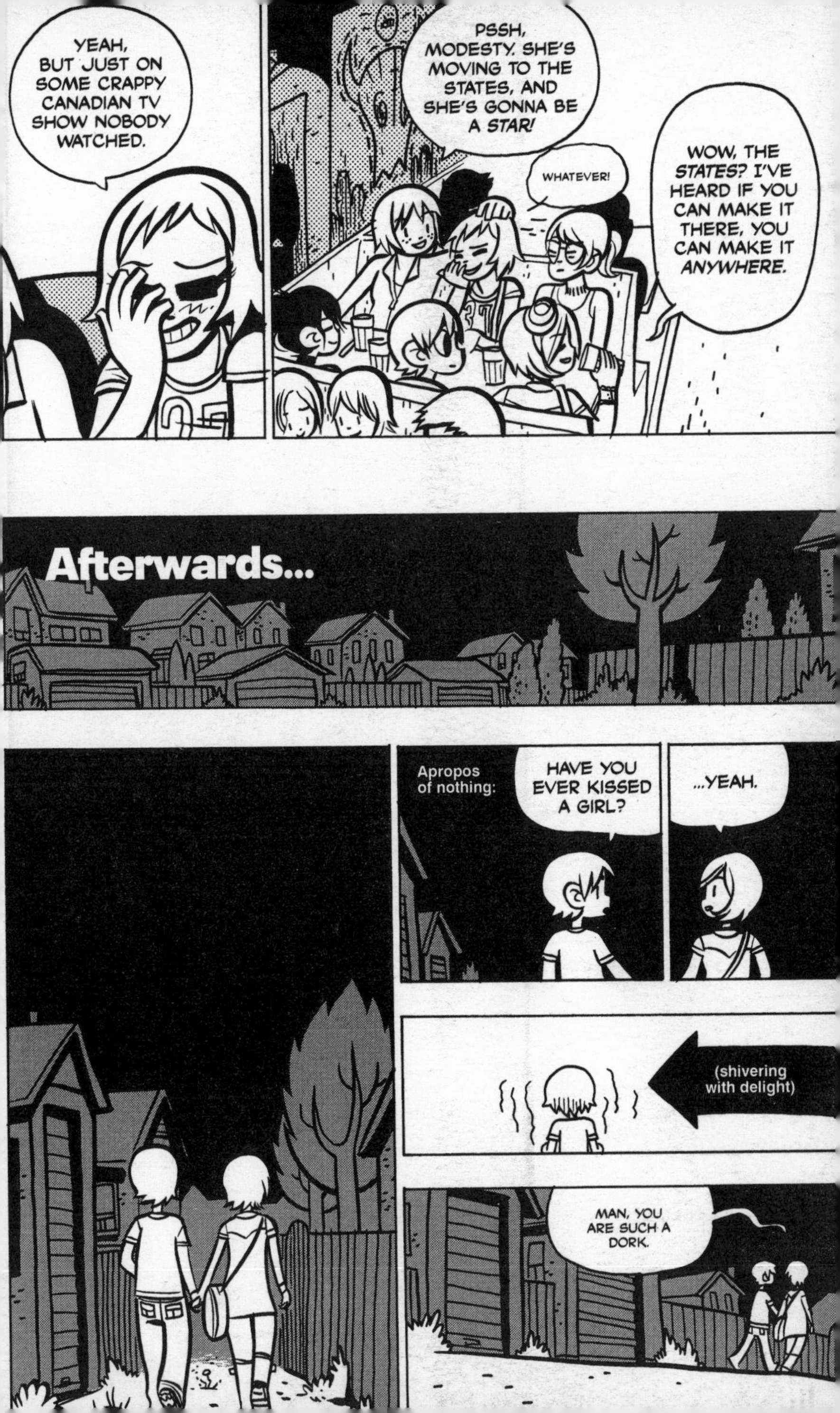
YEAH, BUT JUST ON SOME CRAPPY CANADIAN TV SHOW NOBODY WATCHED.
PSSH, MODESTY. SHE'S MOVING TO THE STATES, AND SHE'S GONNA BE A STAR!
WHATEVER!
WOW, THE STATES? I'VE HEARD IF YOU CAN MAKE IT THERE, YOU CAN MAKE IT ANYWHERE.
Afterwards...
Apropos of nothing:
HAVE YOU EVER KISSED A GIRL?
...YEAH.
(shivering with delight)
MAN, YOU ARE SUCH A DORK.

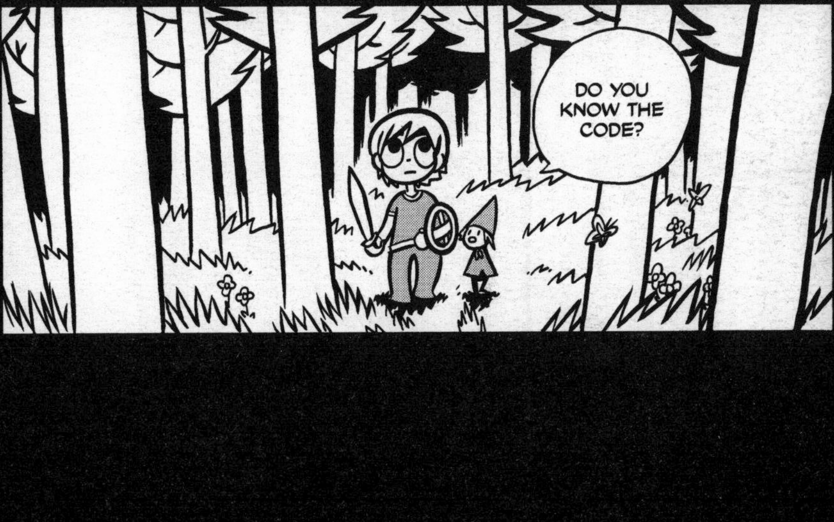
DO YOU KNOW THE CODE?

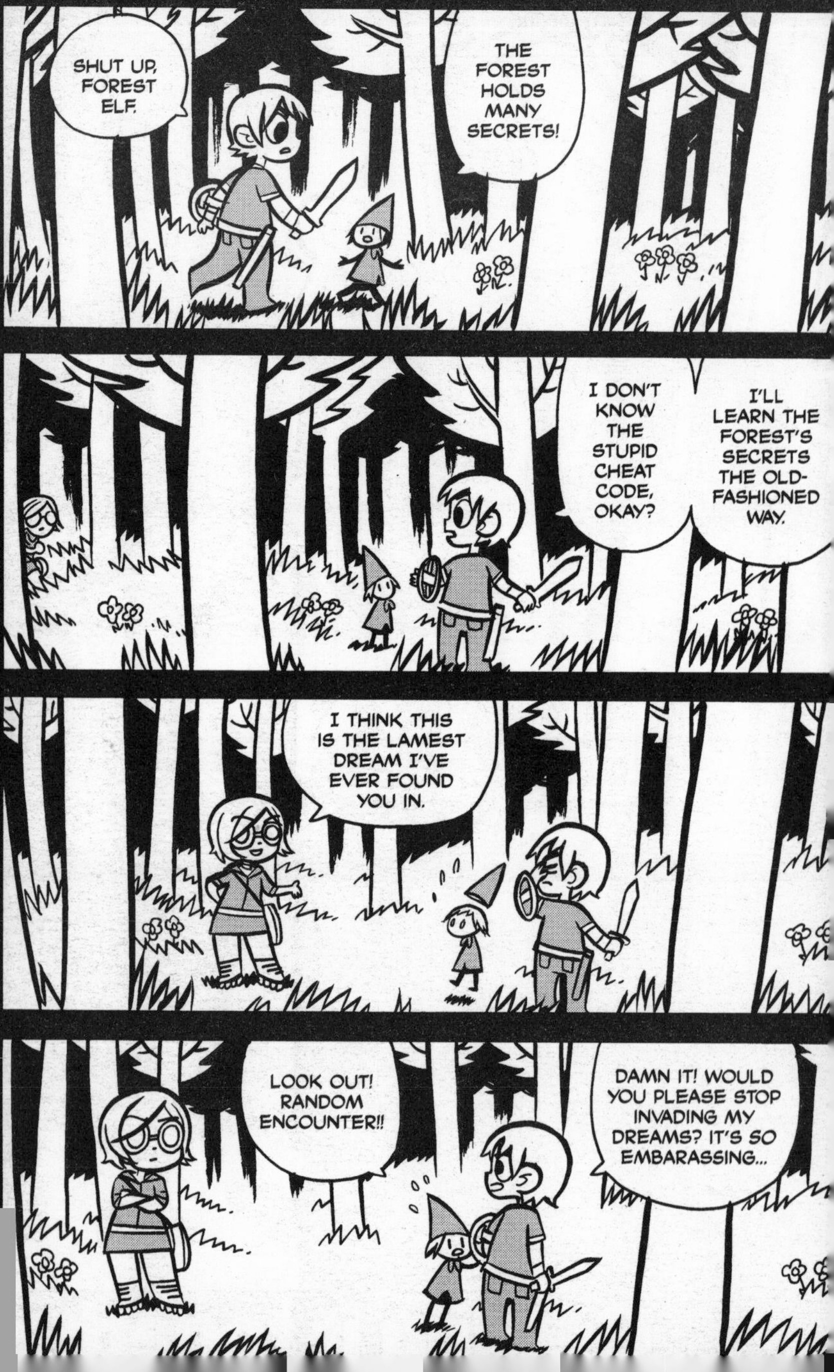
SHUT UP, FOREST ELF.
THE FOREST HOLDS MANY SECRETS!
I DON'T KNOW THE STUPID CHEAT CODE, OKAY?
I'LL LEARN THE FOREST'S SECRETS THE OLD-FASHIONED WAY.
I THINK THIS IS THE LAMEST DREAM I'VE EVER FOUND YOU IN.
LOOK OUT! RANDOM ENCOUNTER!!
DAMN IT! WOULD YOU PLEASE STOP INVADING MY DREAMS? IT'S SO EMBARASSING...

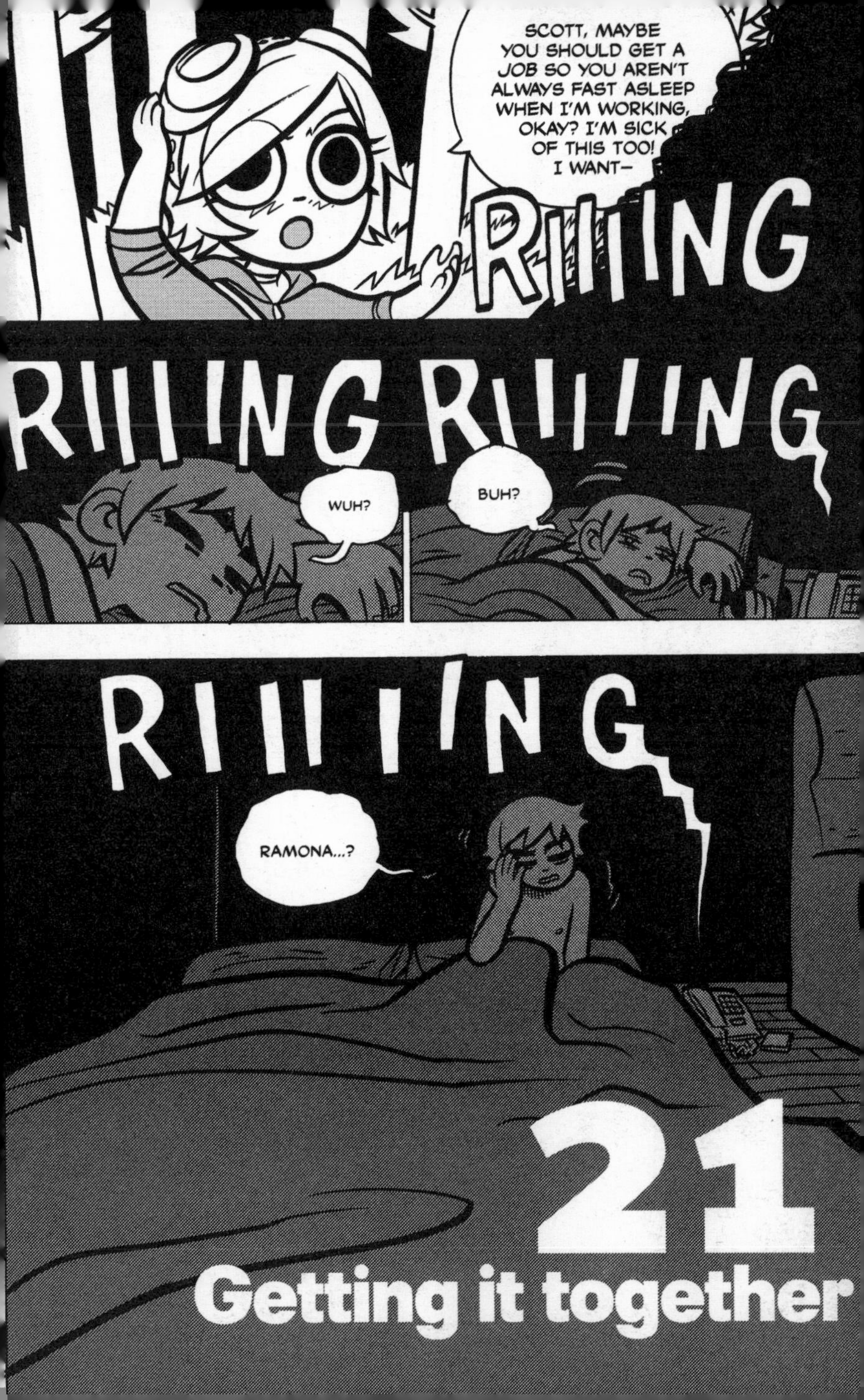

SCOTT, MAYBE YOU SHOULD GET A JOB SO YOU AREN'T ALWAYS FAST ASLEEP WHEN I'M WORKING, OKAY? I'M SICK OF THIS TOO! I WANT–
RIIING
RIIING
RIIIING
WUH?
BUH?
RIIIING
RAMONA...?
21
Getting it together

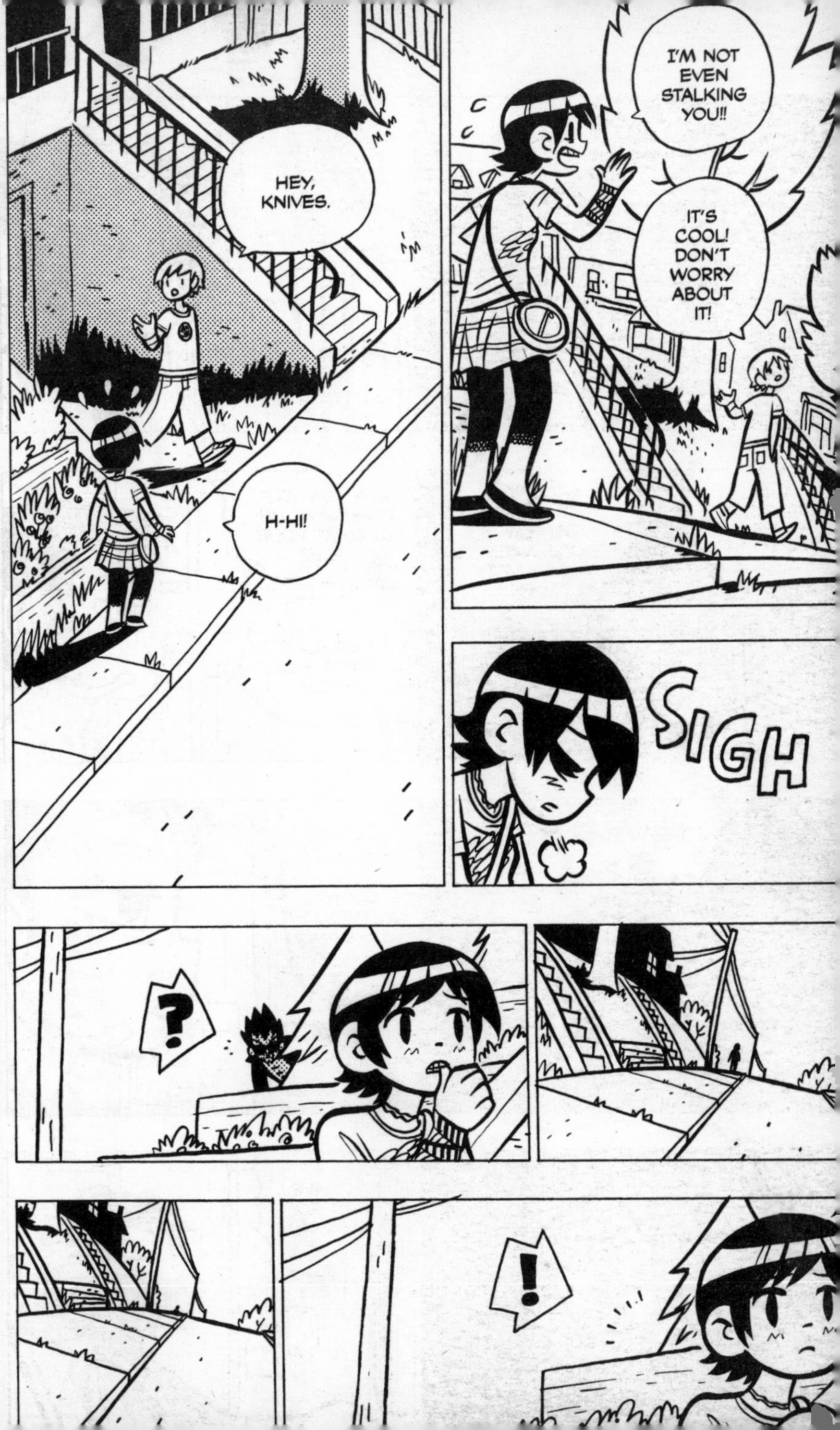
HEY, KNIVES.
H-HI!
I'M NOT EVEN STALKING YOU!!
IT'S COOL! DON'T WORRY ABOUT IT!
SIGH
?
!

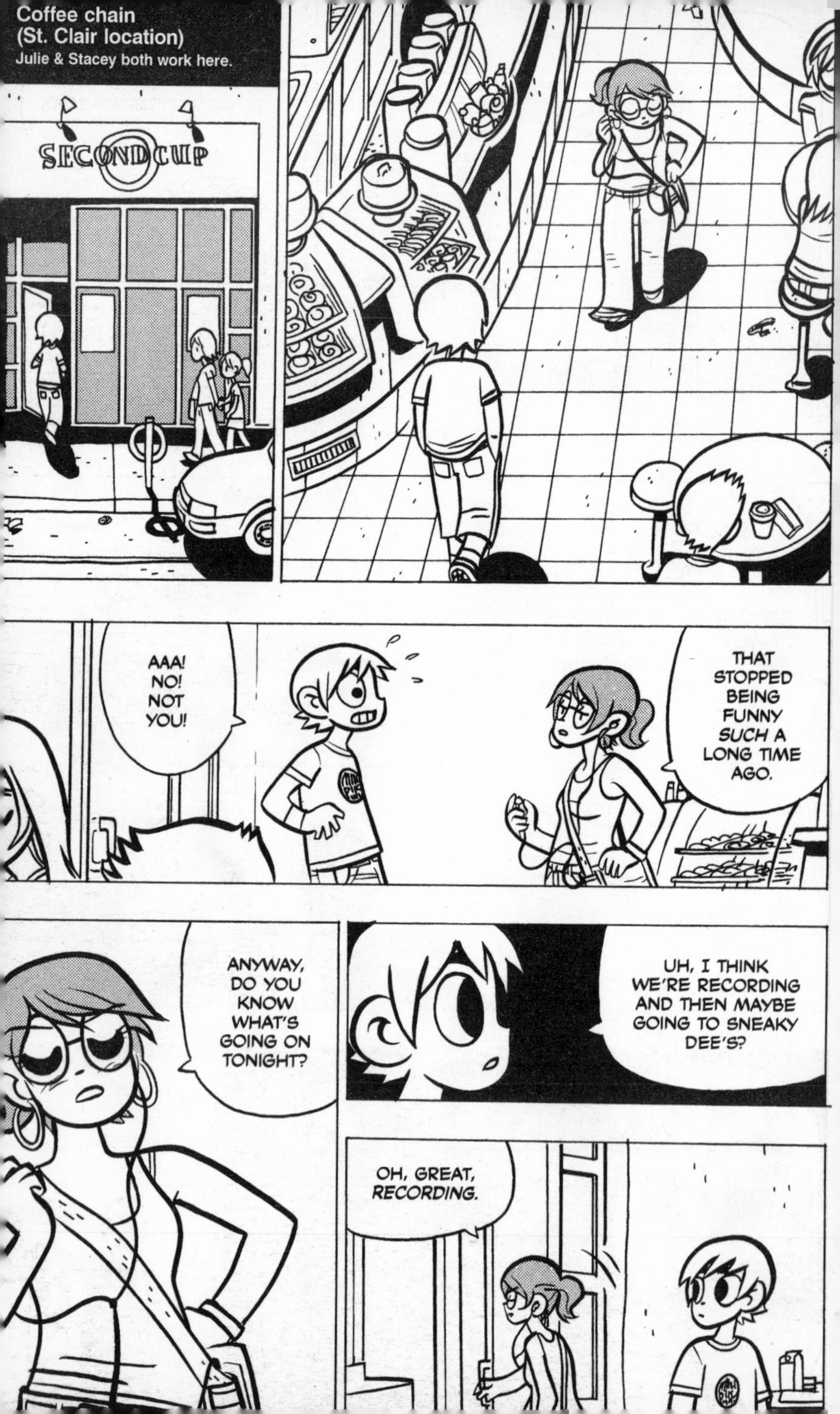
Coffee chain
(St. Clair location)
Julie & Stacey both work here.
SECOND CUP
AAA! NO! NOT YOU!
THAT STOPPED BEING FUNNY *SUCH* A LONG TIME AGO.
ANYWAY, DO YOU KNOW WHAT'S GOING ON TONIGHT?
UH, I THINK WE'RE RECORDING AND THEN MAYBE GOING TO SNEAKY DEE'S?
OH, GREAT, *RECORDING.*

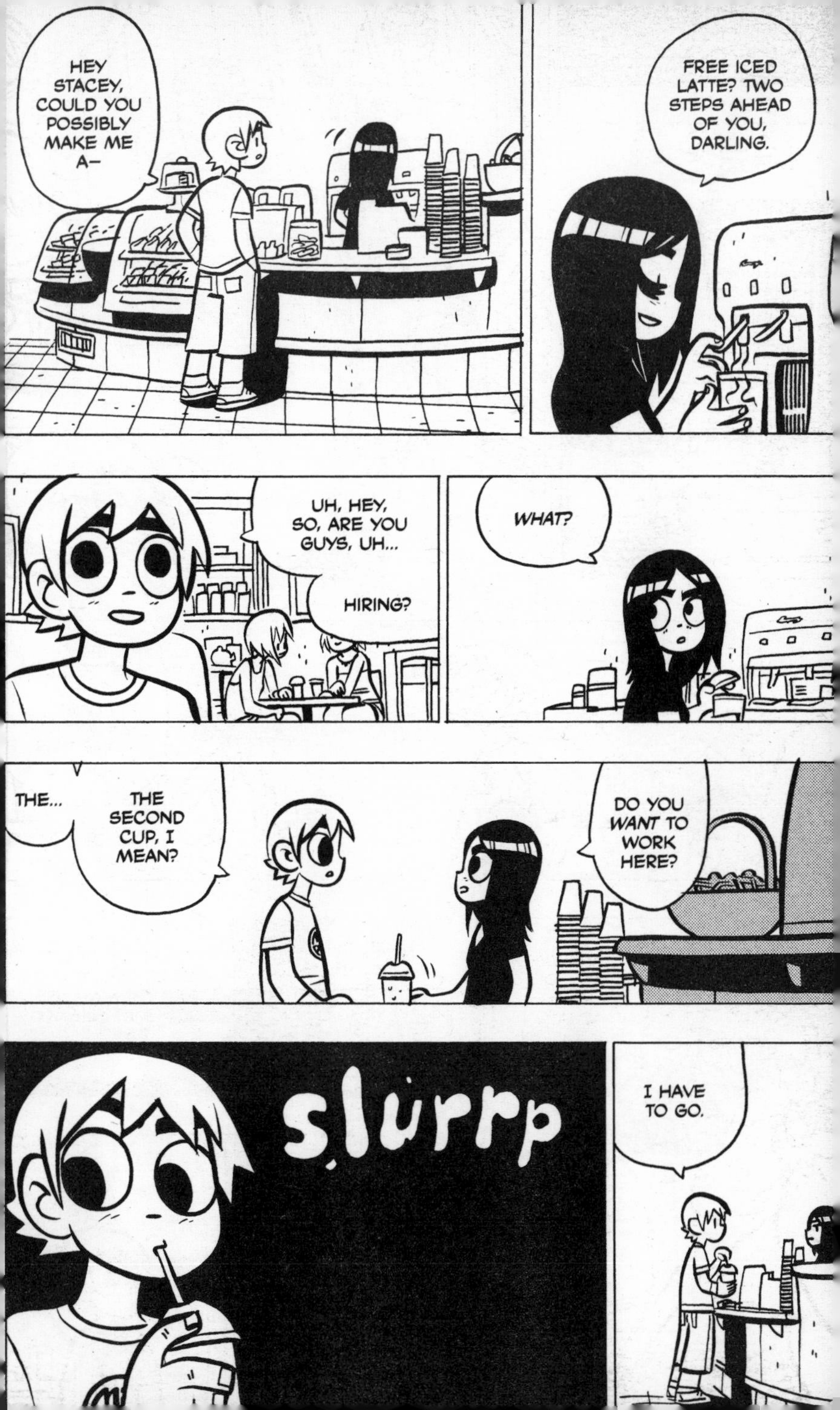
HEY STACEY, COULD YOU POSSIBLY MAKE ME A–
FREE ICED LATTE? TWO STEPS AHEAD OF YOU, DARLING.
UH, HEY, SO, ARE YOU GUYS, UH...
HIRING?
WHAT?
THE...
THE SECOND CUP, I MEAN?
DO YOU WANT TO WORK HERE?
slurrp
I HAVE TO GO.

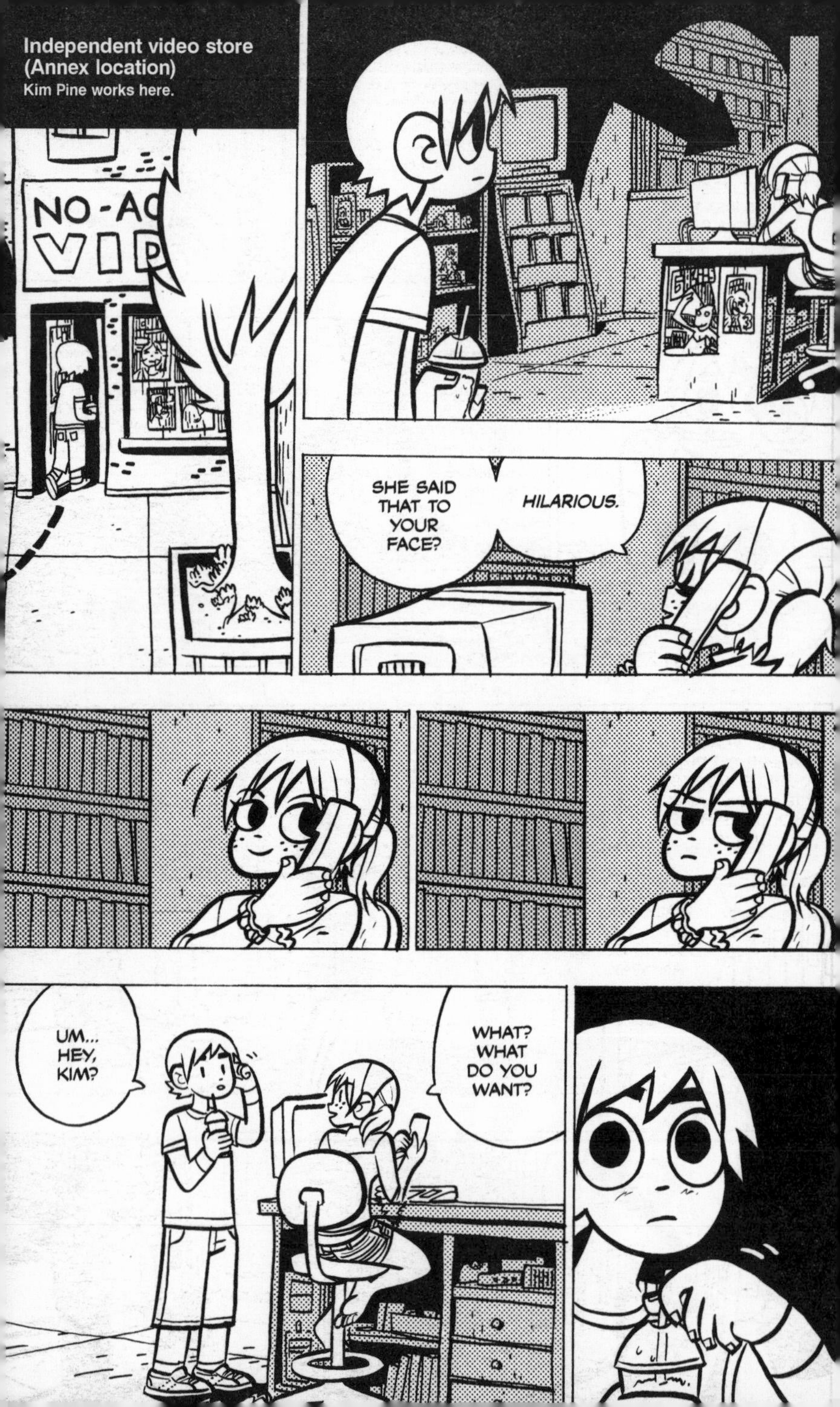

Independent video store
(Annex location)
Kim Pine works here.
NO-AC
VID
SHE SAID THAT TO YOUR FACE?
HILARIOUS.
UM... HEY, KIM?
WHAT? WHAT DO YOU WANT?

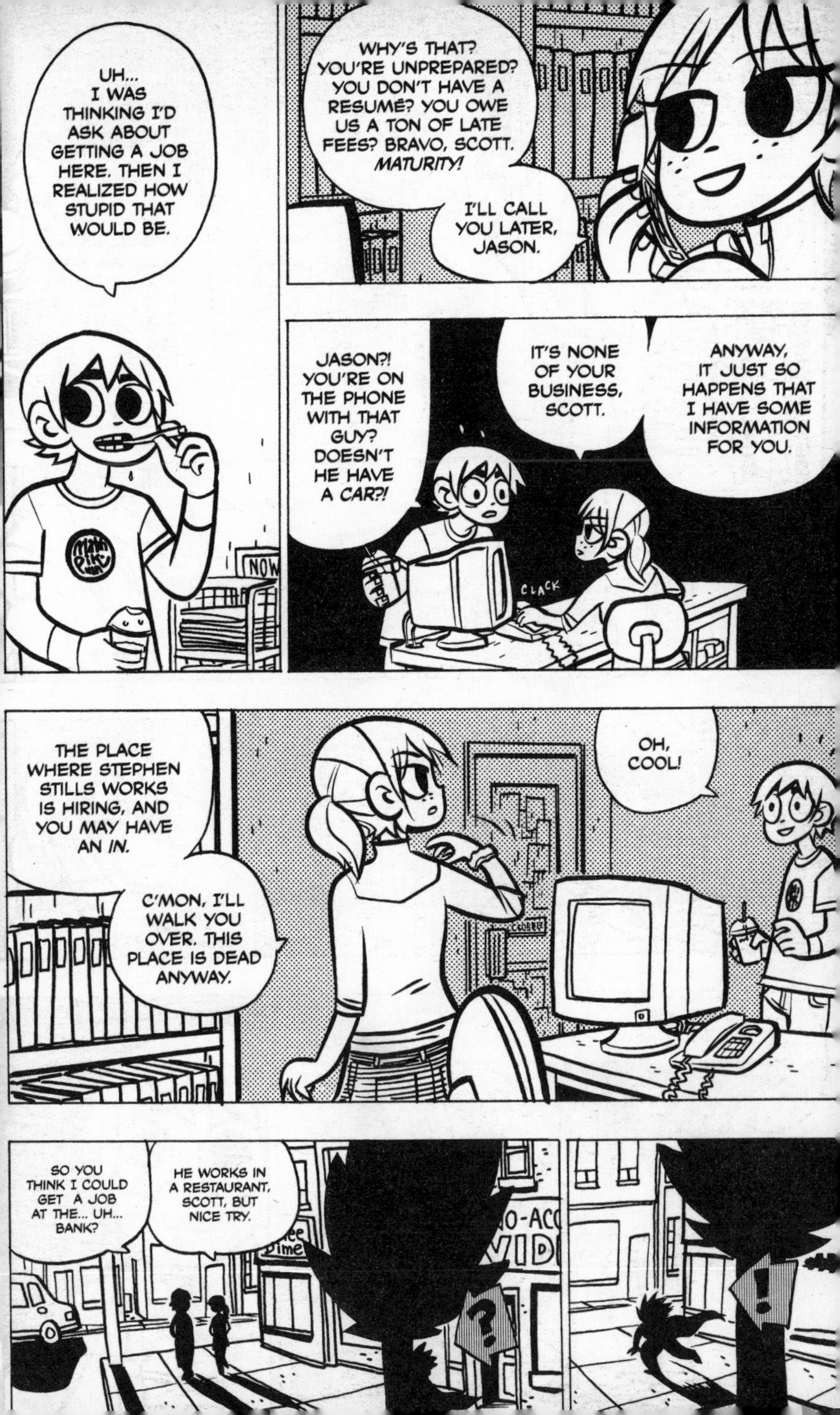
UH... I WAS THINKING I'D ASK ABOUT GETTING A JOB HERE. THEN I REALIZED HOW STUPID THAT WOULD BE.
WHY'S THAT? YOU'RE UNPREPARED? YOU DON'T HAVE A RESUMÉ? YOU OWE US A TON OF LATE FEES? BRAVO, SCOTT. *MATURITY!*
I'LL CALL YOU LATER, JASON.
JASON?! YOU'RE ON THE PHONE WITH THAT GUY? DOESN'T HE HAVE A *CAR?!*
IT'S NONE OF YOUR BUSINESS, SCOTT.
ANYWAY, IT JUST SO HAPPENS THAT I HAVE SOME INFORMATION FOR YOU.
NOW
CLACK
THE PLACE WHERE STEPHEN STILLS WORKS IS HIRING, AND YOU MAY HAVE AN *IN.*
C'MON, I'LL WALK YOU OVER. THIS PLACE IS DEAD ANYWAY.
OH, COOL!
SO YOU THINK I COULD GET A JOB AT THE... UH... BANK?
HE WORKS IN A RESTAURANT, SCOTT, BUT NICE TRY.
?
!

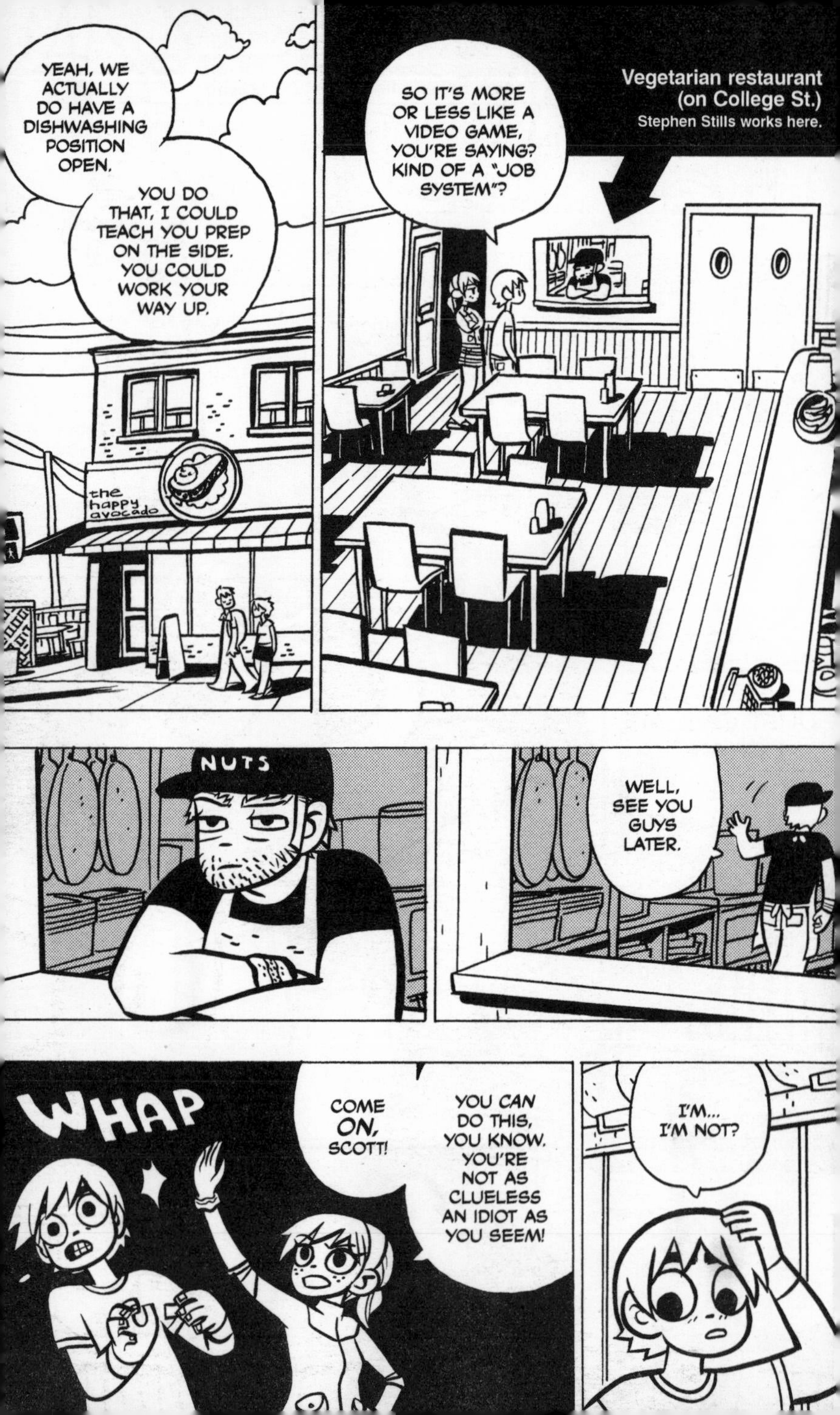
YEAH, WE ACTUALLY DO HAVE A DISHWASHING POSITION OPEN.
YOU DO THAT, I COULD TEACH YOU PREP ON THE SIDE. YOU COULD WORK YOUR WAY UP.
the happy avocado
Vegetarian restaurant (on College St.)
Stephen Stills works here.
SO IT'S MORE OR LESS LIKE A VIDEO GAME, YOU'RE SAYING? KIND OF A "JOB SYSTEM"?
NUTS
WELL, SEE YOU GUYS LATER.
WHAP
COME ON, SCOTT!
YOU CAN DO THIS, YOU KNOW. YOU'RE NOT AS CLUELESS AN IDIOT AS YOU SEEM!
I'M... I'M NOT?

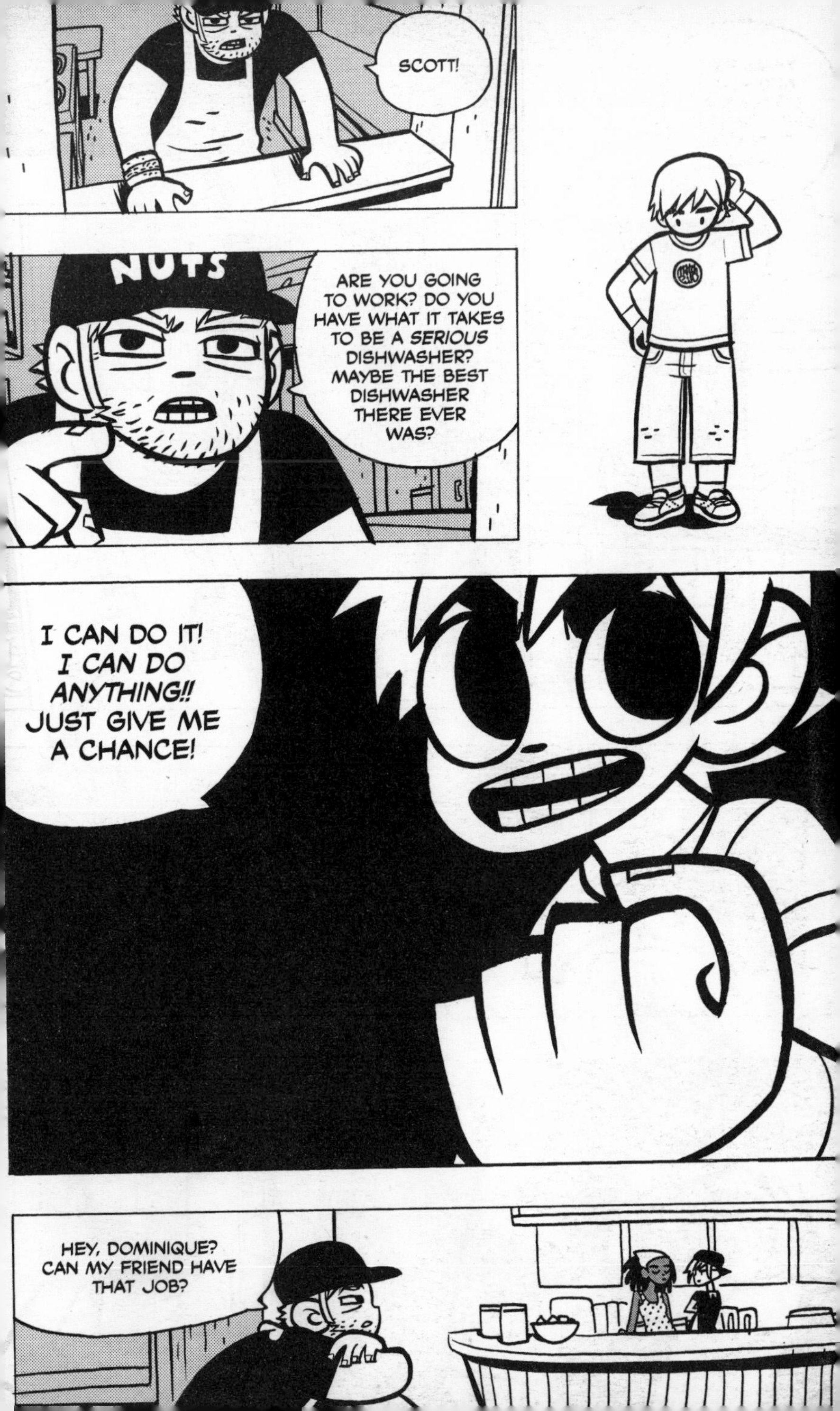
SCOTT!
ARE YOU GOING TO WORK? DO YOU HAVE WHAT IT TAKES TO BE A *SERIOUS* DISHWASHER? MAYBE THE BEST DISHWASHER THERE EVER WAS?
NUTS
I CAN DO IT! *I CAN DO ANYTHING!!* JUST GIVE ME A CHANCE!
HEY, DOMINIQUE? CAN MY FRIEND HAVE THAT JOB?

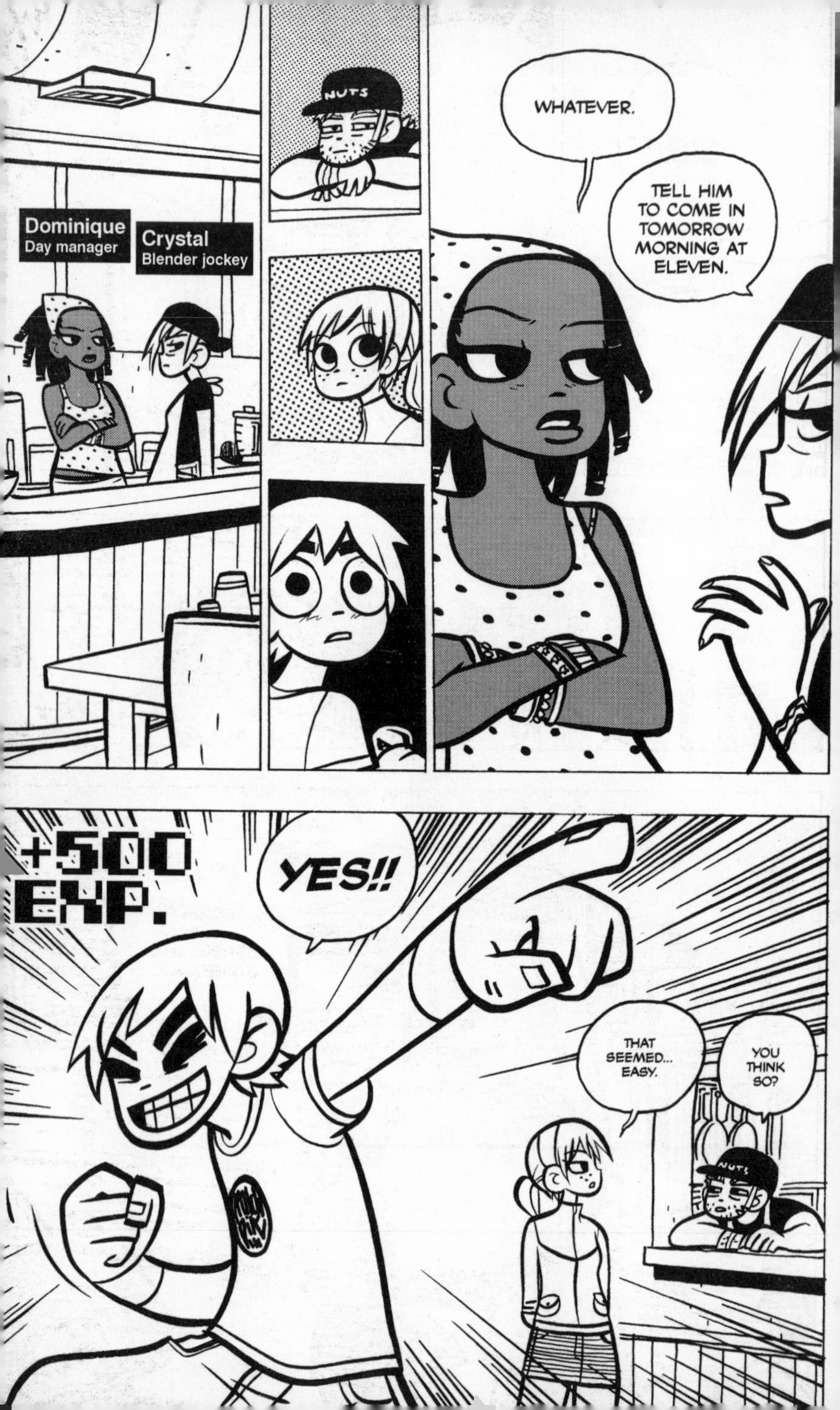

Dominique
Day manager
Crystal
Blender jockey
NUTS
WHATEVER.
TELL HIM TO COME IN TOMORROW MORNING AT ELEVEN.
+500 EXP.
YES!!
THAT SEEMED... EASY.
YOU THINK SO?

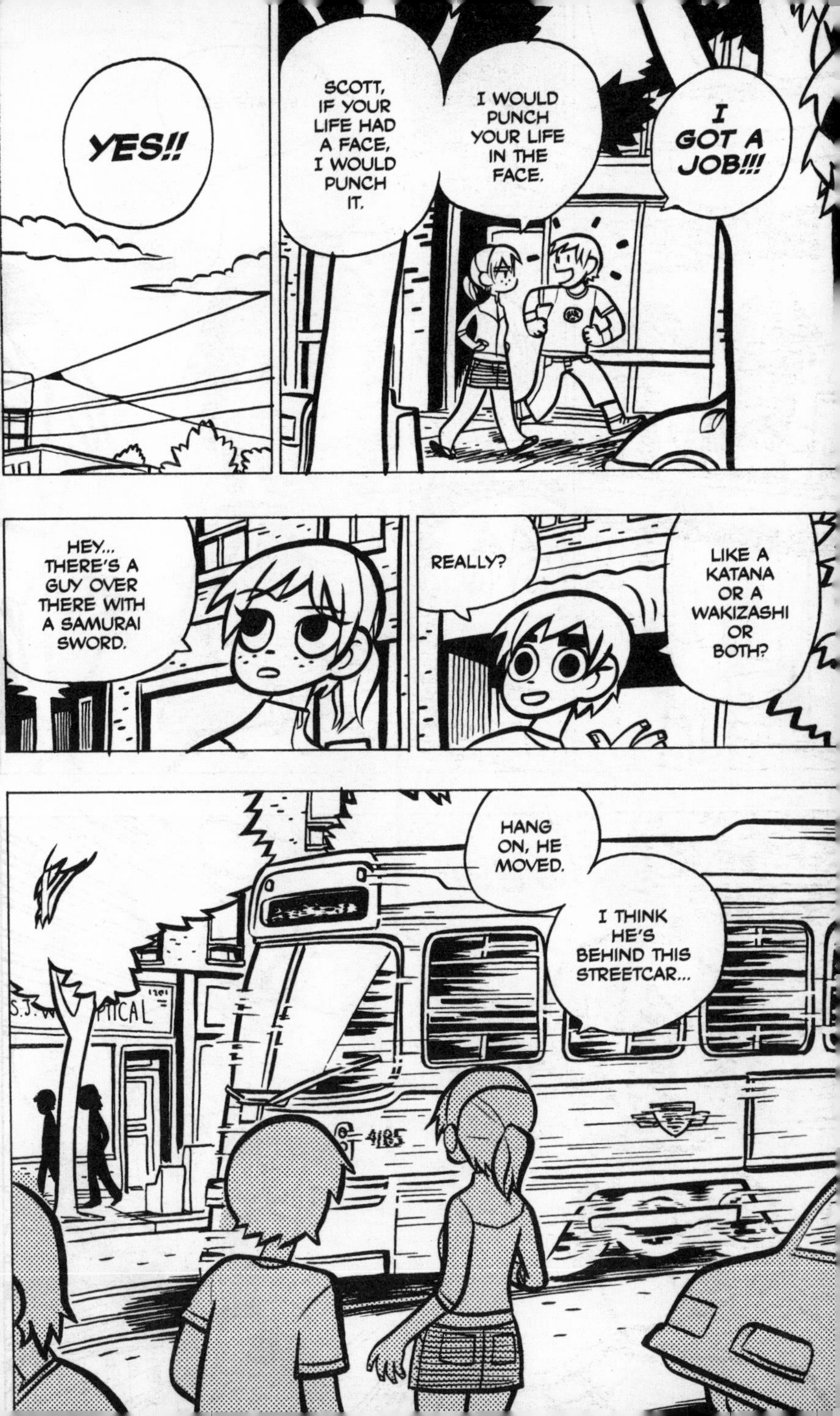
YES!!
SCOTT, IF YOUR LIFE HAD A FACE, I WOULD PUNCH IT.
I WOULD PUNCH YOUR LIFE IN THE FACE.
I GOT A JOB!!!
HEY... THERE'S A GUY OVER THERE WITH A SAMURAI SWORD.
REALLY?
LIKE A KATANA OR A WAKIZASHI OR BOTH?
HANG ON, HE MOVED.
I THINK HE'S BEHIND THIS STREETCAR...
S.J. W PTICAL
1201
4185

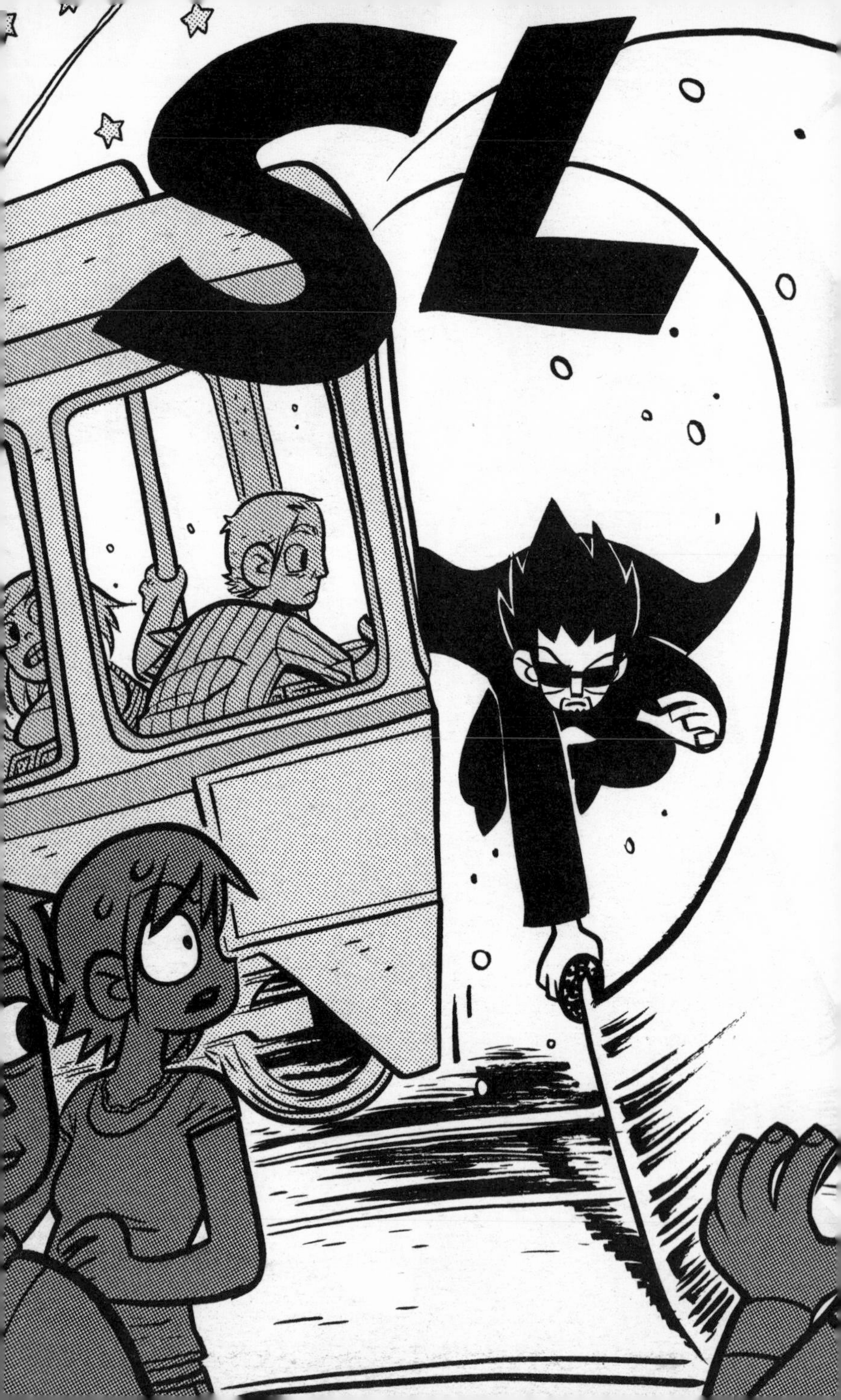
SL

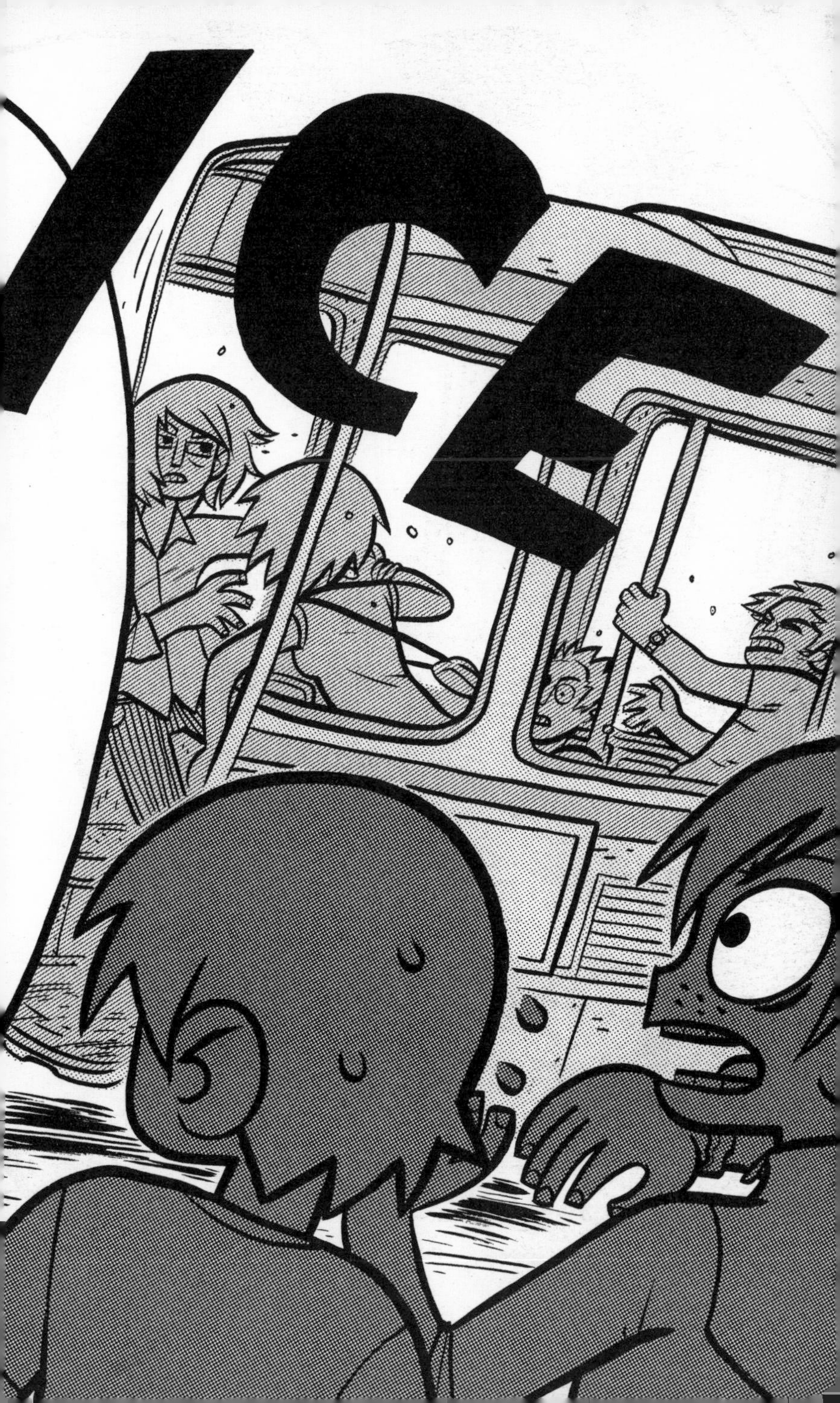

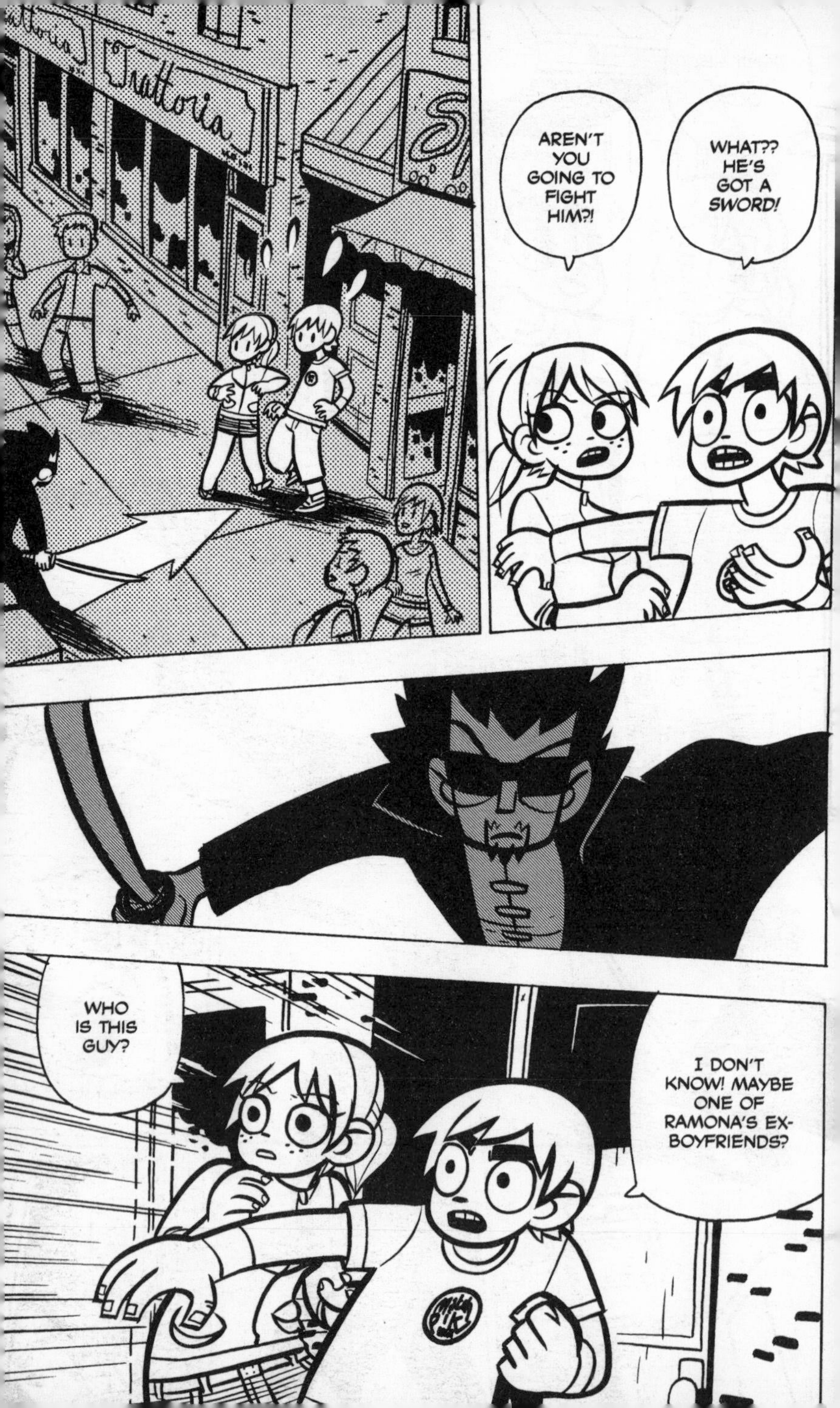
Trattoria
AREN'T YOU GOING TO FIGHT HIM?!
WHAT?? HE'S GOT A SWORD!
WHO IS THIS GUY?
I DON'T KNOW! MAYBE ONE OF RAMONA'S EX-BOYFRIENDS?

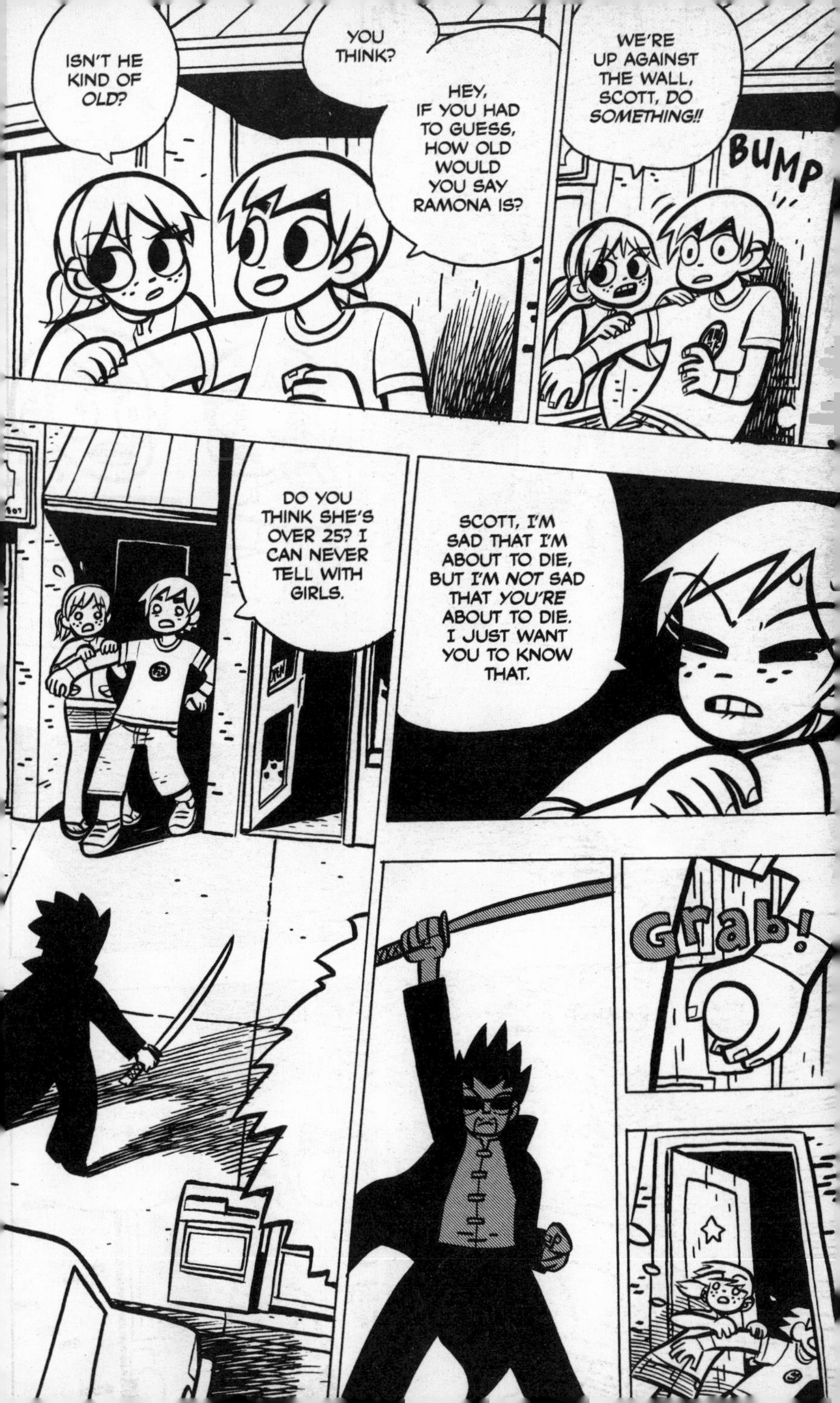

ISN'T HE KIND OF *OLD?*
YOU THINK?
HEY, IF YOU HAD TO GUESS, HOW OLD WOULD YOU SAY RAMONA IS?
WE'RE UP AGAINST THE WALL, SCOTT, *DO SOMETHING!!*
BUMP
DO YOU THINK SHE'S OVER 25? I CAN NEVER TELL WITH GIRLS.
SCOTT, I'M SAD THAT I'M ABOUT TO DIE, BUT I'M *NOT* SAD THAT *YOU'RE* ABOUT TO DIE. I JUST WANT YOU TO KNOW THAT.
Grab!

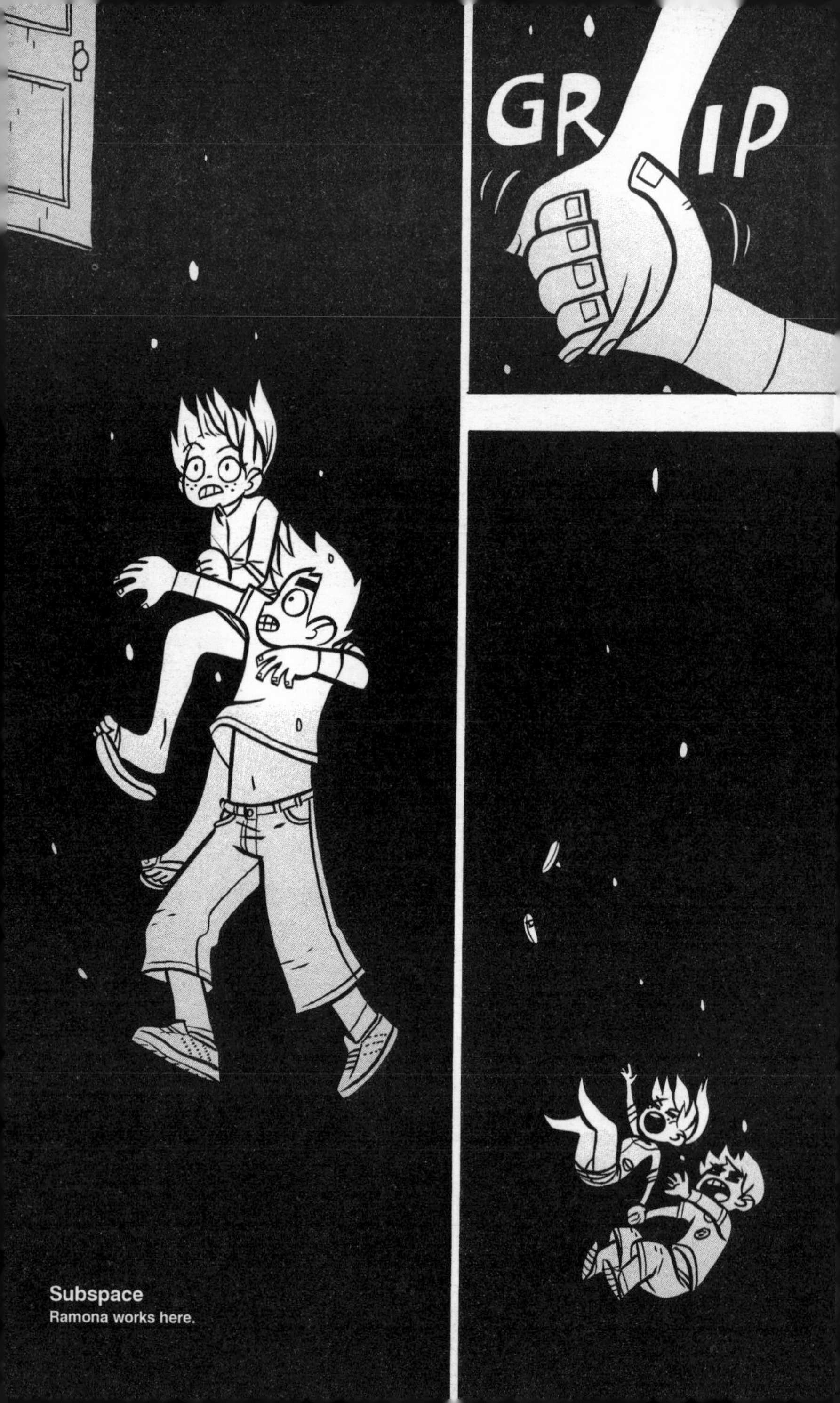
GR IP
Subspace
Ramona works here.

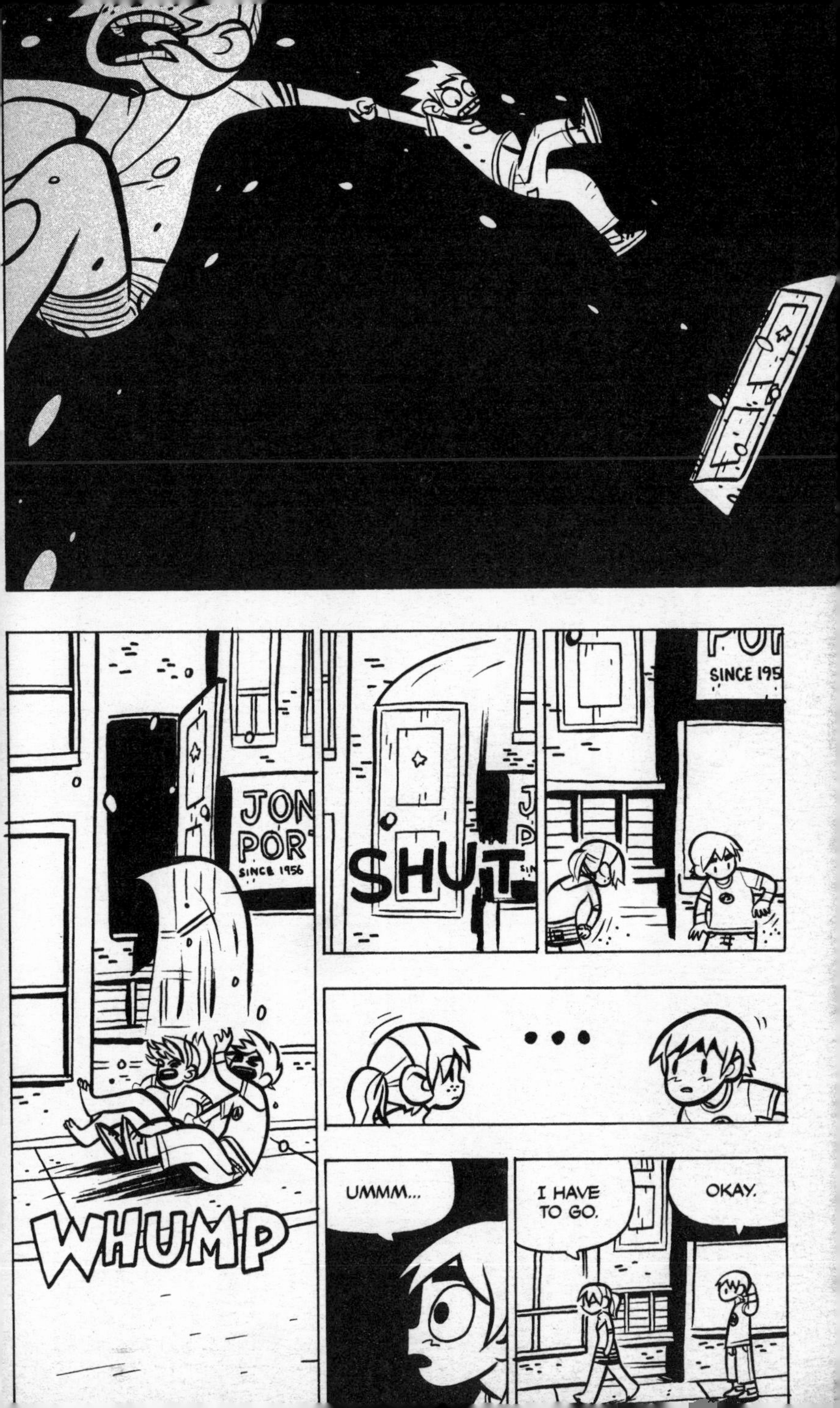
JON
POR
SINCE 1956
WHUMP
SHUT
SINCE 195
...
UMMM...
I HAVE TO GO.
OKAY.

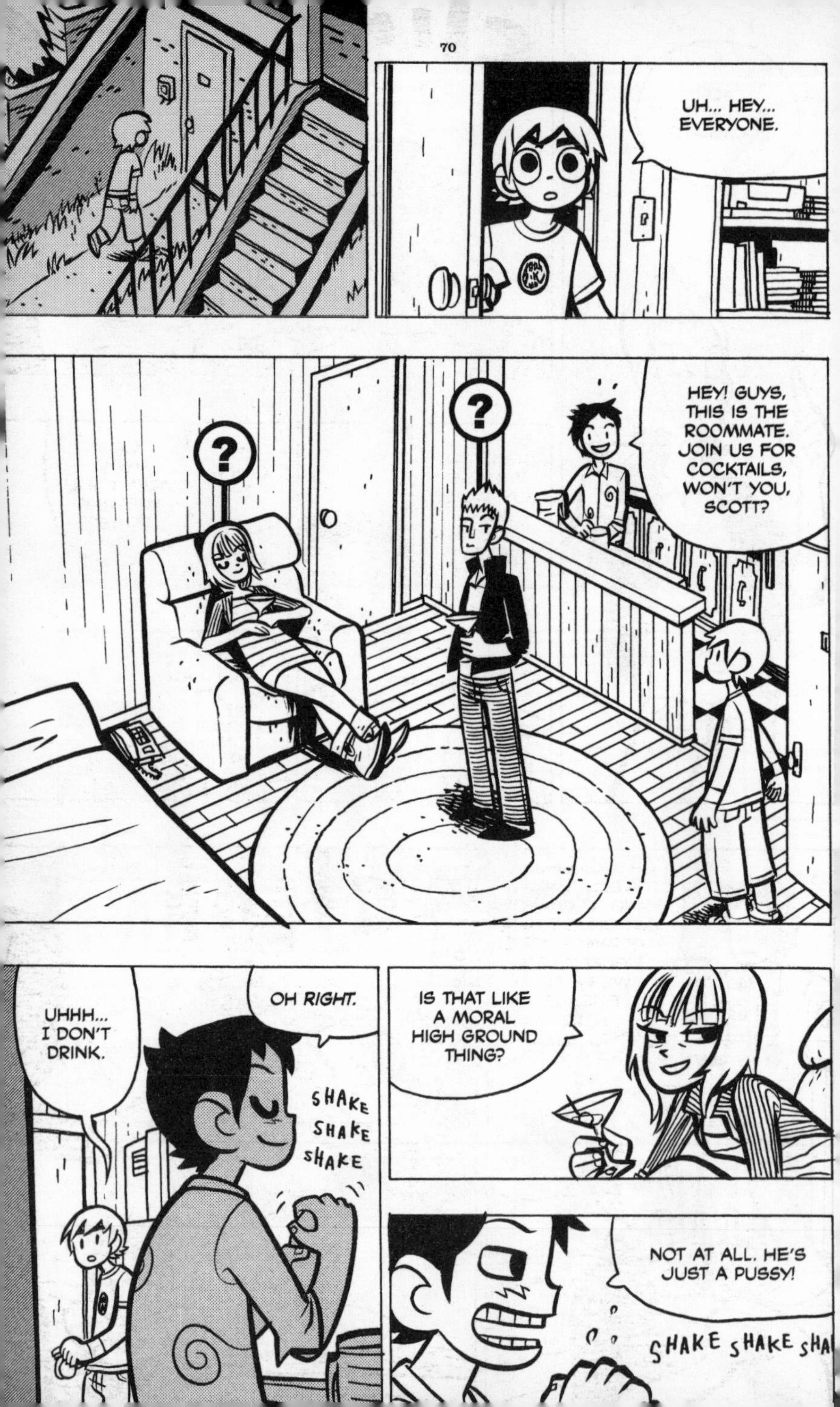
UH... HEY... EVERYONE.
?
?
HEY! GUYS, THIS IS THE ROOMMATE. JOIN US FOR COCKTAILS, WON'T YOU, SCOTT?
UHHH... I DON'T DRINK.
OH RIGHT.
SHAKE SHAKE SHAKE
IS THAT LIKE A MORAL HIGH GROUND THING?
NOT AT ALL. HE'S JUST A PUSSY!
SHAKE SHAKE SHA

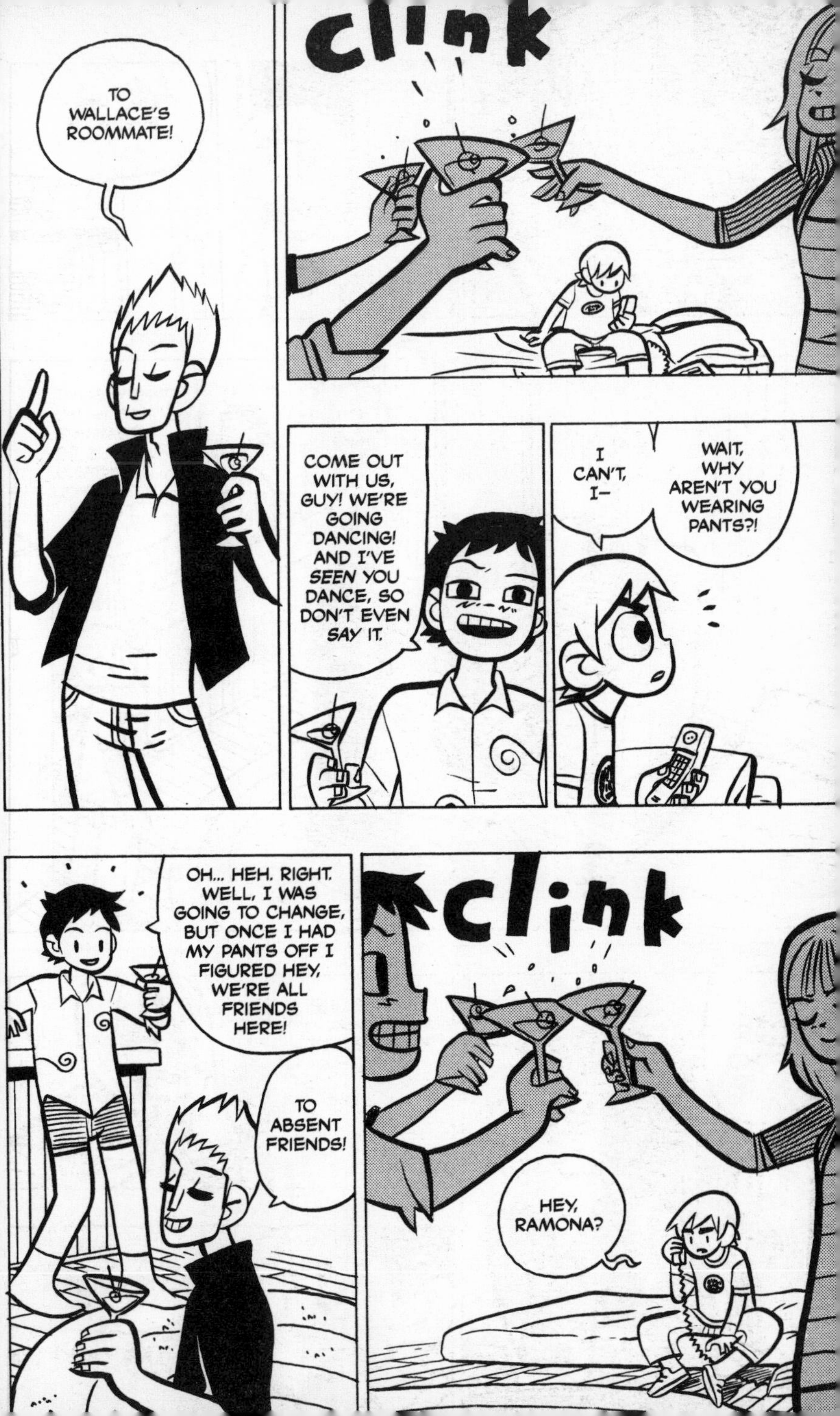
TO WALLACE'S ROOMMATE!
Clink
COME OUT WITH US, GUY! WE'RE GOING DANCING! AND I'VE SEEN YOU DANCE, SO DON'T EVEN SAY IT.
I CAN'T, I–
WAIT, WHY AREN'T YOU WEARING PANTS?!
OH... HEH. RIGHT. WELL, I WAS GOING TO CHANGE, BUT ONCE I HAD MY PANTS OFF I FIGURED HEY, WE'RE ALL FRIENDS HERE!
TO ABSENT FRIENDS!
clink
HEY, RAMONA?

72

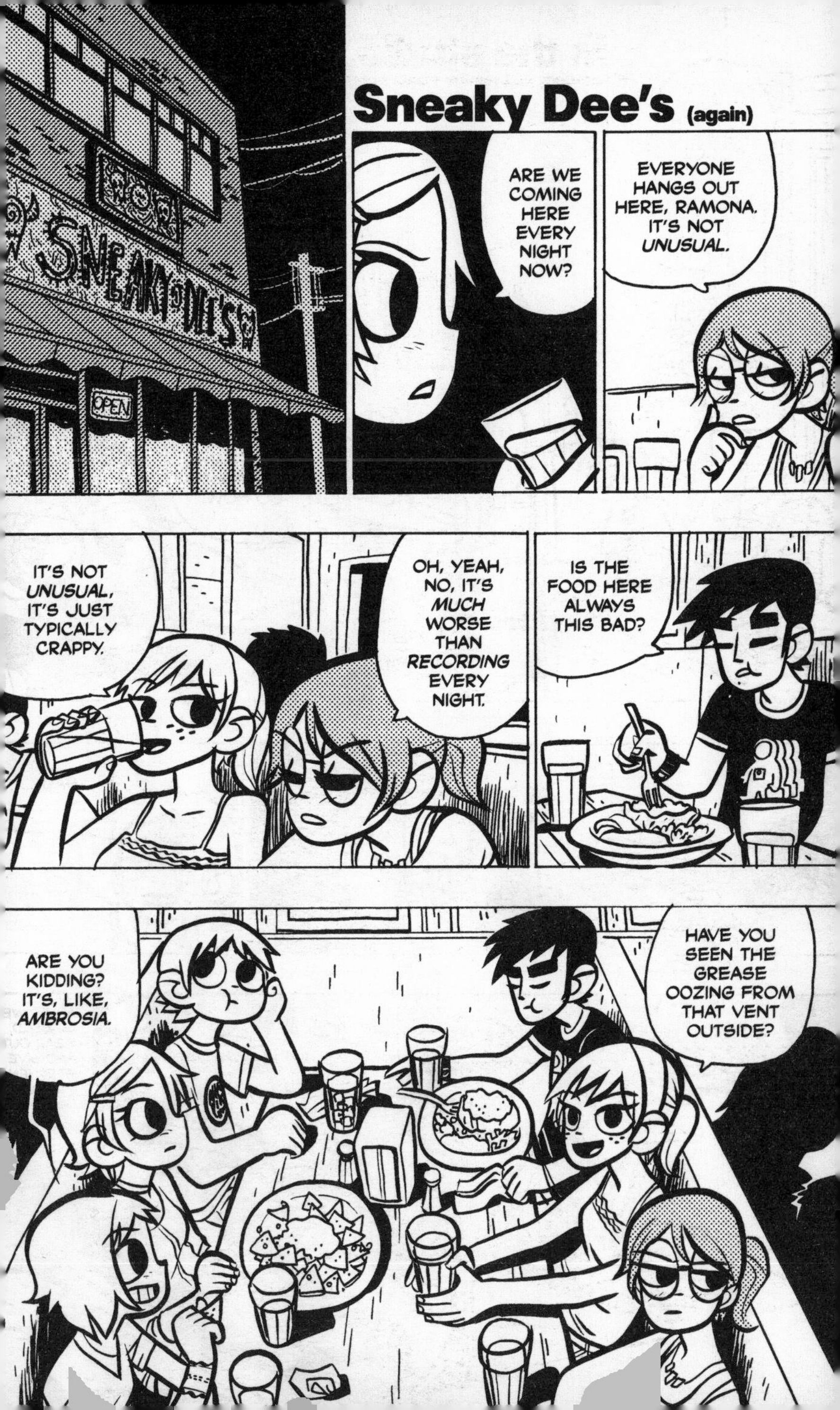

Sneaky Dee's (again)
SNEAKY DEE'S
OPEN
ARE WE COMING HERE EVERY NIGHT NOW?
EVERYONE HANGS OUT HERE, RAMONA. IT'S NOT *UNUSUAL.*
IT'S NOT *UNUSUAL,* IT'S JUST TYPICALLY CRAPPY.
OH, YEAH, NO, IT'S *MUCH* WORSE THAN *RECORDING* EVERY NIGHT.
IS THE FOOD HERE ALWAYS THIS BAD?
ARE YOU KIDDING? IT'S, LIKE, *AMBROSIA.*
HAVE YOU SEEN THE GREASE OOZING FROM THAT VENT OUTSIDE?

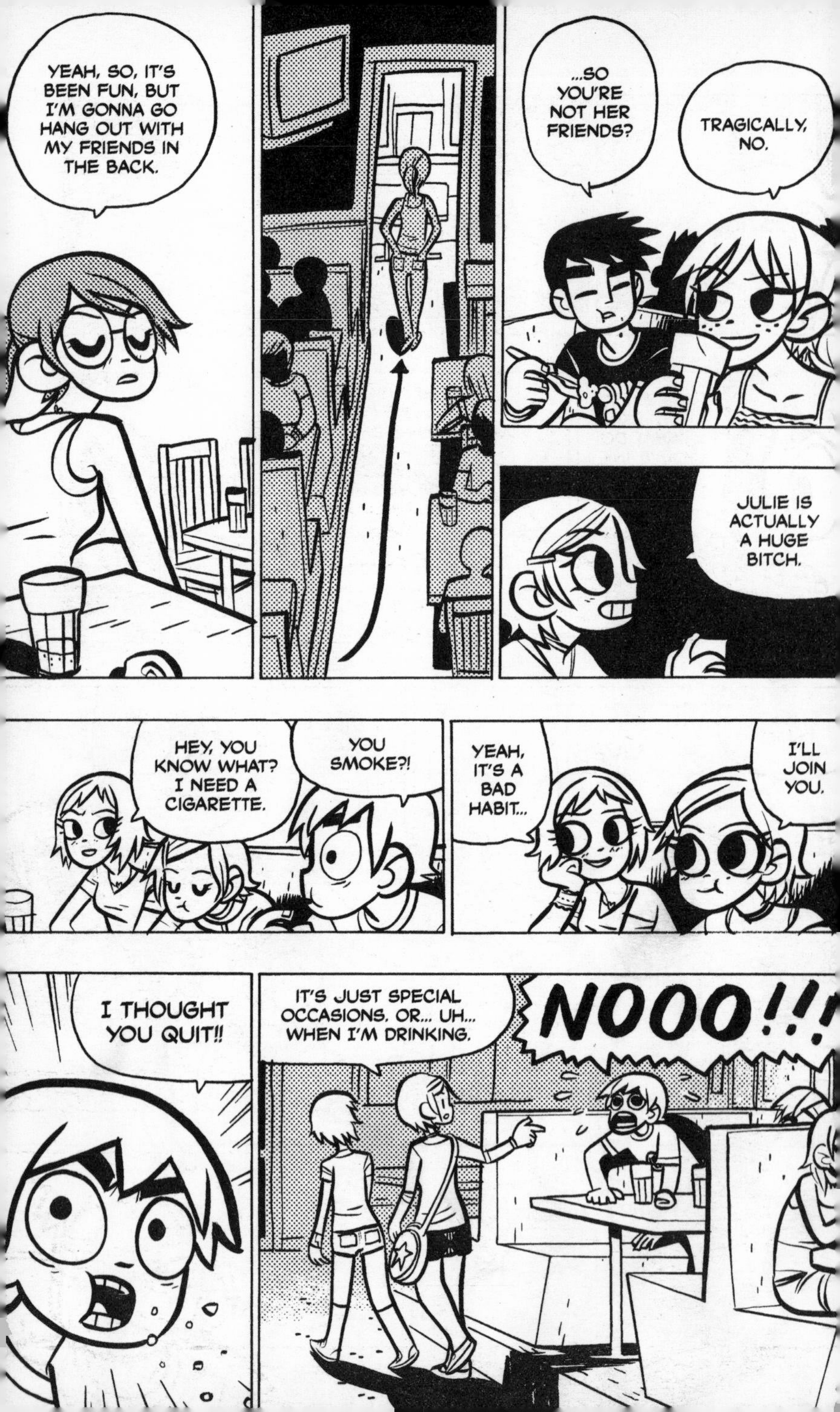
YEAH, SO, IT'S BEEN FUN, BUT I'M GONNA GO HANG OUT WITH MY FRIENDS IN THE BACK.
...SO YOU'RE NOT HER FRIENDS?
TRAGICALLY, NO.
JULIE IS ACTUALLY A HUGE BITCH.
HEY, YOU KNOW WHAT? I NEED A CIGARETTE.
YOU SMOKE?!
YEAH, IT'S A BAD HABIT...
I'LL JOIN YOU.
I THOUGHT YOU QUIT!!
IT'S JUST SPECIAL OCCASIONS. OR... UH... WHEN I'M DRINKING.
NOOO!!!

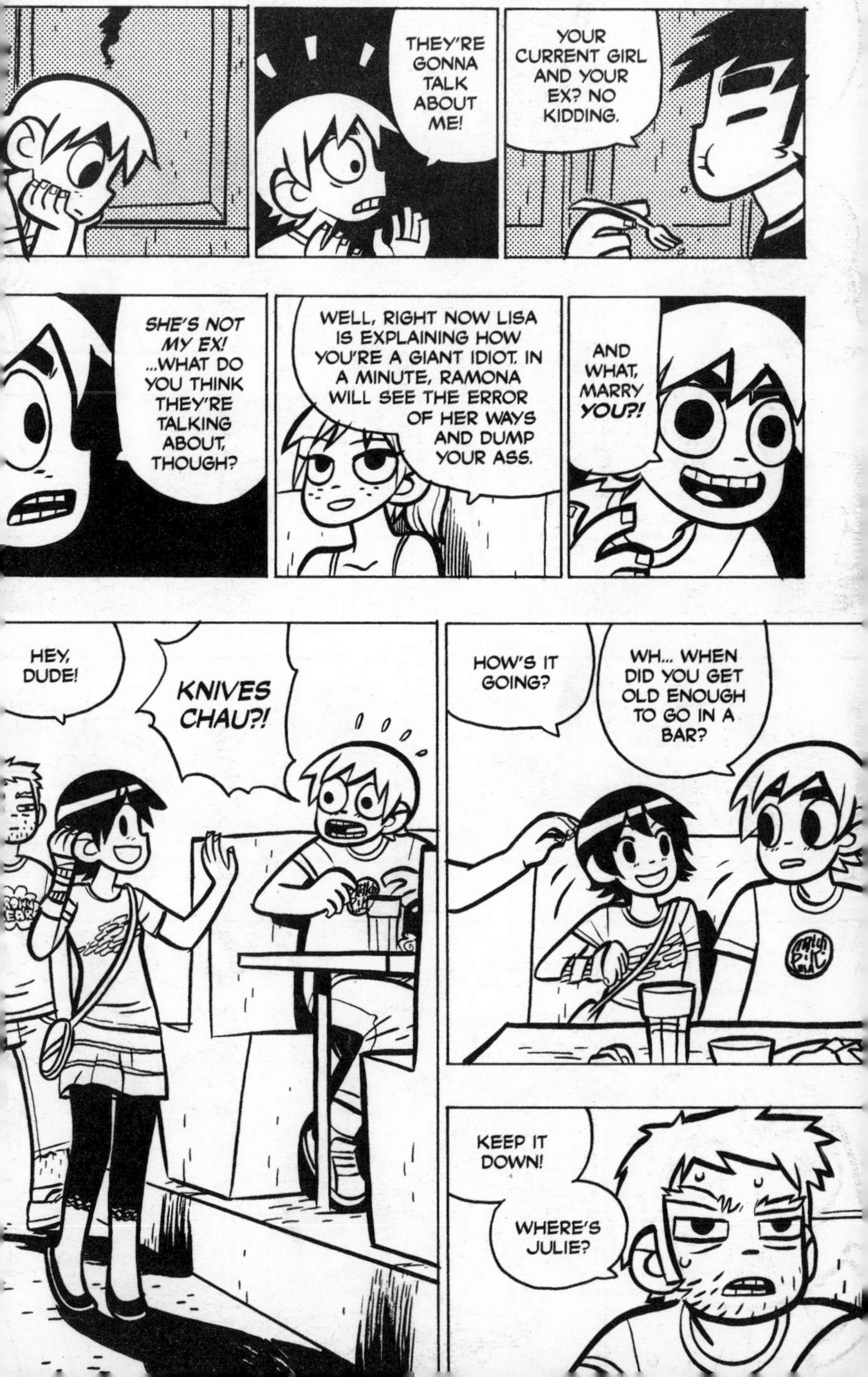
THEY'RE GONNA TALK ABOUT ME!
YOUR CURRENT GIRL AND YOUR EX? NO KIDDING.
SHE'S NOT MY EX! ...WHAT DO YOU THINK THEY'RE TALKING ABOUT, THOUGH?
WELL, RIGHT NOW LISA IS EXPLAINING HOW YOU'RE A GIANT IDIOT. IN A MINUTE, RAMONA WILL SEE THE ERROR OF HER WAYS AND DUMP YOUR ASS.
AND WHAT, MARRY YOU?!
HEY, DUDE!
KNIVES CHAU?!
HOW'S IT GOING?
WH... WHEN DID YOU GET OLD ENOUGH TO GO IN A BAR?
KEEP IT DOWN!
WHERE'S JULIE?

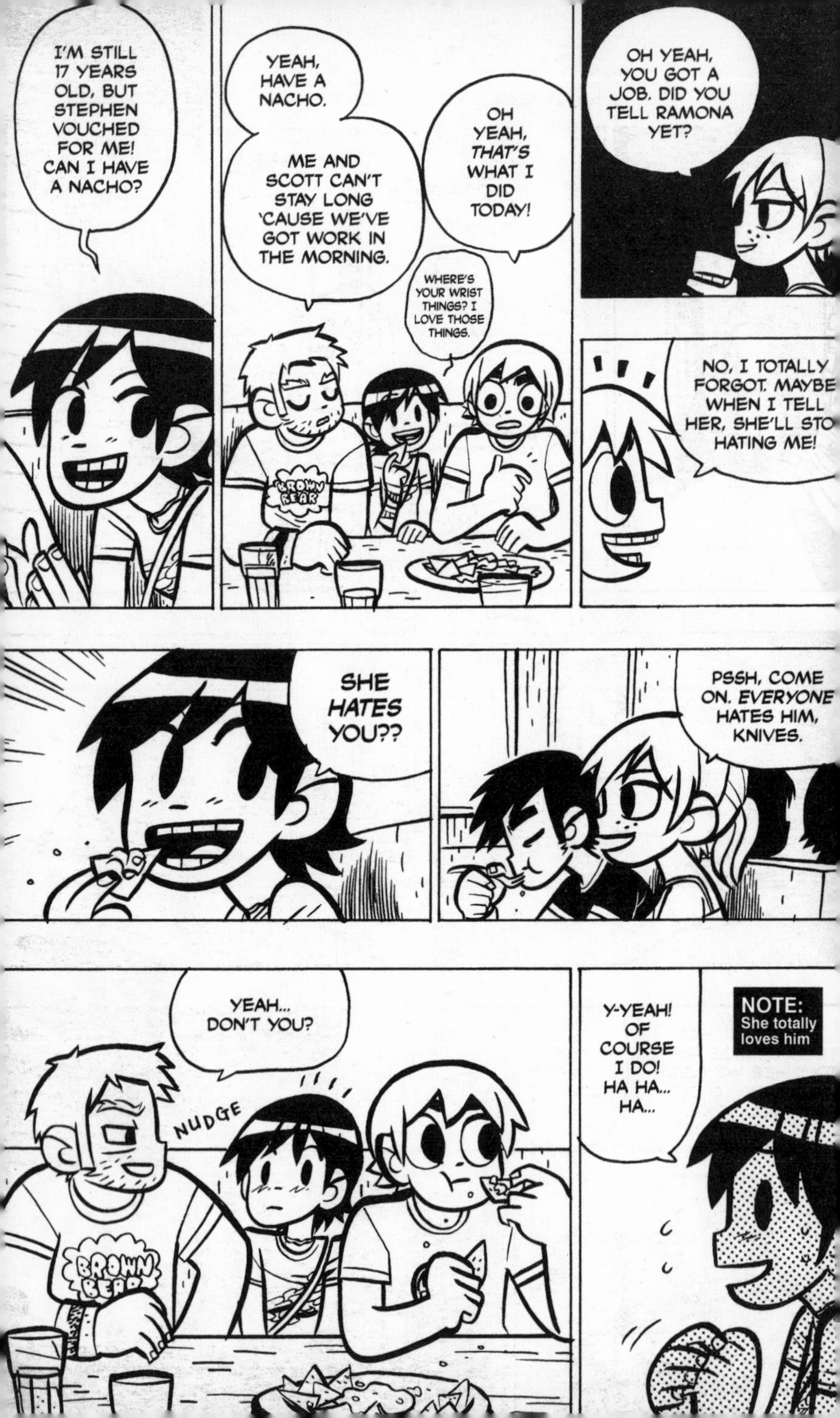
I'M STILL 17 YEARS OLD, BUT STEPHEN VOUCHED FOR ME! CAN I HAVE A NACHO?
YEAH, HAVE A NACHO.
ME AND SCOTT CAN'T STAY LONG 'CAUSE WE'VE GOT WORK IN THE MORNING.
OH YEAH, THAT'S WHAT I DID TODAY!
WHERE'S YOUR WRIST THINGS? I LOVE THOSE THINGS.
BROWN BEAR
OH YEAH, YOU GOT A JOB. DID YOU TELL RAMONA YET?
NO, I TOTALLY FORGOT. MAYBE WHEN I TELL HER, SHE'LL STO HATING ME!
SHE HATES YOU??
PSSH, COME ON. EVERYONE HATES HIM, KNIVES.
YEAH... DON'T YOU?
NUDGE
BROWN BEAR
Y-YEAH! OF COURSE I DO! HA HA... HA...
NOTE: She totally loves him

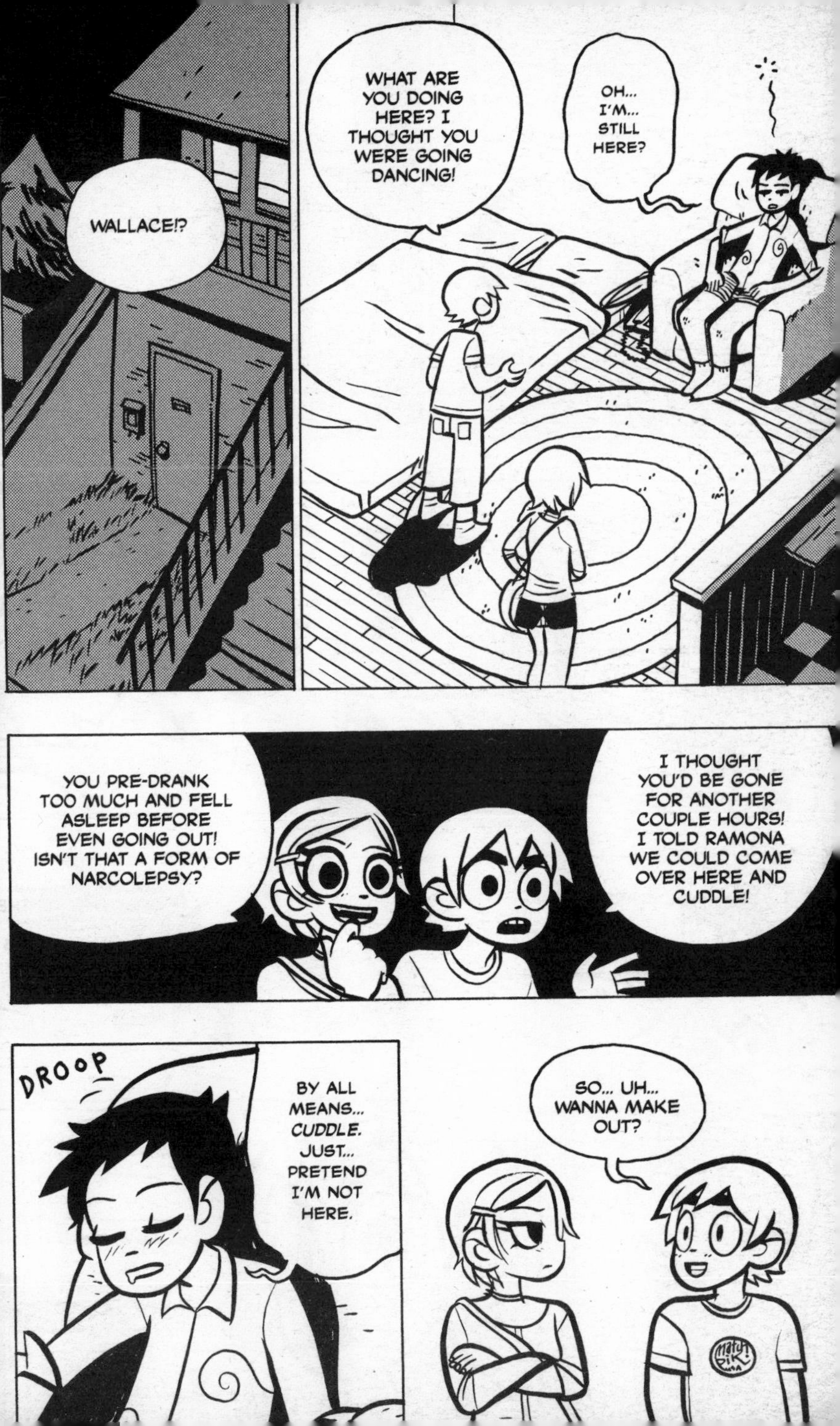
WALLACE!?
WHAT ARE YOU DOING HERE? I THOUGHT YOU WERE GOING DANCING!
OH... I'M... STILL HERE?
YOU PRE-DRANK TOO MUCH AND FELL ASLEEP BEFORE EVEN GOING OUT! ISN'T THAT A FORM OF NARCOLEPSY?
I THOUGHT YOU'D BE GONE FOR ANOTHER COUPLE HOURS! I TOLD RAMONA WE COULD COME OVER HERE AND CUDDLE!
DROOP
BY ALL MEANS... CUDDLE. JUST... PRETEND I'M NOT HERE.
SO... UH... WANNA MAKE OUT?

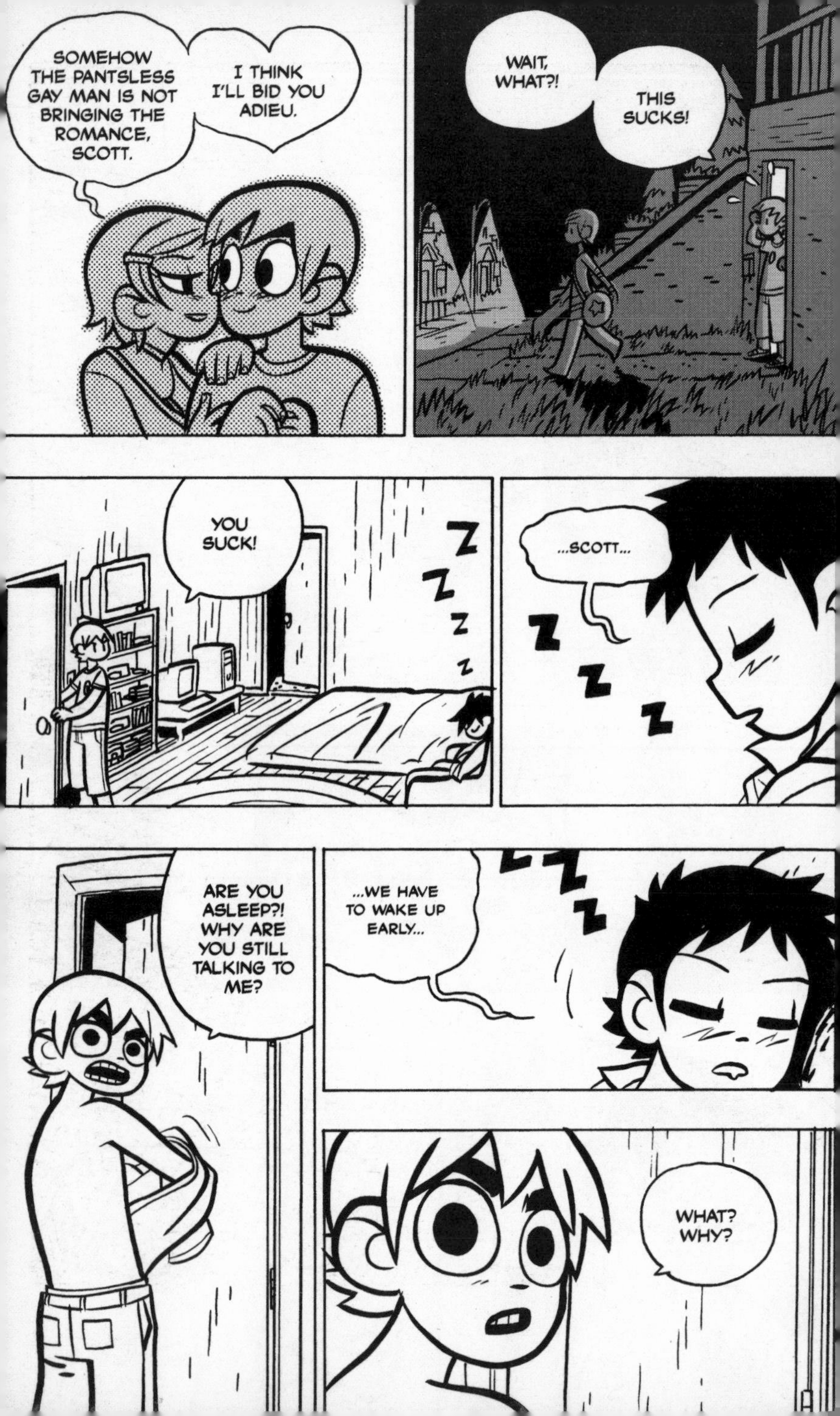
SOMEHOW THE PANTSLESS GAY MAN IS NOT BRINGING THE ROMANCE, SCOTT.
I THINK I'LL BID YOU ADIEU.
WAIT, WHAT?!
THIS SUCKS!
YOU SUCK!
Z Z Z Z
...SCOTT...
Z Z Z
ARE YOU ASLEEP?! WHY ARE YOU STILL TALKING TO ME?
...WE HAVE TO WAKE UP EARLY...
WHAT? WHY?

22 Comes a time

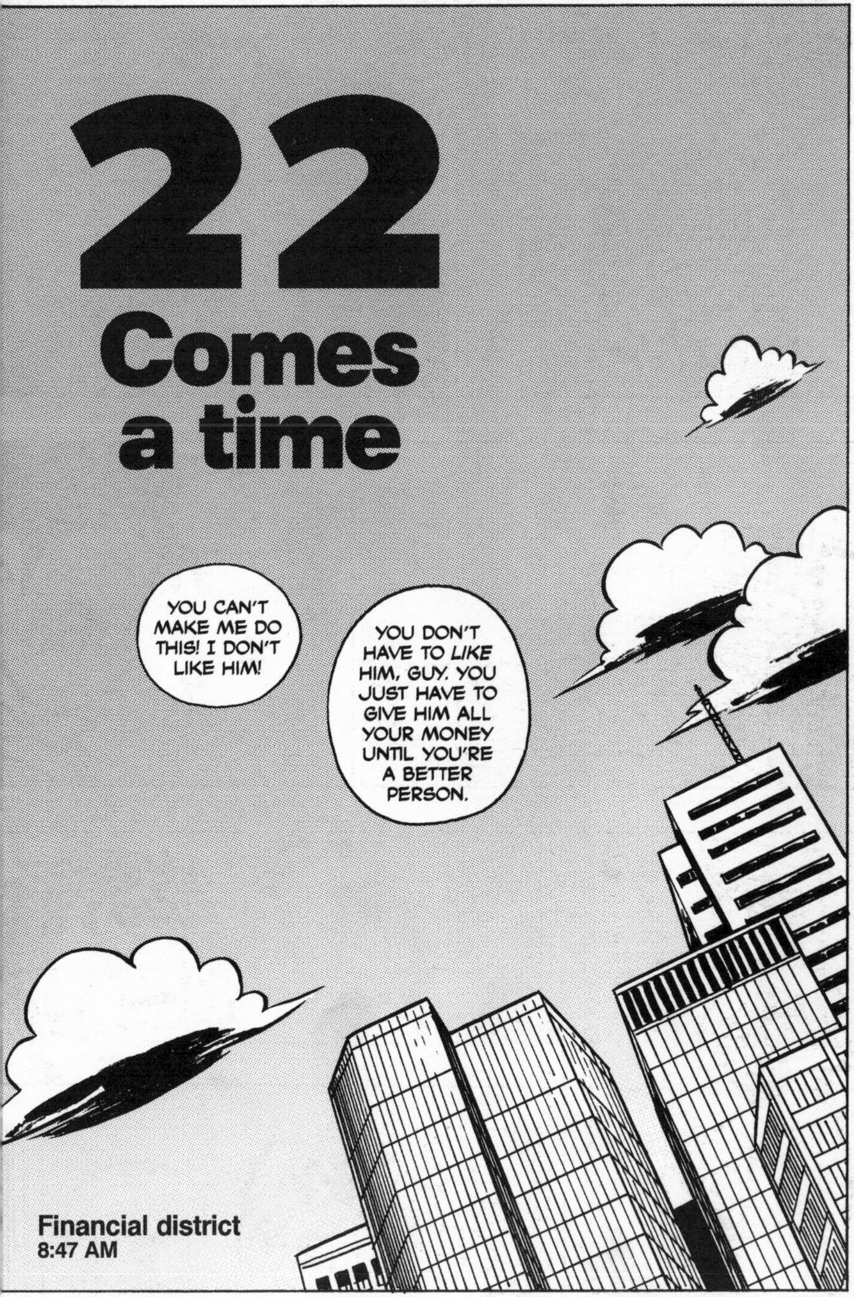
YOU CAN'T MAKE ME DO THIS! I DON'T LIKE HIM!
YOU DON'T HAVE TO *LIKE* HIM, GUY. YOU JUST HAVE TO GIVE HIM ALL YOUR MONEY UNTIL YOU'RE A BETTER PERSON.
Financial district
8:47 AM

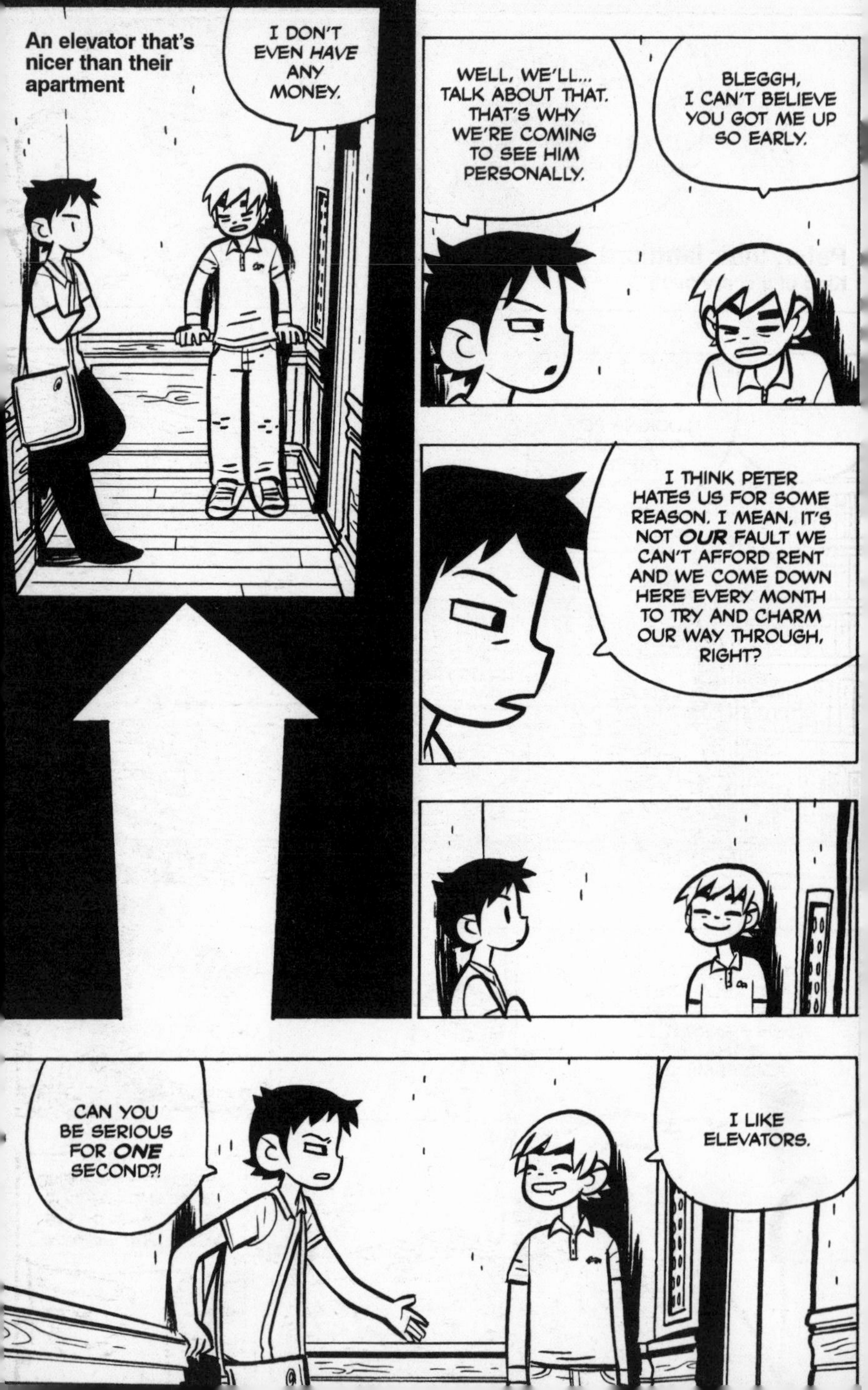
An elevator that's nicer than their apartment
I DON'T EVEN *HAVE* ANY MONEY.
WELL, WE'LL... TALK ABOUT THAT. THAT'S WHY WE'RE COMING TO SEE HIM PERSONALLY.
BLEGGH, I CAN'T BELIEVE YOU GOT ME UP SO EARLY.
I THINK PETER HATES US FOR SOME REASON. I MEAN, IT'S NOT ***OUR*** FAULT WE CAN'T AFFORD RENT AND WE COME DOWN HERE EVERY MONTH TO TRY AND CHARM OUR WAY THROUGH, RIGHT?
CAN YOU BE SERIOUS FOR ***ONE*** SECOND?!
I LIKE ELEVATORS.

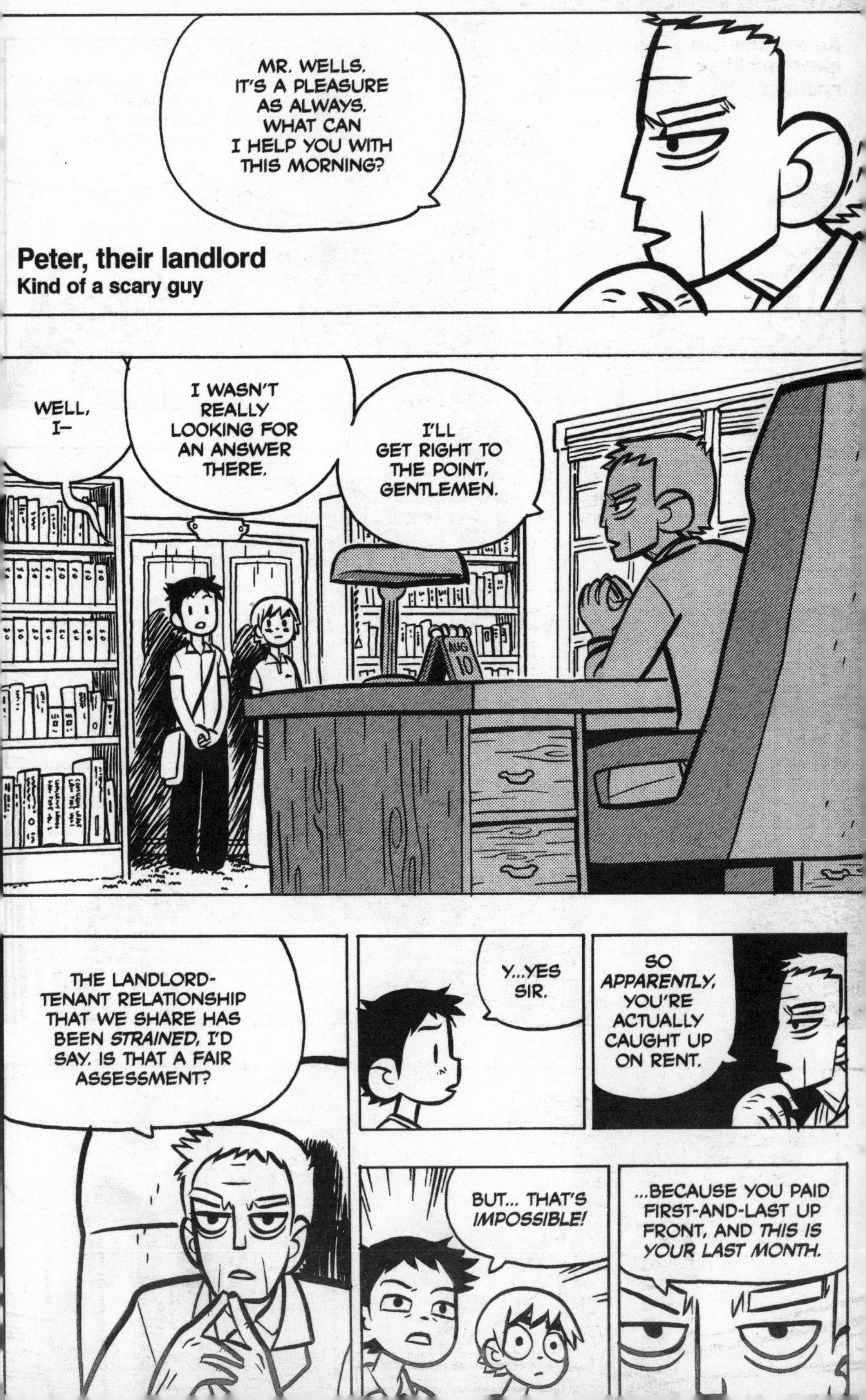
MR. WELLS. IT'S A PLEASURE AS ALWAYS. WHAT CAN I HELP YOU WITH THIS MORNING?
Peter, their landlord
Kind of a scary guy
WELL, I–
I WASN'T REALLY LOOKING FOR AN ANSWER THERE.
I'LL GET RIGHT TO THE POINT, GENTLEMEN.
AUG 10
THE LANDLORD-TENANT RELATIONSHIP THAT WE SHARE HAS BEEN *STRAINED*, I'D SAY. IS THAT A FAIR ASSESSMENT?
Y...YES SIR.
SO *APPARENTLY*, YOU'RE ACTUALLY CAUGHT UP ON RENT.
BUT... THAT'S *IMPOSSIBLE!*
...BECAUSE YOU PAID FIRST-AND-LAST UP FRONT, AND *THIS IS YOUR LAST MONTH*.

86

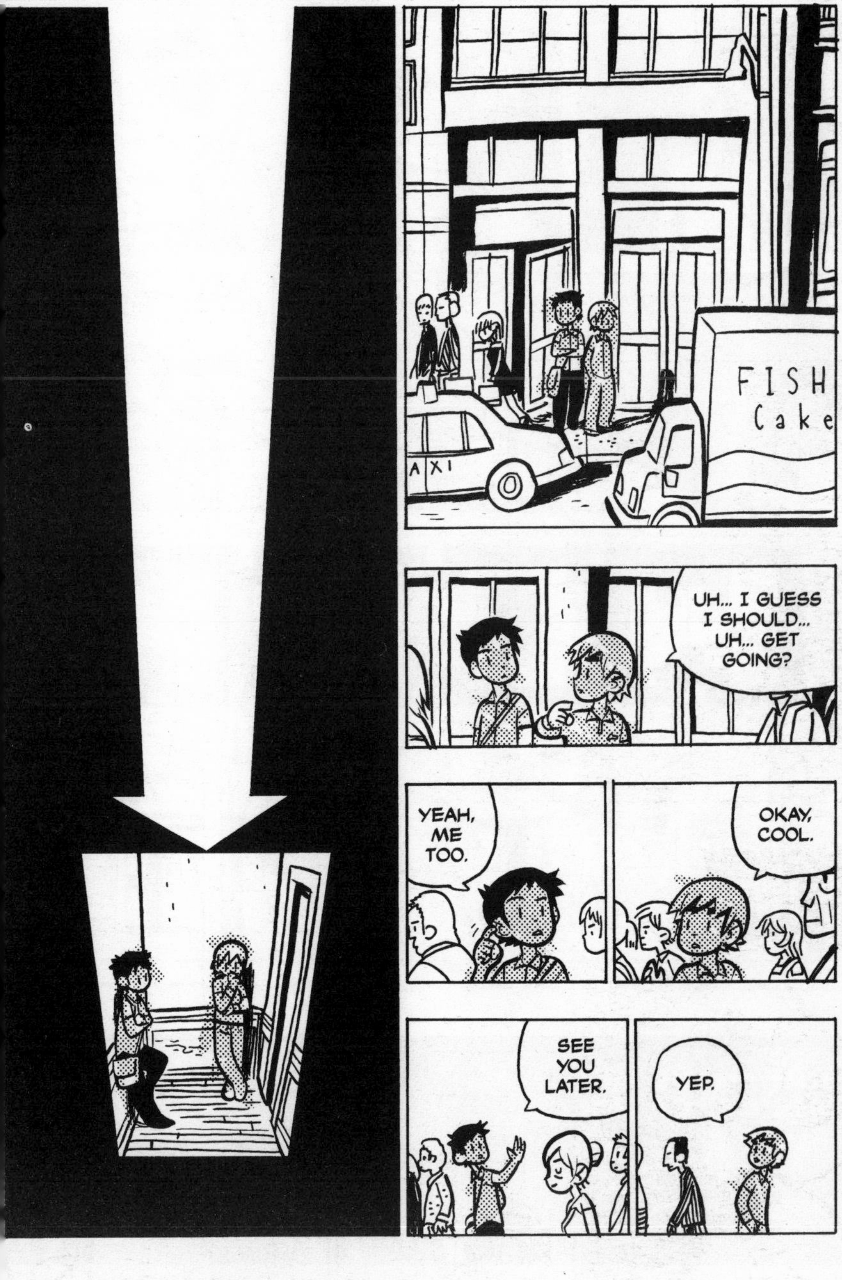
FISH
Cake
AXI
UH... I GUESS I SHOULD... UH... GET GOING?
YEAH, ME TOO.
OKAY, COOL.
SEE YOU LATER.
YEP.

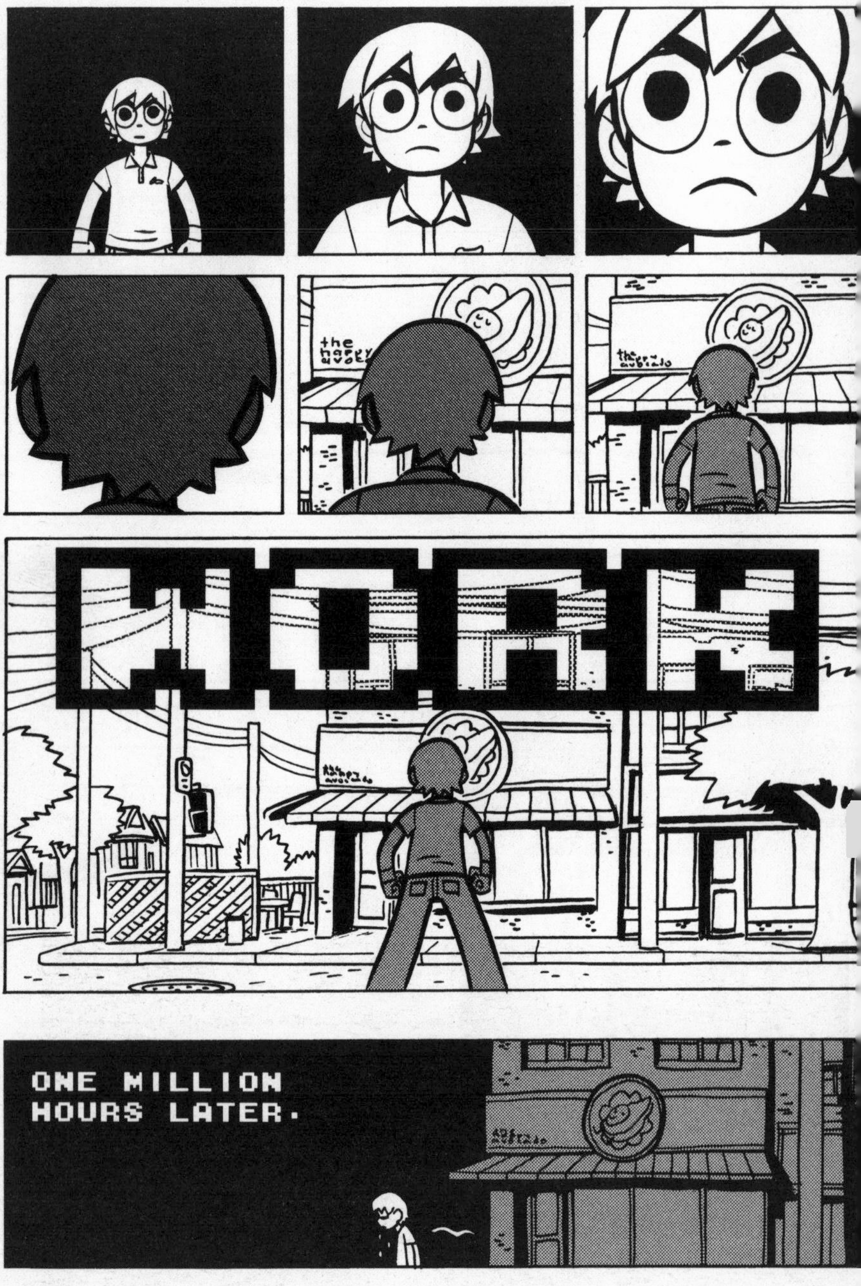
WORK
ONE MILLION
HOURS LATER.

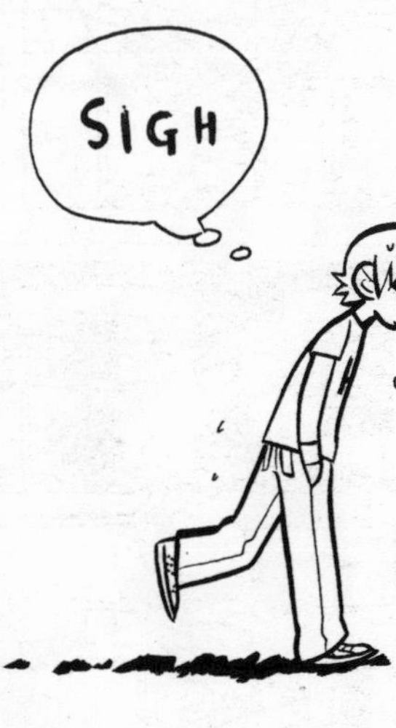
SIGH

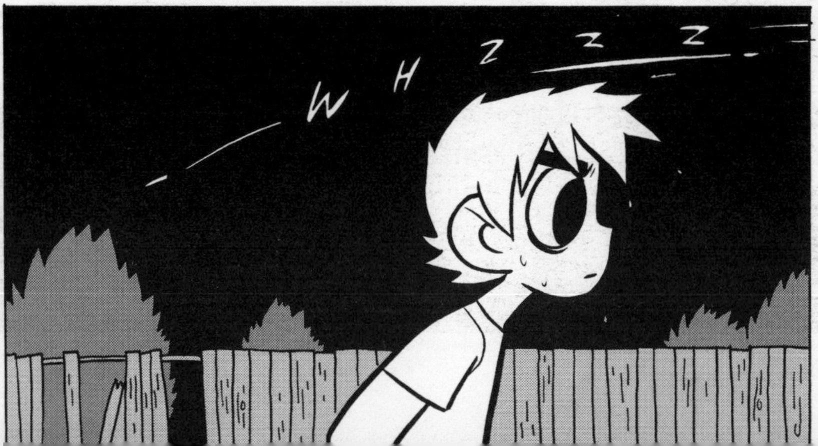
WHZZZ

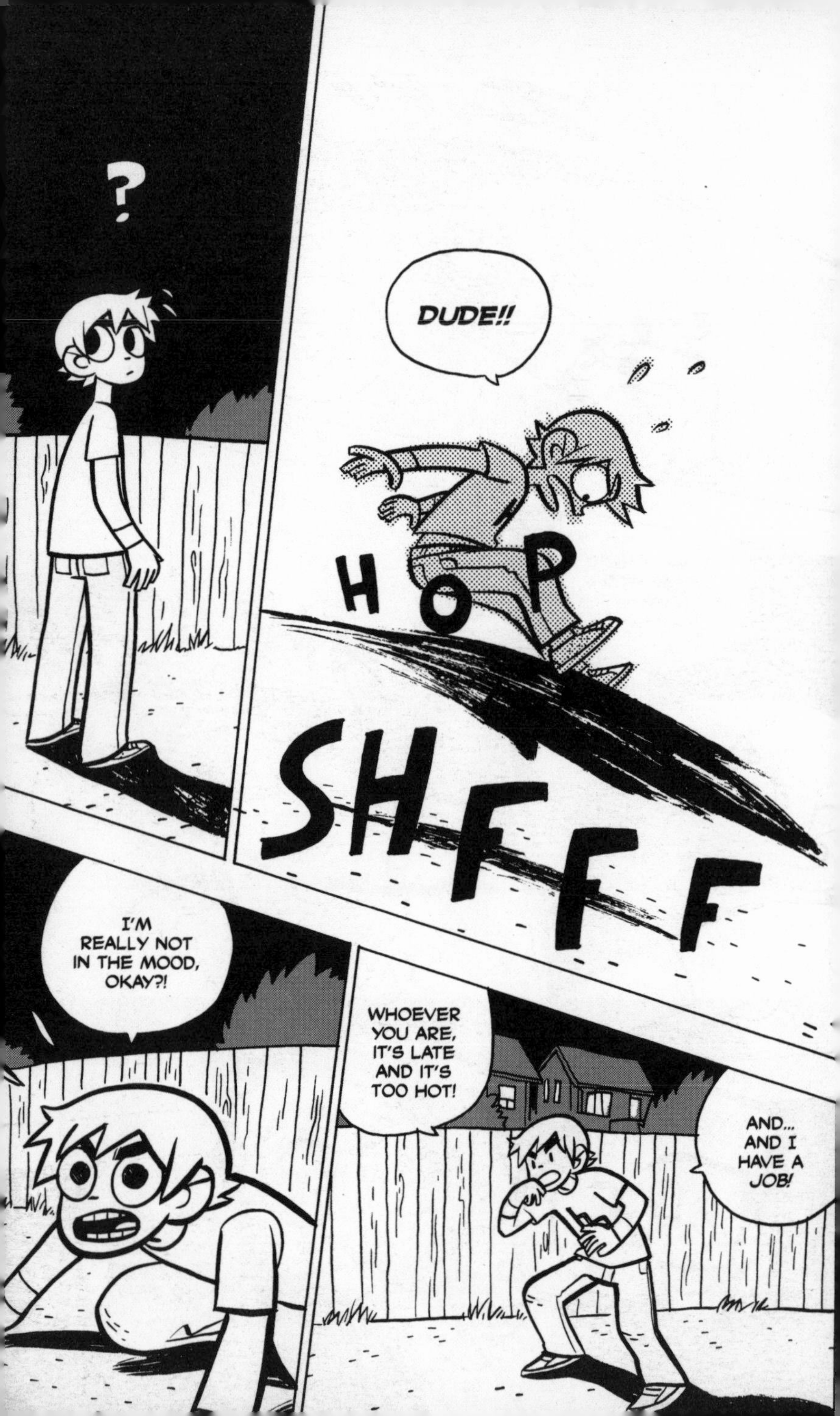
?
DUDE!!
HOP
SHFFF
I'M REALLY NOT IN THE MOOD, OKAY?!
WHOEVER YOU ARE, IT'S LATE AND IT'S TOO HOT!
AND... AND I HAVE A JOB!

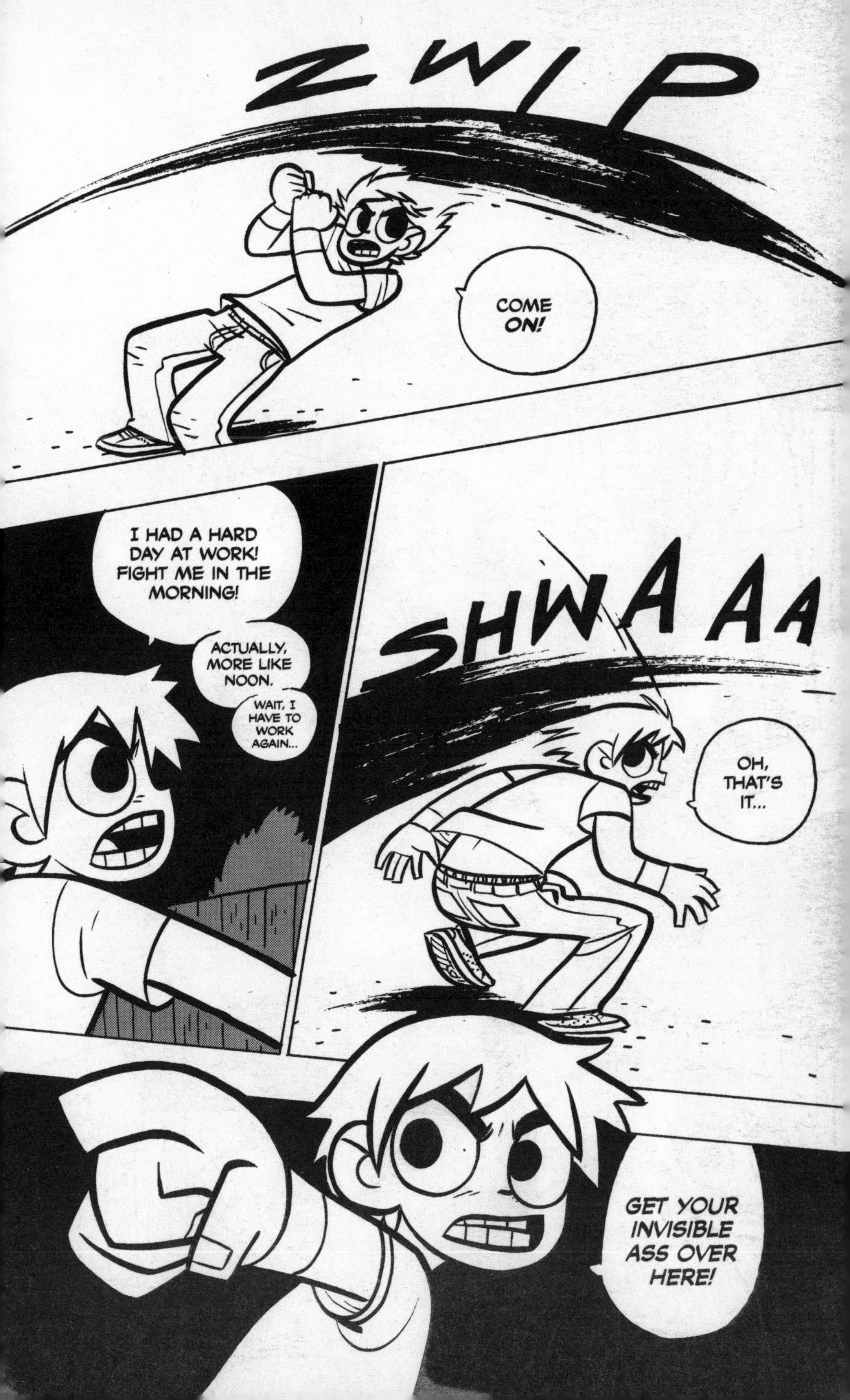
ZWIP
COME ON!
I HAD A HARD DAY AT WORK! FIGHT ME IN THE MORNING!
ACTUALLY, MORE LIKE NOON.
WAIT, I HAVE TO WORK AGAIN...
SHWAAAA
OH, THAT'S IT...
GET YOUR INVISIBLE ASS OVER HERE!

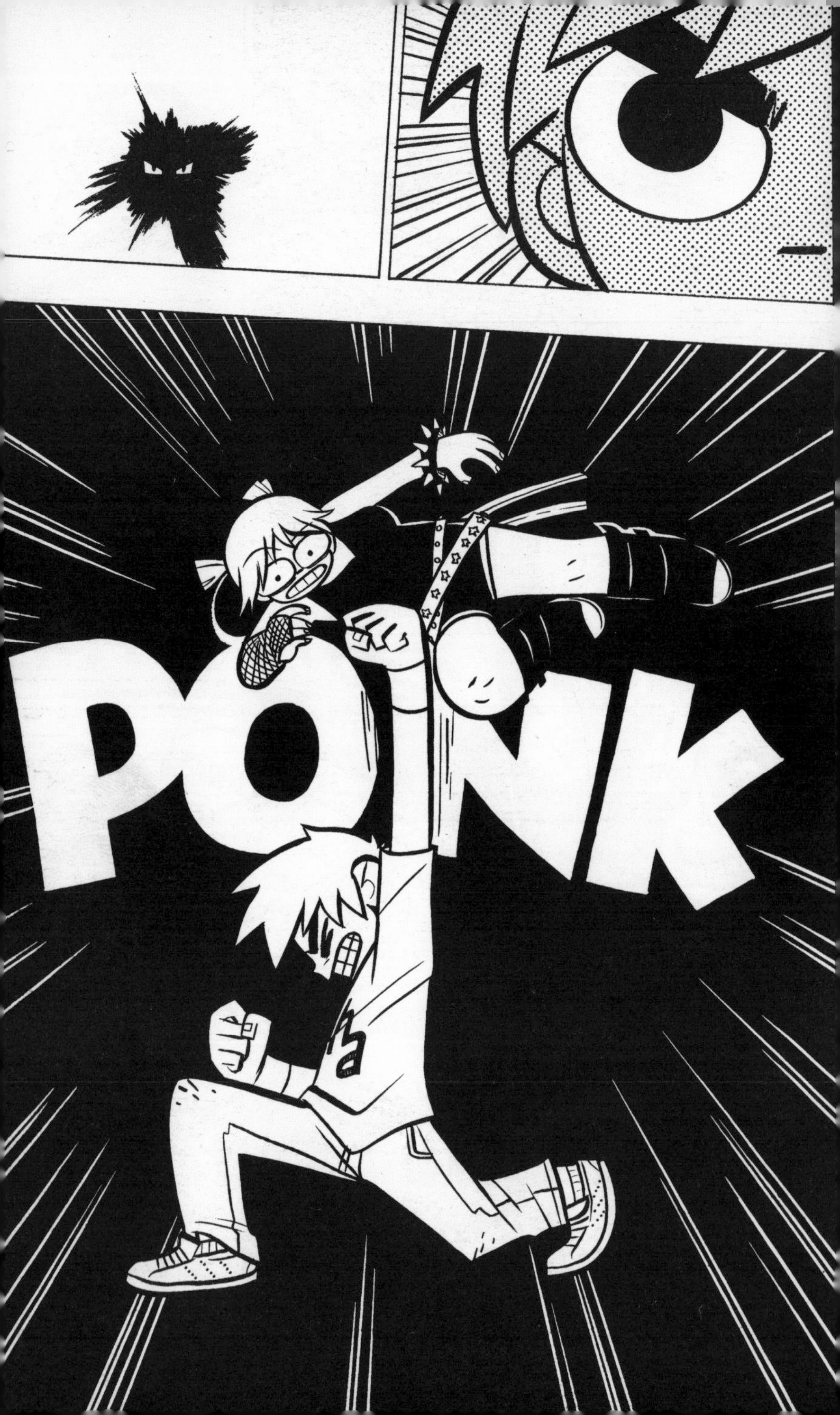
POINK

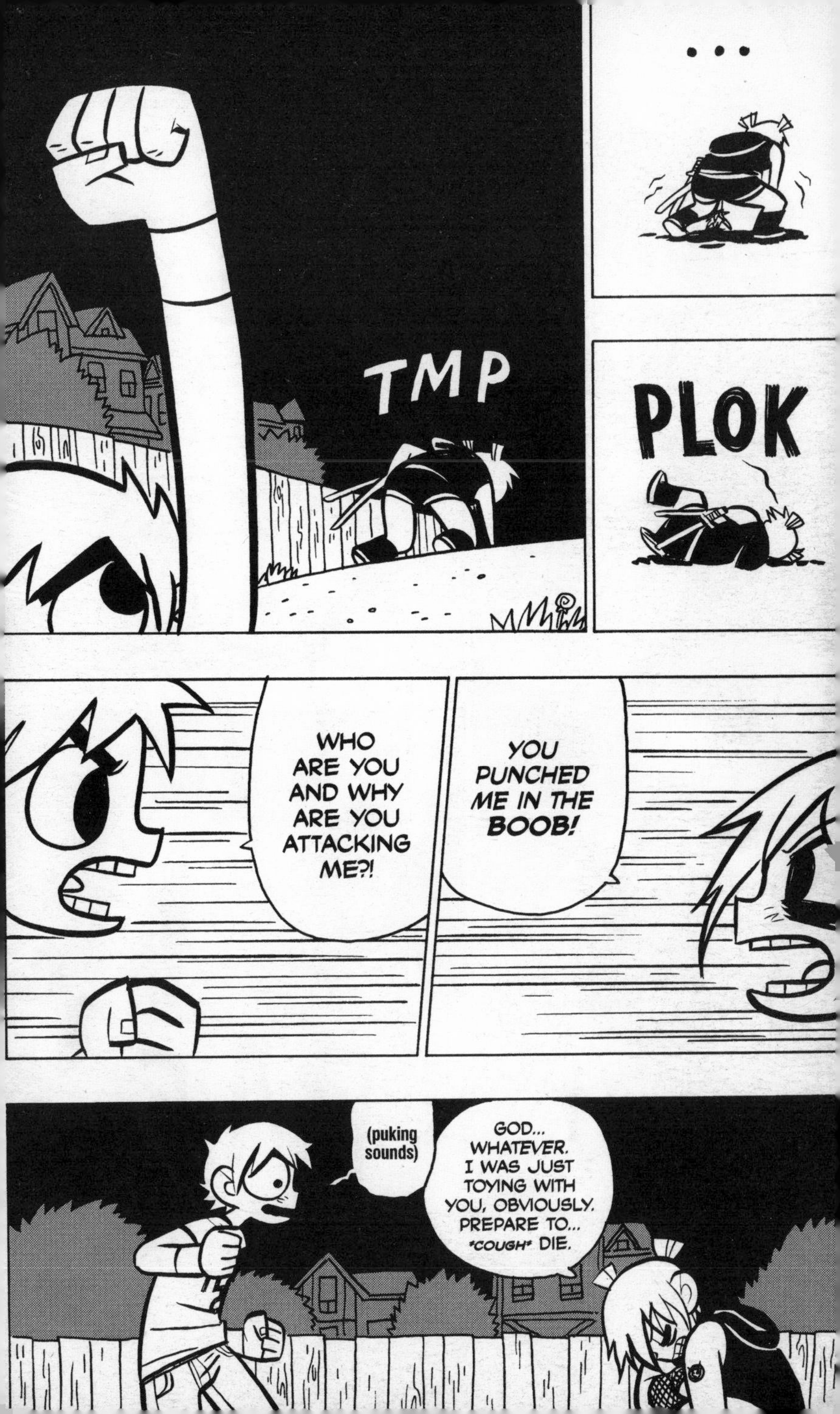
...
TMP
PLOK
WHO ARE YOU AND WHY ARE YOU ATTACKING ME?!
YOU PUNCHED ME IN THE BOOB!
(puking sounds)
GOD... WHATEVER. I WAS JUST TOYING WITH YOU, OBVIOUSLY. PREPARE TO... *COUGH* DIE.

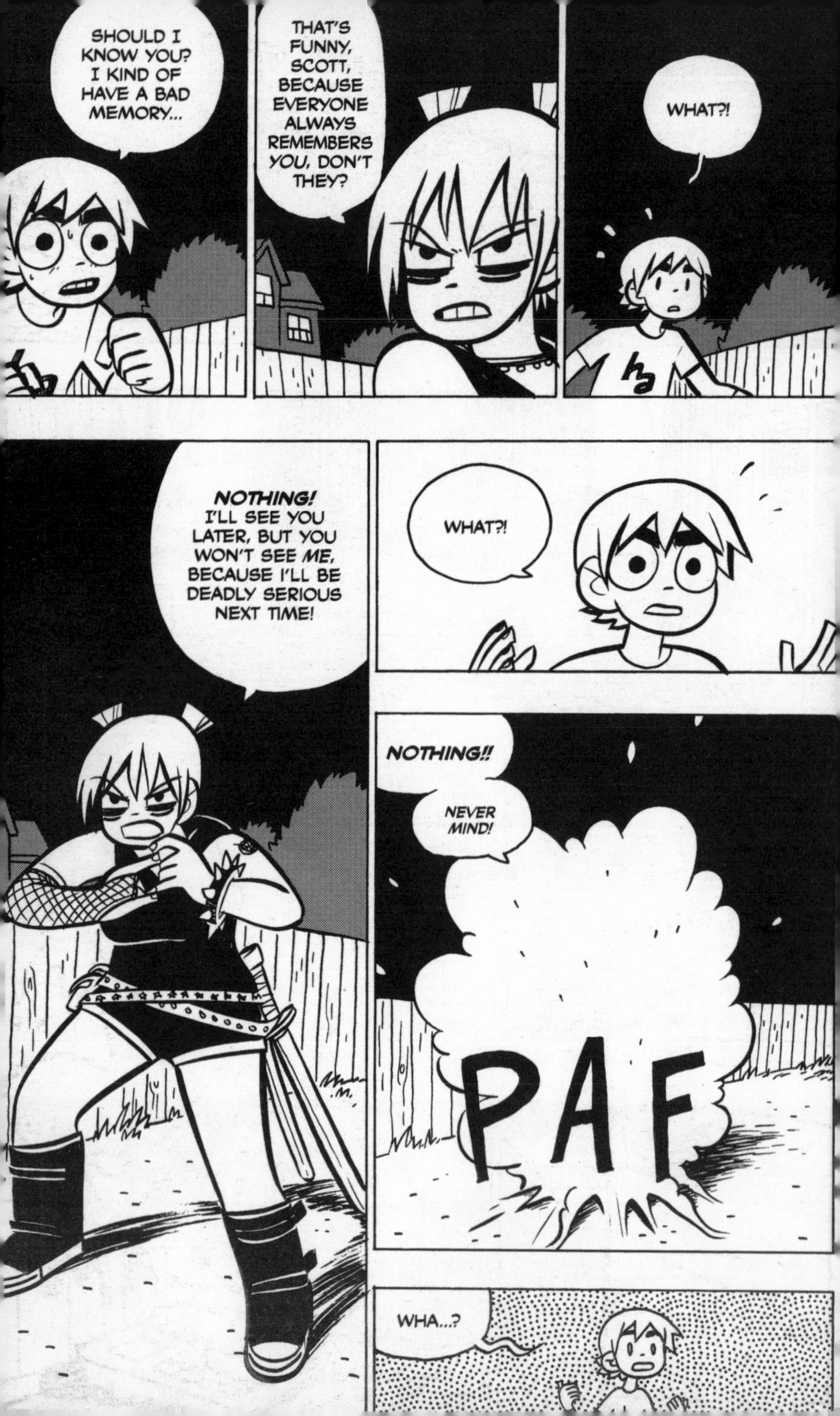
SHOULD I KNOW YOU? I KIND OF HAVE A BAD MEMORY...
THAT'S FUNNY, SCOTT, BECAUSE EVERYONE ALWAYS REMEMBERS *YOU*, DON'T THEY?
WHAT?!
NOTHING! I'LL SEE YOU LATER, BUT YOU WON'T SEE *ME*, BECAUSE I'LL BE DEADLY SERIOUS NEXT TIME!
WHAT?!
NOTHING!!
NEVER MIND!
PAF
WHA...?

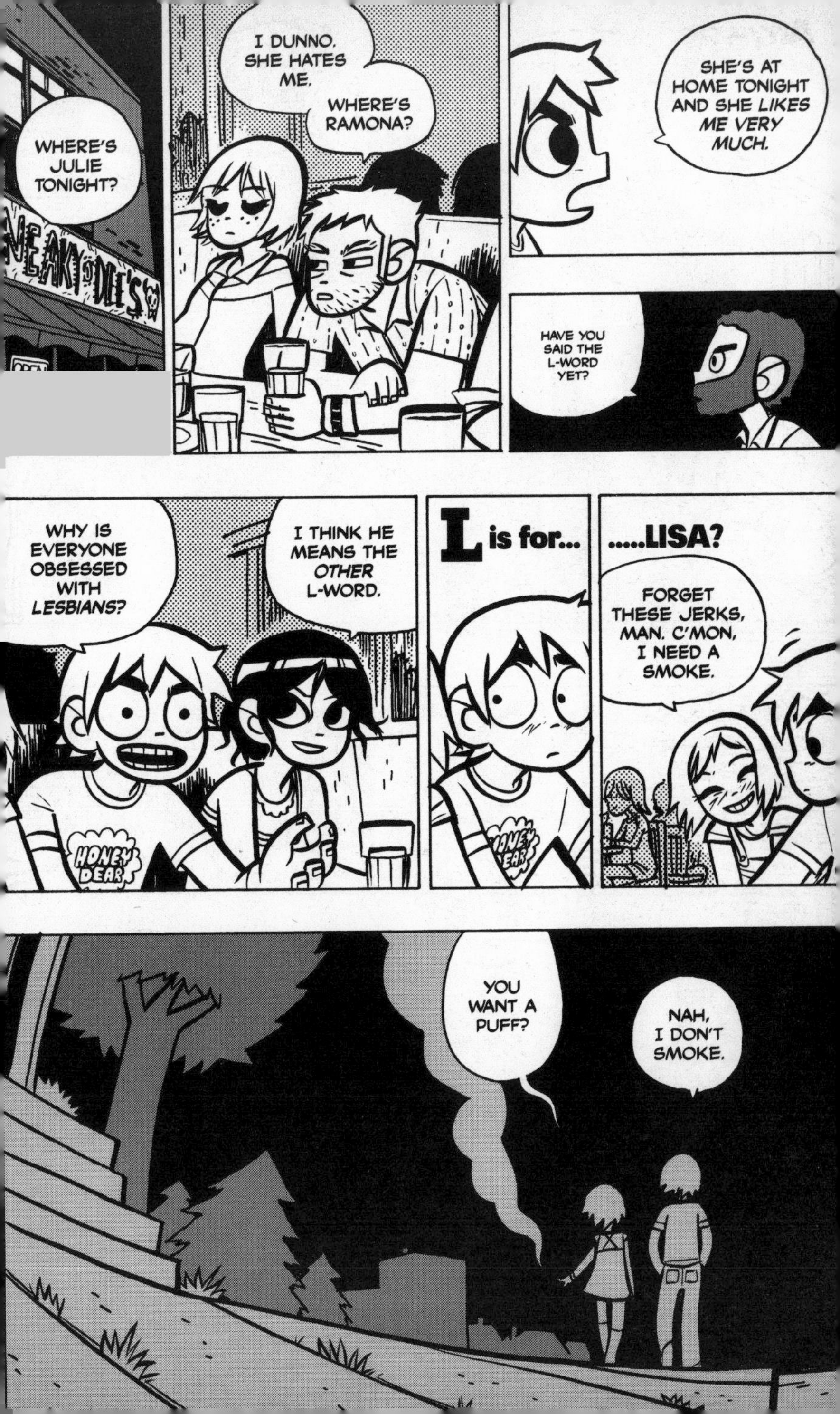

WHERE'S JULIE TONIGHT?
NEAKY DEE'S
I DUNNO. SHE HATES ME.
WHERE'S RAMONA?
SHE'S AT HOME TONIGHT AND SHE LIKES ME VERY MUCH.
HAVE YOU SAID THE L-WORD YET?
WHY IS EVERYONE OBSESSED WITH LESBIANS?
I THINK HE MEANS THE OTHER L-WORD.
HONEY DEAR
L is for...
.....LISA?
FORGET THESE JERKS, MAN. C'MON, I NEED A SMOKE.
YOU WANT A PUFF?
NAH, I DON'T SMOKE.

99

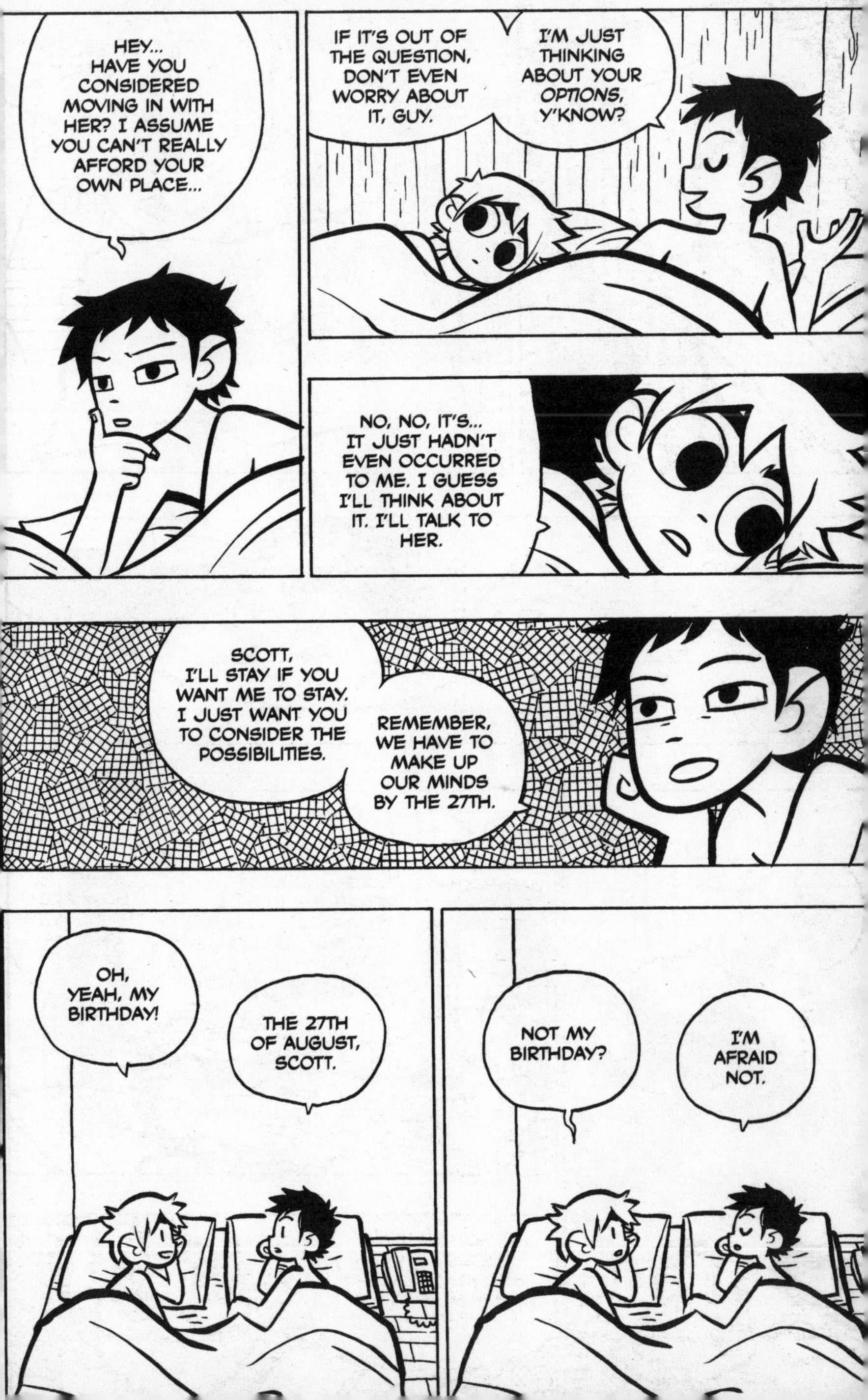
HEY... HAVE YOU CONSIDERED MOVING IN WITH HER? I ASSUME YOU CAN'T REALLY AFFORD YOUR OWN PLACE...
IF IT'S OUT OF THE QUESTION, DON'T EVEN WORRY ABOUT IT, GUY.
I'M JUST THINKING ABOUT YOUR *OPTIONS*, Y'KNOW?
NO, NO, IT'S... IT JUST HADN'T EVEN OCCURRED TO ME. I GUESS I'LL THINK ABOUT IT. I'LL TALK TO HER.
SCOTT, I'LL STAY IF YOU WANT ME TO STAY. I JUST WANT YOU TO CONSIDER THE POSSIBILITIES.
REMEMBER, WE HAVE TO MAKE UP OUR MINDS BY THE 27TH.
OH, YEAH, MY BIRTHDAY!
THE 27TH OF AUGUST, SCOTT.
NOT MY BIRTHDAY?
I'M AFRAID NOT.

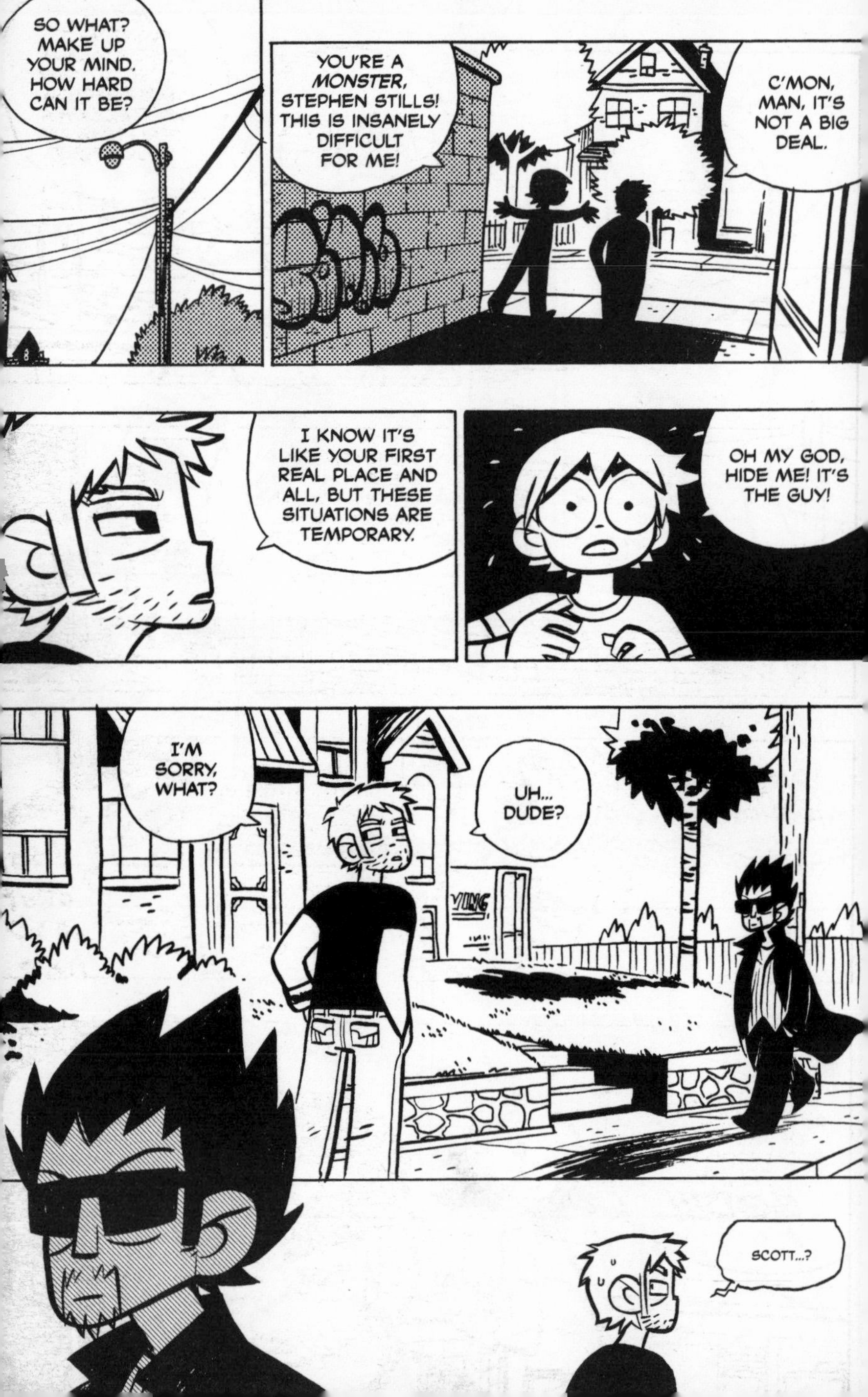
SO WHAT? MAKE UP YOUR MIND. HOW HARD CAN IT BE?
YOU'RE A *MONSTER*, STEPHEN STILLS! THIS IS INSANELY DIFFICULT FOR ME!
C'MON, MAN, IT'S NOT A BIG DEAL.
I KNOW IT'S LIKE YOUR FIRST REAL PLACE AND ALL, BUT THESE SITUATIONS ARE TEMPORARY.
OH MY GOD, HIDE ME! IT'S THE GUY!
I'M SORRY, WHAT?
UH... DUDE?
SCOTT...?

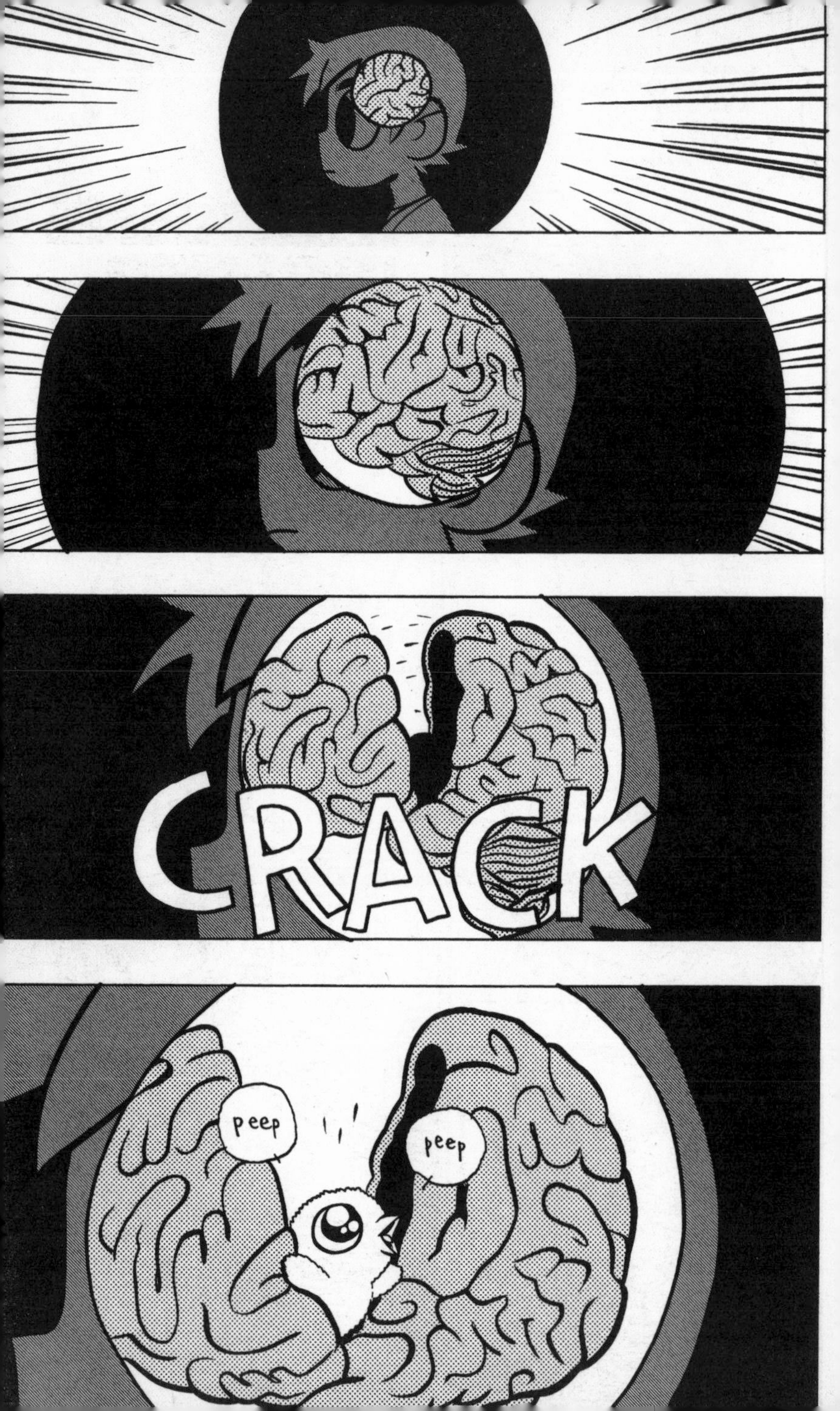
CRACK
peep
peep

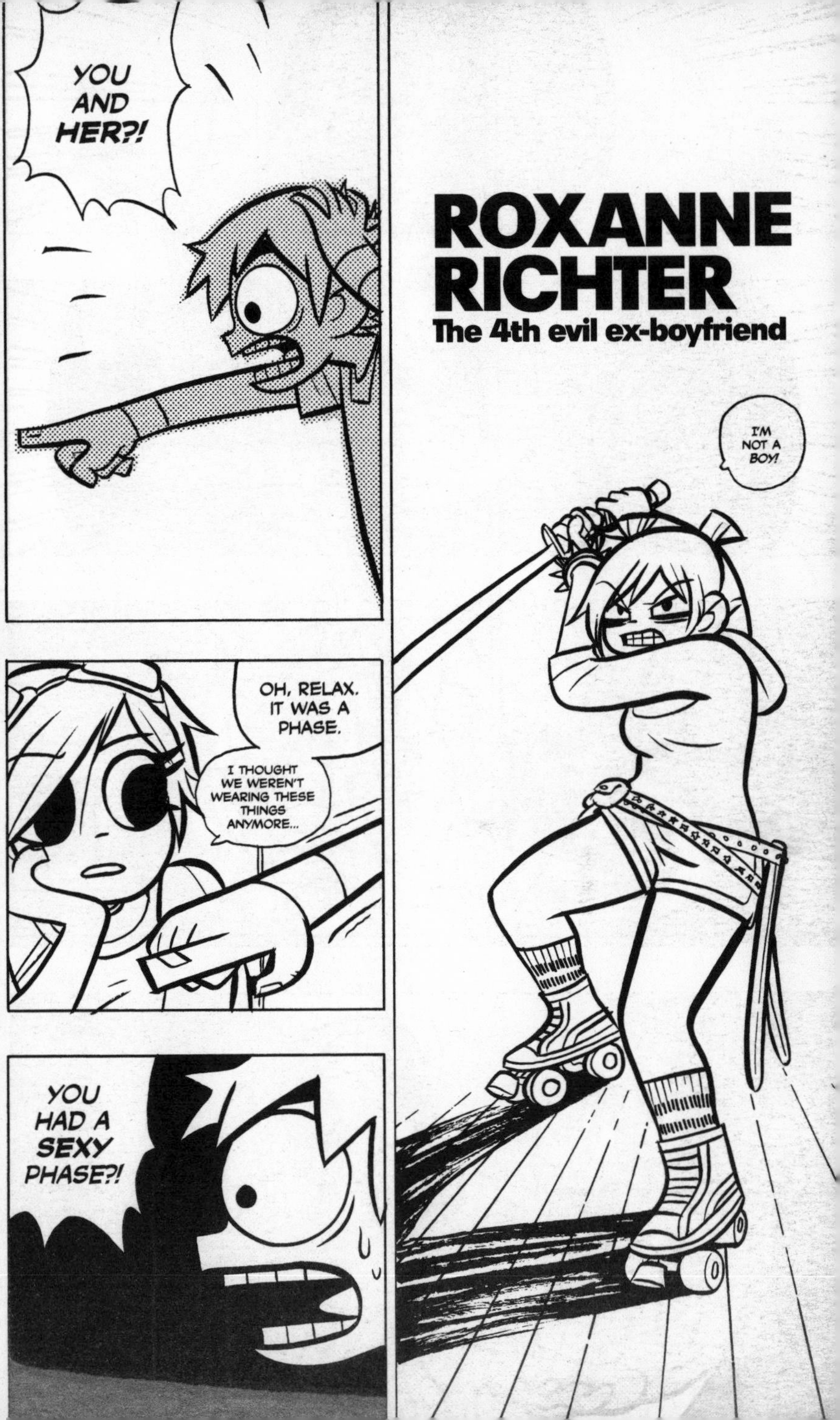
YOU AND HER?!
ROXANNE RICHTER
The 4th evil ex-boyfriend
I'M NOT A BOY!
OH, RELAX. IT WAS A PHASE.
I THOUGHT WE WEREN'T WEARING THESE THINGS ANYMORE...
YOU HAD A SEXY PHASE?!

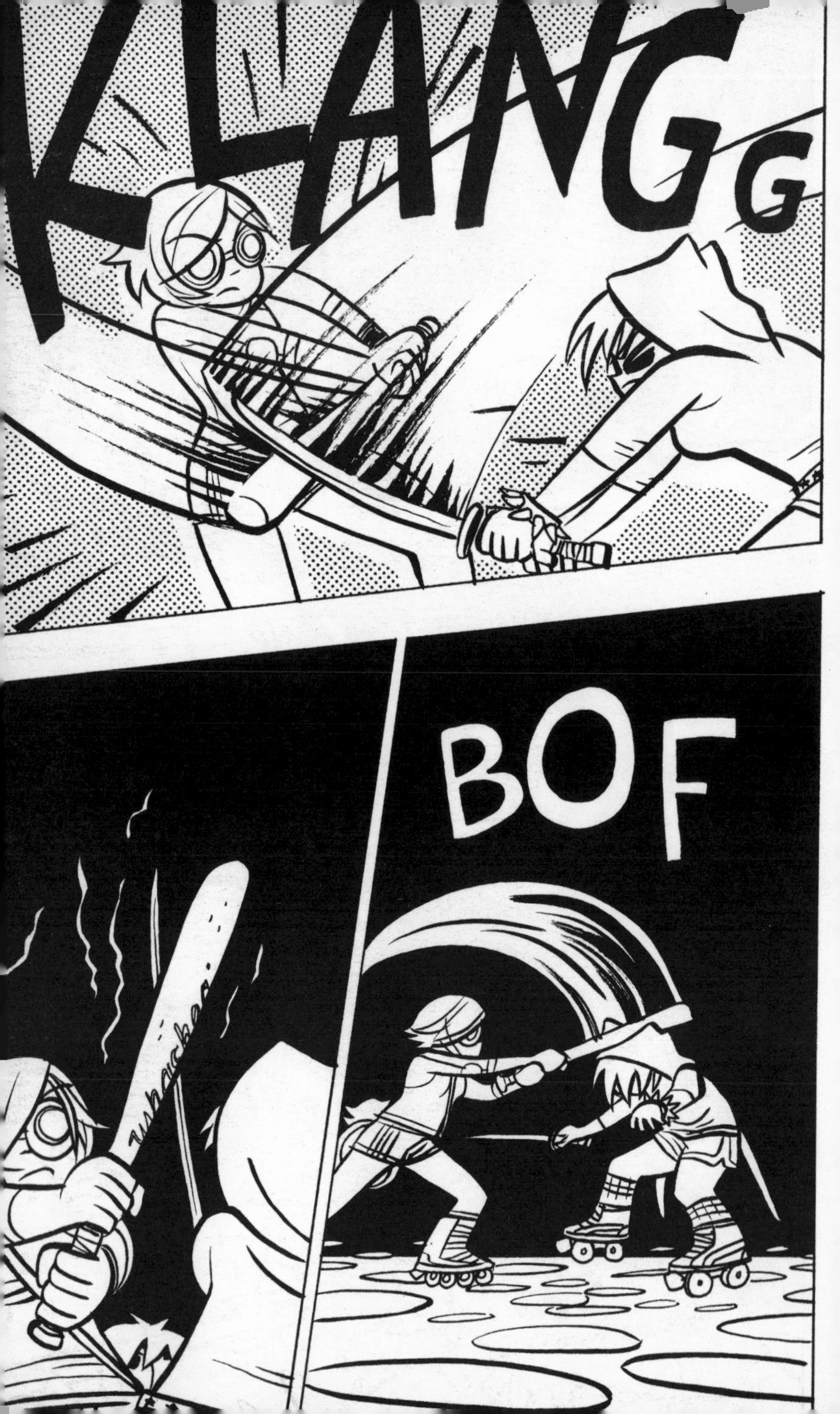
KLANGG
whacker
BOF

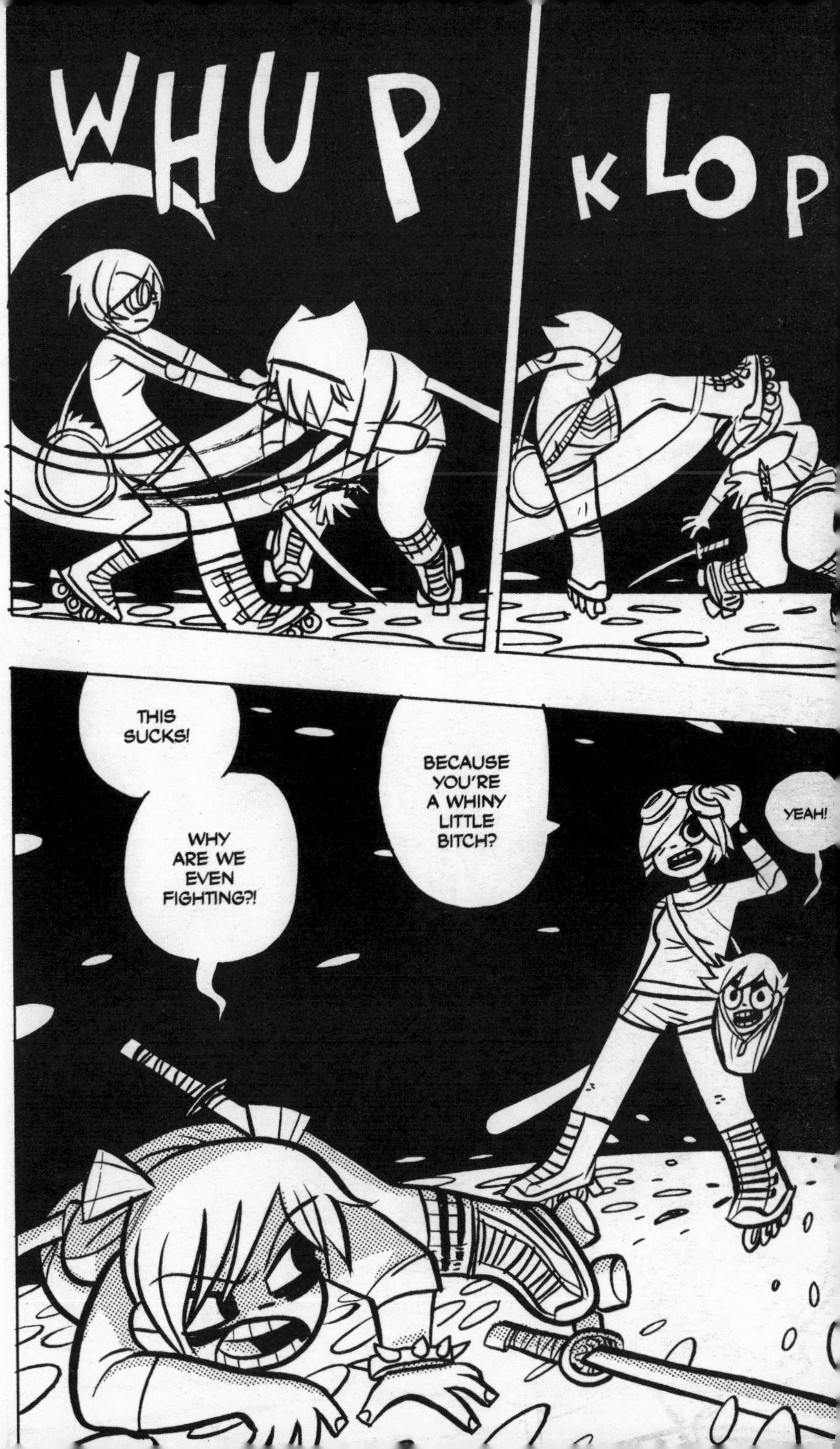
WHUP
KLOP
THIS SUCKS!
WHY ARE WE EVEN FIGHTING?!
BECAUSE YOU'RE A WHINY LITTLE BITCH?
YEAH!

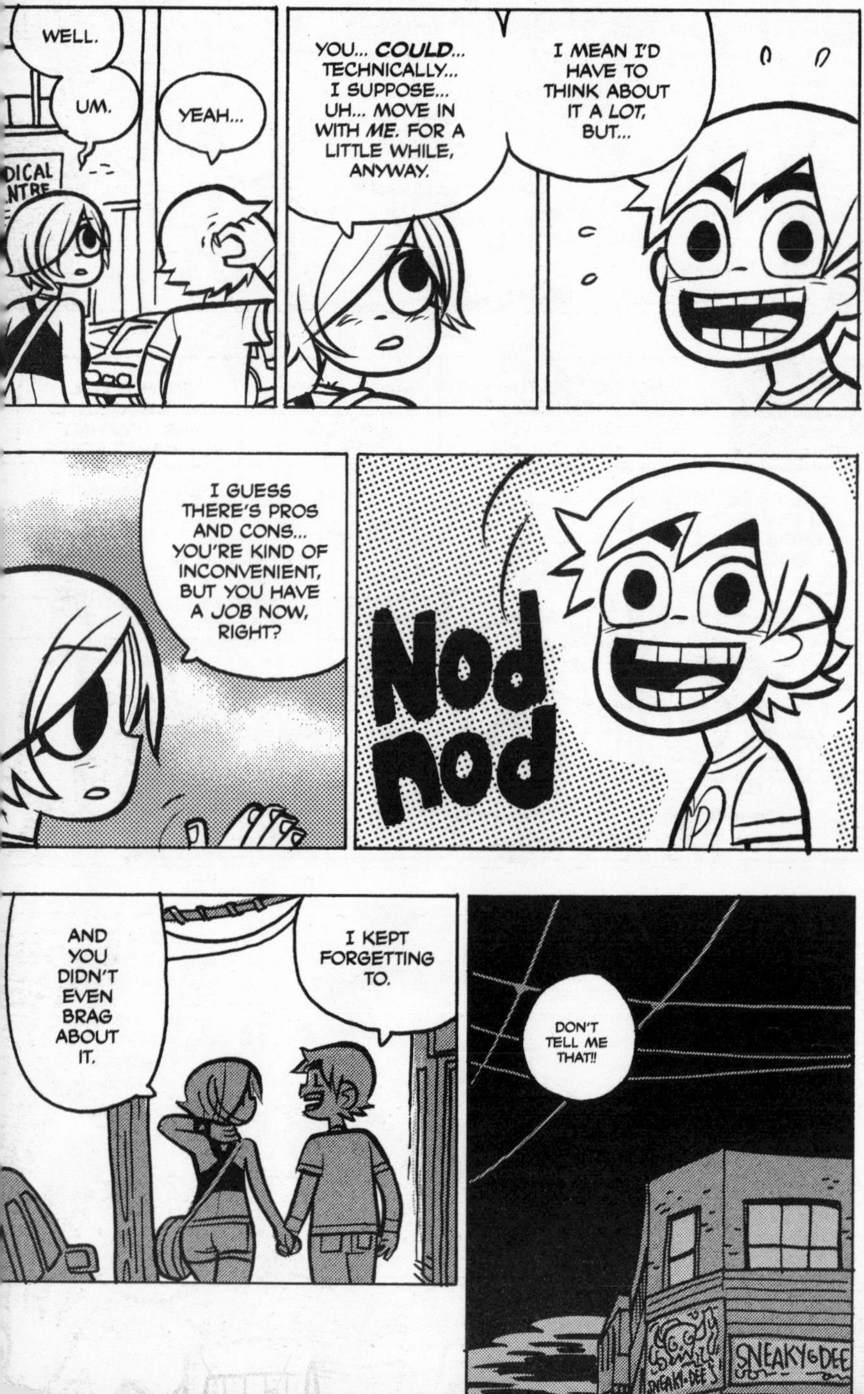
WELL.
UM.
YEAH...
DICAL
NTRE
YOU... COULD... TECHNICALLY... I SUPPOSE... UH... MOVE IN WITH ME. FOR A LITTLE WHILE, ANYWAY.
I MEAN I'D HAVE TO THINK ABOUT IT A LOT, BUT...
I GUESS THERE'S PROS AND CONS... YOU'RE KIND OF INCONVENIENT, BUT YOU HAVE A JOB NOW, RIGHT?
Nod nod
AND YOU DIDN'T EVEN BRAG ABOUT IT.
I KEPT FORGETTING TO.
DON'T TELL ME THAT!!
SNEAKY DEE'S
SNEAKY DEE

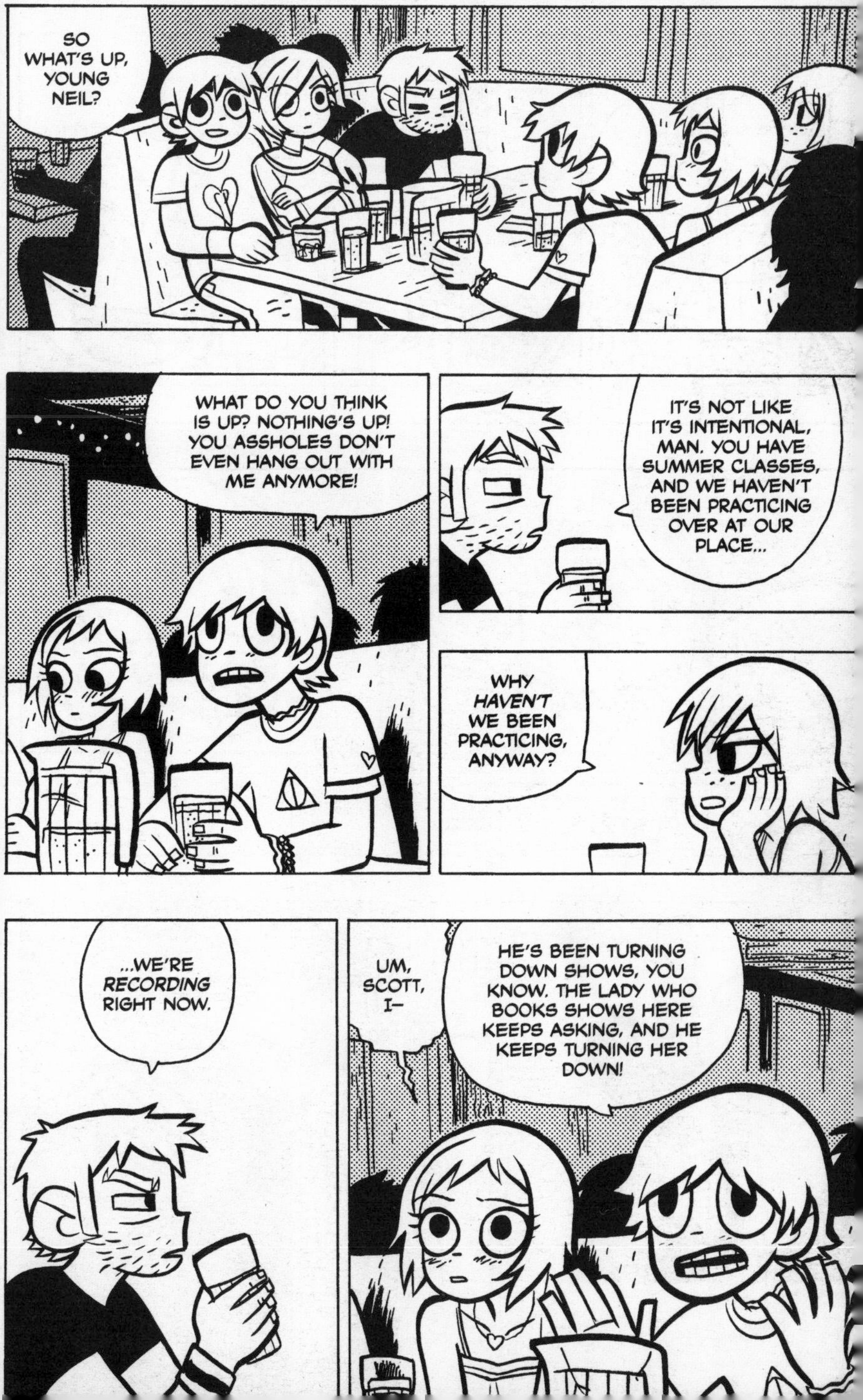
SO WHAT'S UP, YOUNG NEIL?
WHAT DO YOU THINK IS UP? NOTHING'S UP! YOU ASSHOLES DON'T EVEN HANG OUT WITH ME ANYMORE!
IT'S NOT LIKE IT'S INTENTIONAL, MAN. YOU HAVE SUMMER CLASSES, AND WE HAVEN'T BEEN PRACTICING OVER AT OUR PLACE...
WHY *HAVEN'T* WE BEEN PRACTICING, ANYWAY?
...WE'RE *RECORDING* RIGHT NOW.
UM, SCOTT, I–
HE'S BEEN TURNING DOWN SHOWS, YOU KNOW. THE LADY WHO BOOKS SHOWS HERE KEEPS ASKING, AND HE KEEPS TURNING HER DOWN!

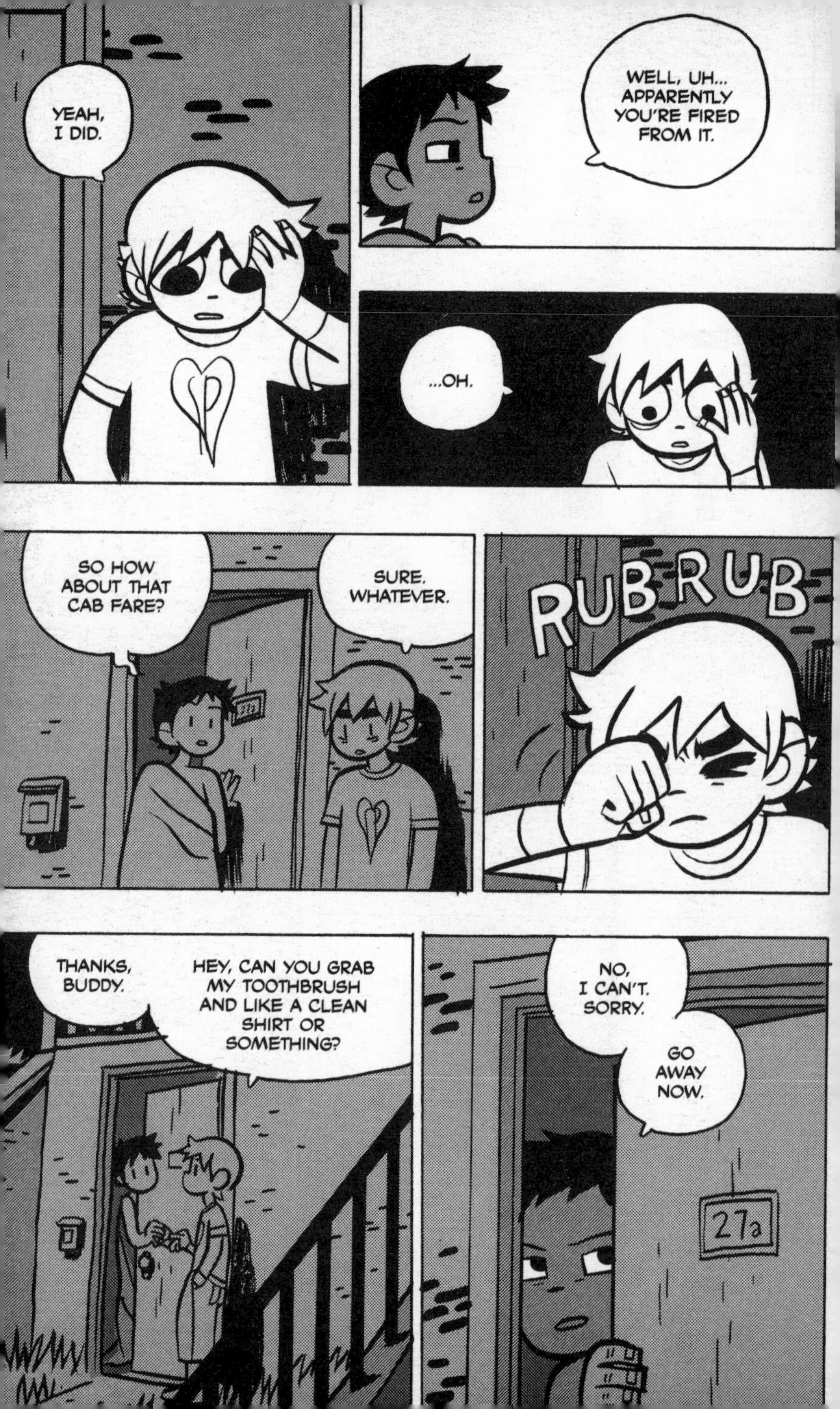

YEAH, I DID.
WELL, UH... APPARENTLY YOU'RE FIRED FROM IT.
...OH.
SO HOW ABOUT THAT CAB FARE?
SURE. WHATEVER.
RUB RUB
THANKS, BUDDY.
HEY, CAN YOU GRAB MY TOOTHBRUSH AND LIKE A CLEAN SHIRT OR SOMETHING?
NO, I CAN'T. SORRY.
GO AWAY NOW.
27a

THOUGHT

CONTENTS OF SCOTT PILGRIM'S POCKETS

candy wrapper
rock
couch w/face of dog
lint
guitar pick
???
single penny
also lint
$10 (from wallace)

271-3406
Lisa M.

AAAA AARAA GGHHRR BBLGHRF

(deep breath)

AAAHII EERRRGH HHRAAFFGBL

Lisa's sister's apartment

2 AM-ish

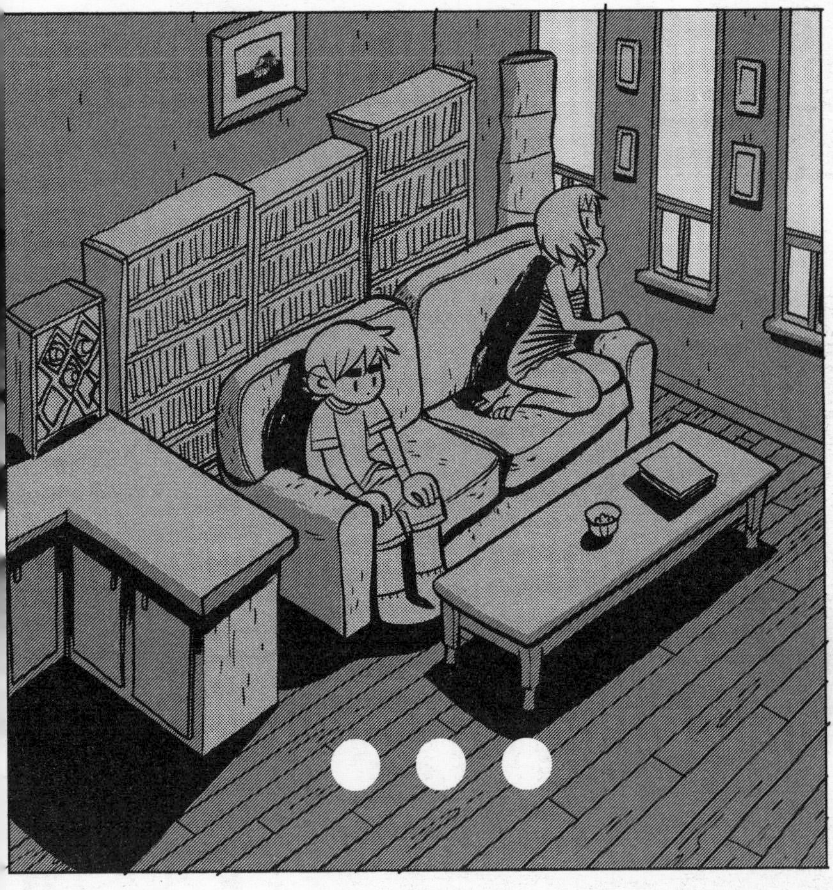

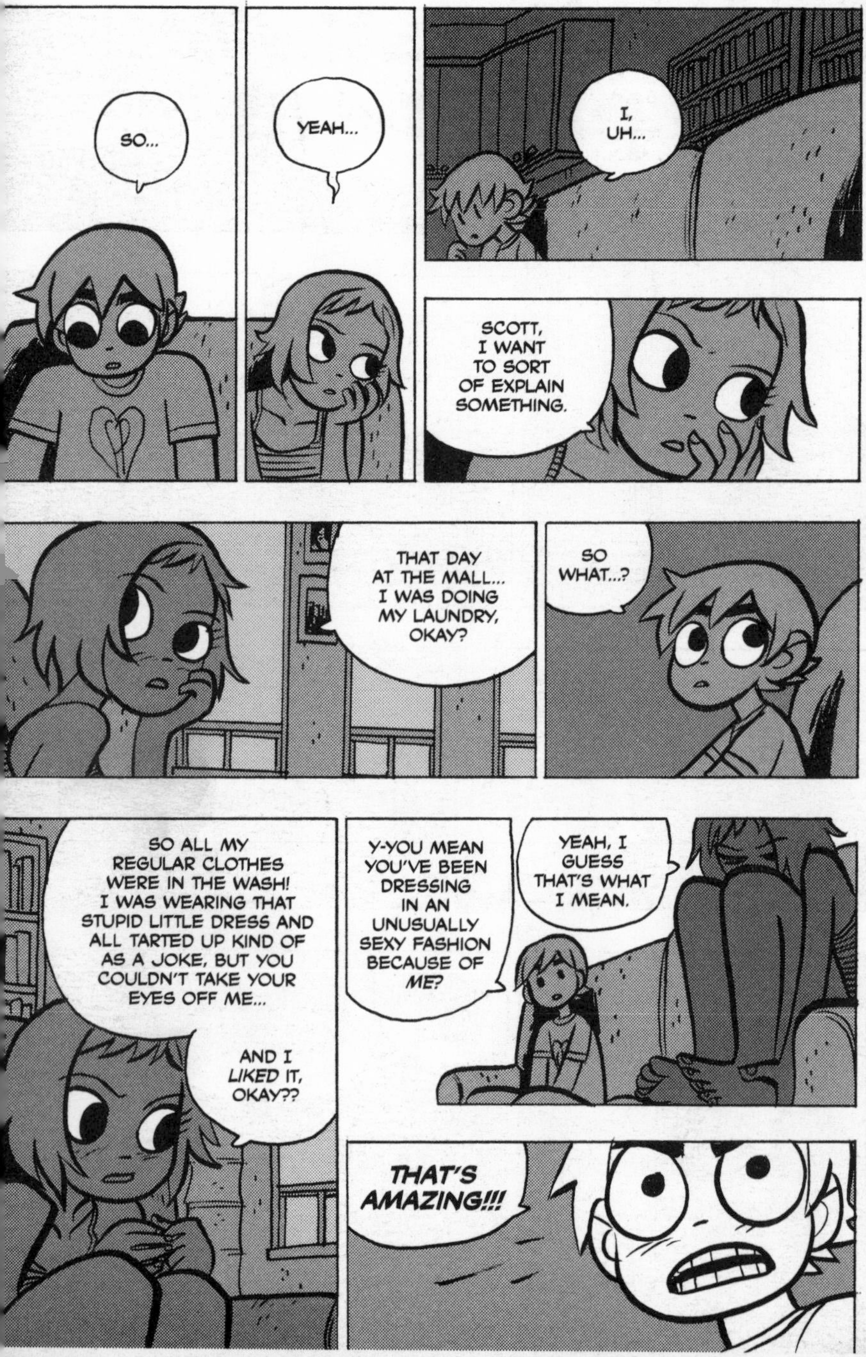
SO...
YEAH...
I, UH...
SCOTT, I WANT TO SORT OF EXPLAIN SOMETHING.
THAT DAY AT THE MALL... I WAS DOING MY LAUNDRY, OKAY?
SO WHAT...?
SO ALL MY REGULAR CLOTHES WERE IN THE WASH! I WAS WEARING THAT STUPID LITTLE DRESS AND ALL TARTED UP KIND OF AS A JOKE, BUT YOU COULDN'T TAKE YOUR EYES OFF ME...
AND I *LIKED* IT, OKAY??
Y-YOU MEAN YOU'VE BEEN DRESSING IN AN UNUSUALLY SEXY FASHION BECAUSE OF *ME?*
YEAH, I GUESS THAT'S WHAT I MEAN.
THAT'S AMAZING!!!

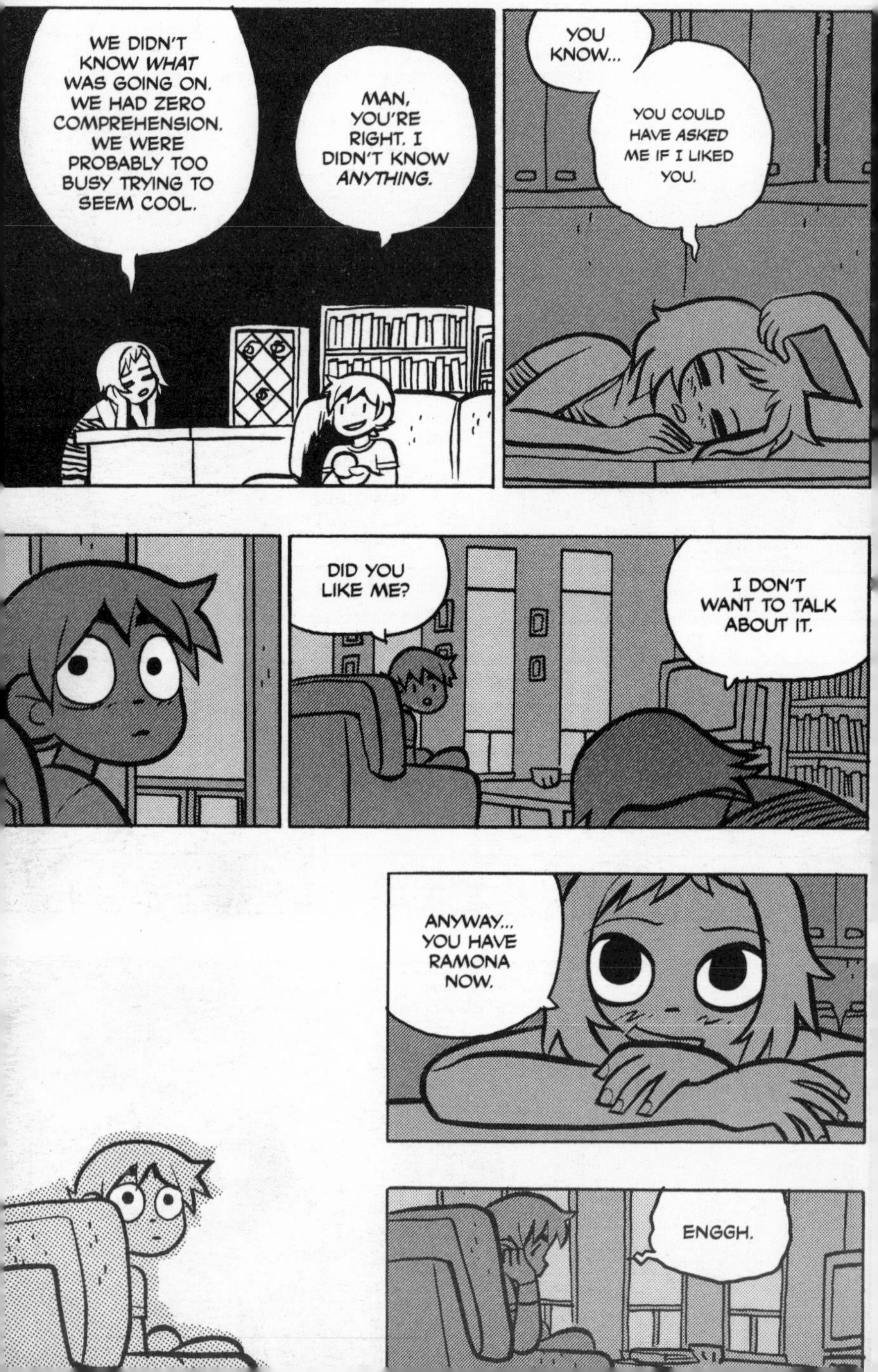
WE DIDN'T KNOW *WHAT* WAS GOING ON. WE HAD ZERO COMPREHENSION. WE WERE PROBABLY TOO BUSY TRYING TO SEEM COOL.
MAN, YOU'RE RIGHT. I DIDN'T KNOW *ANYTHING.*
YOU KNOW...
YOU COULD HAVE *ASKED* ME IF I LIKED YOU.
DID YOU LIKE ME?
I DON'T WANT TO TALK ABOUT IT.
ANYWAY... YOU HAVE RAMONA NOW.
ENGGH.

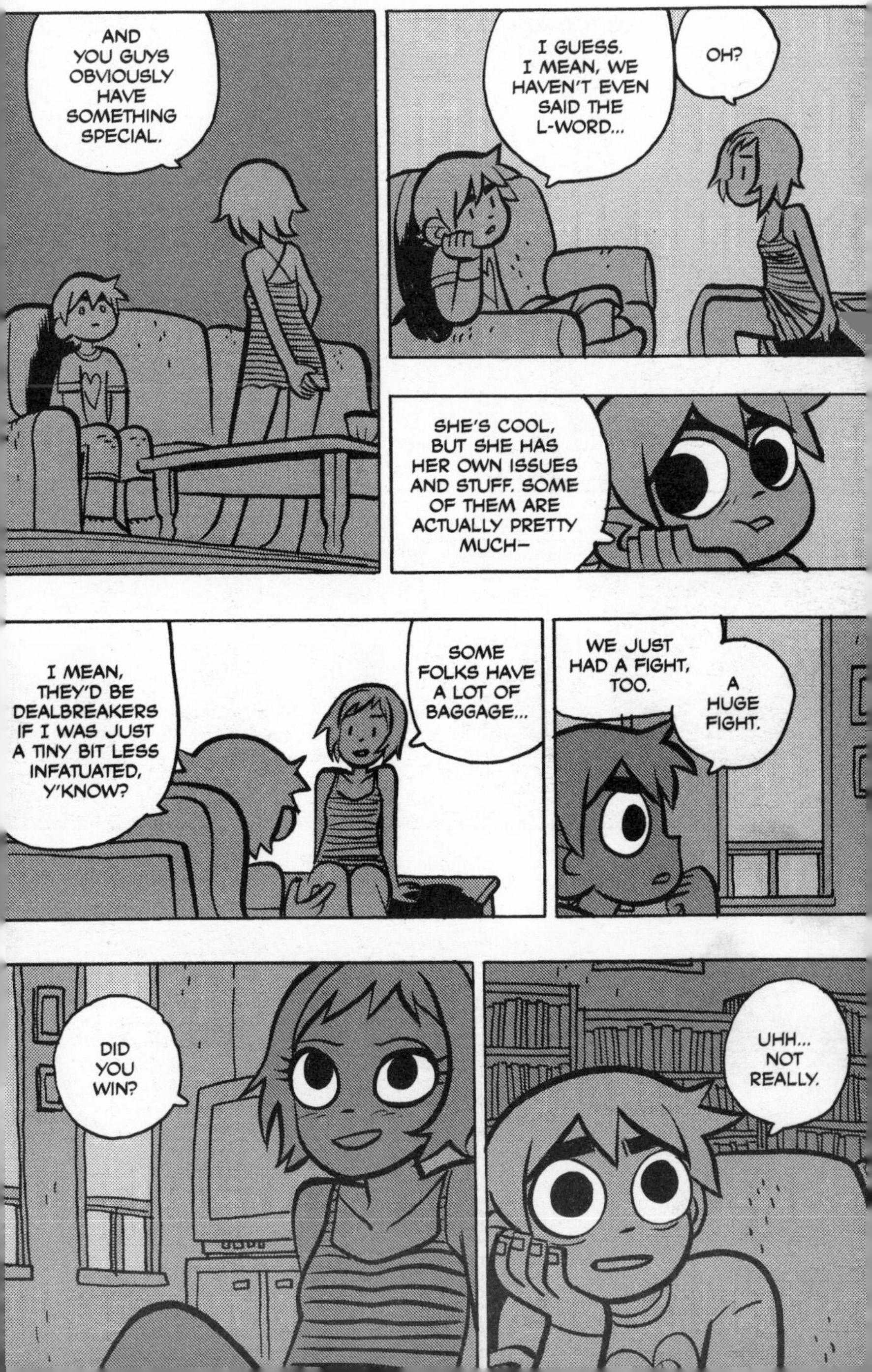
AND YOU GUYS OBVIOUSLY HAVE SOMETHING SPECIAL.
I GUESS. I MEAN, WE HAVEN'T EVEN SAID THE L-WORD...
OH?
SHE'S COOL, BUT SHE HAS HER OWN ISSUES AND STUFF. SOME OF THEM ARE ACTUALLY PRETTY MUCH–
I MEAN, THEY'D BE DEALBREAKERS IF I WAS JUST A TINY BIT LESS INFATUATED, Y'KNOW?
SOME FOLKS HAVE A LOT OF BAGGAGE...
WE JUST HAD A FIGHT, TOO.
A HUGE FIGHT.
DID YOU WIN?
UHH... NOT REALLY.

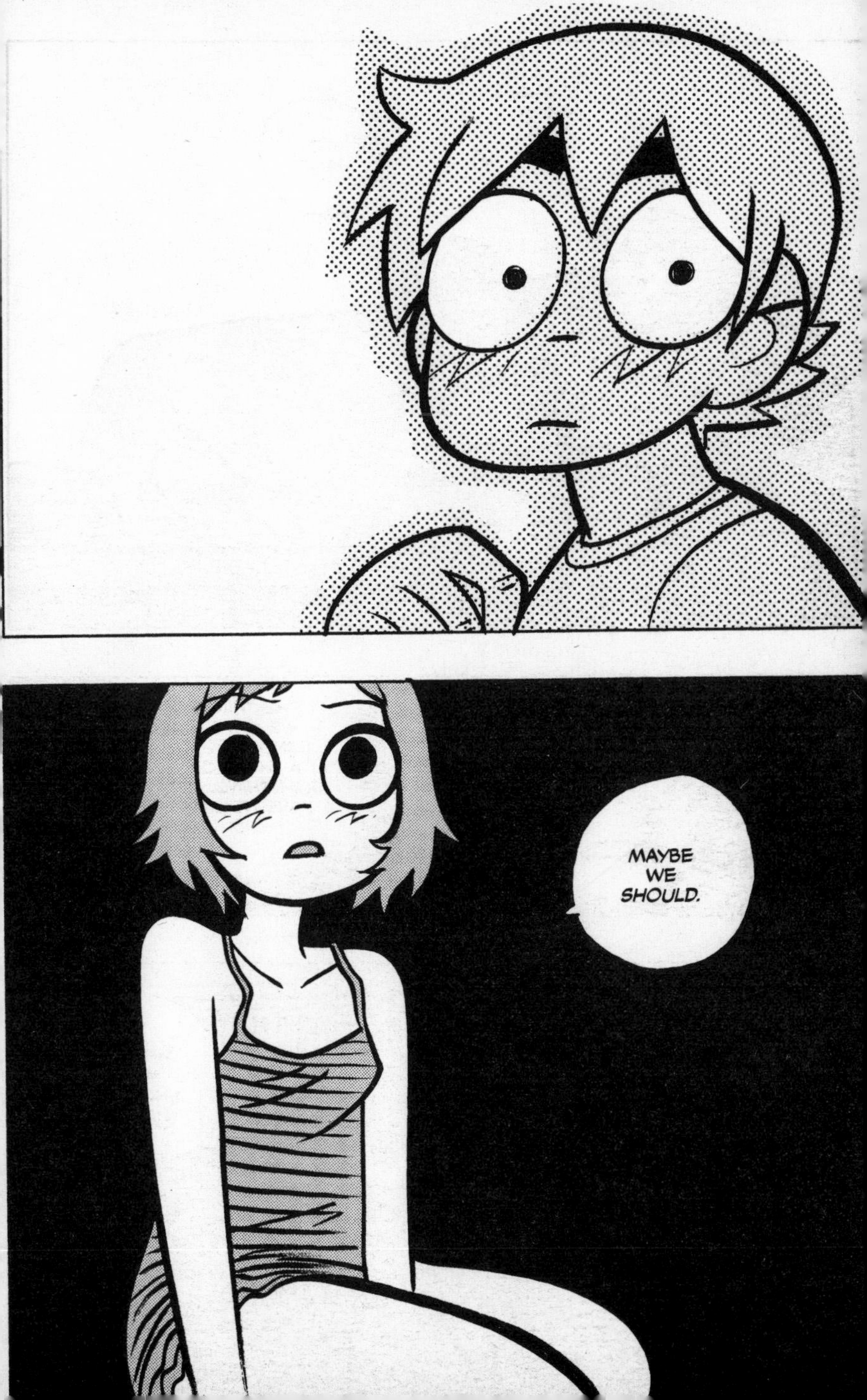
MAYBE WE SHOULD.

24 Terrible vision

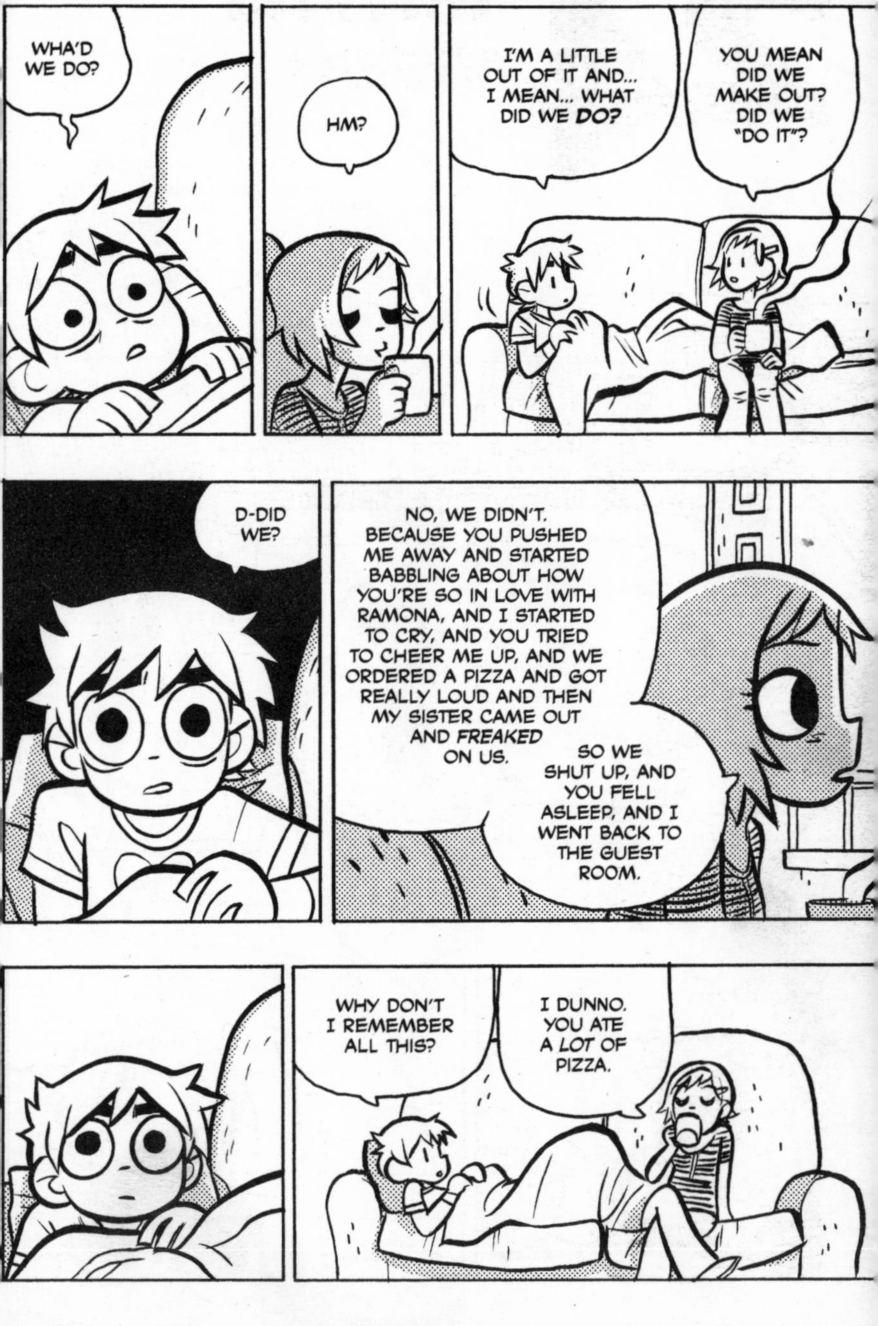
WHA'D WE DO?
HM?
I'M A LITTLE OUT OF IT AND... I MEAN... WHAT DID WE DO?
YOU MEAN DID WE MAKE OUT? DID WE "DO IT"?
D-DID WE?
NO, WE DIDN'T. BECAUSE YOU PUSHED ME AWAY AND STARTED BABBLING ABOUT HOW YOU'RE SO IN LOVE WITH RAMONA, AND I STARTED TO CRY, AND YOU TRIED TO CHEER ME UP, AND WE ORDERED A PIZZA AND GOT REALLY LOUD AND THEN MY SISTER CAME OUT AND FREAKED ON US.
SO WE SHUT UP, AND YOU FELL ASLEEP, AND I WENT BACK TO THE GUEST ROOM.
WHY DON'T I REMEMBER ALL THIS?
I DUNNO. YOU ATE A LOT OF PIZZA.

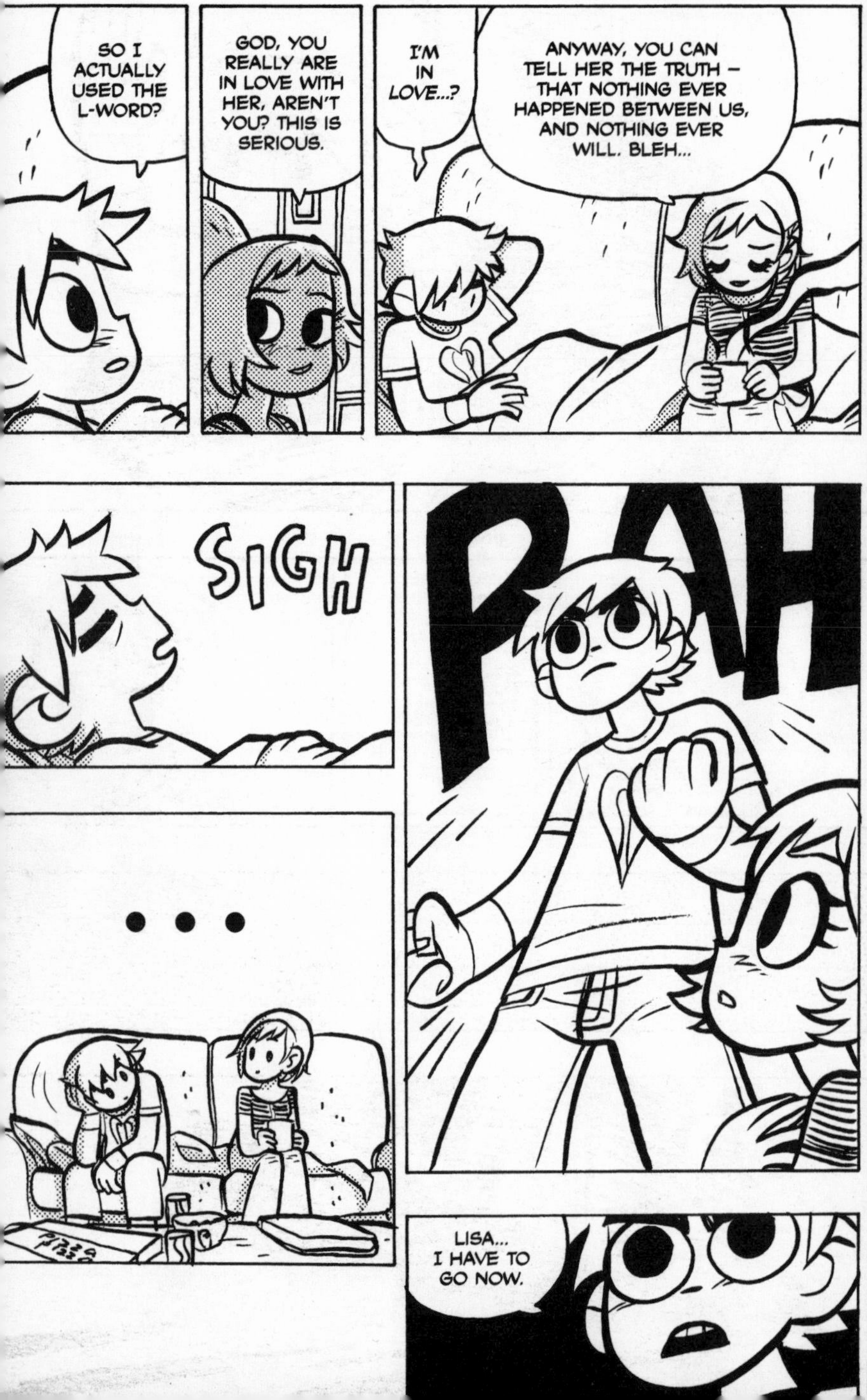
SO I ACTUALLY USED THE L-WORD?
GOD, YOU REALLY ARE IN LOVE WITH HER, AREN'T YOU? THIS IS SERIOUS.
I'M IN LOVE...?
ANYWAY, YOU CAN TELL HER THE TRUTH – THAT NOTHING EVER HAPPENED BETWEEN US, AND NOTHING EVER WILL. BLEH...
SIGH
• • •
RAH
LISA... I HAVE TO GO NOW.

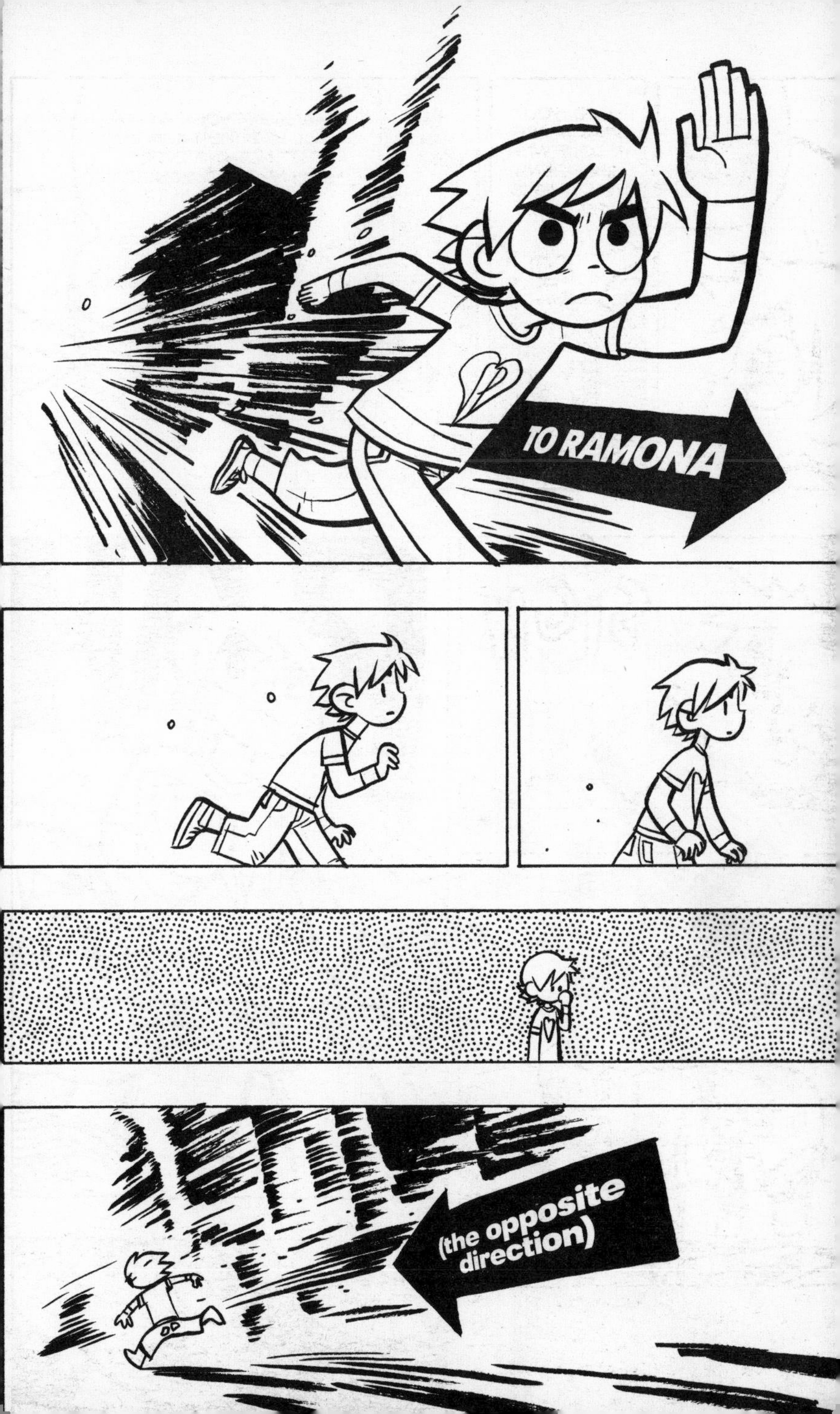
TO RAMONA
(the opposite direction)

AND THAT MUST HAVE CAUSED MY DAD'S BRAIN TO...

SPLIT

...BREAK IN HALF, REPLACED BY A PURELY MECHANICAL ENGINE OF REVENGE!

SO *HE* MUST BE THE ONE WHO DEFACED MY SHRINE!

SLASH

HE PROBABLY WANTS TO CUT YOUR HEAD OFF WITH HIS PRIZED ANTIQUE SAMURAI SWORDS!

MAN, MY DAD IS *SO* LAME.

WELL THAT'S JUST *GREAT*.

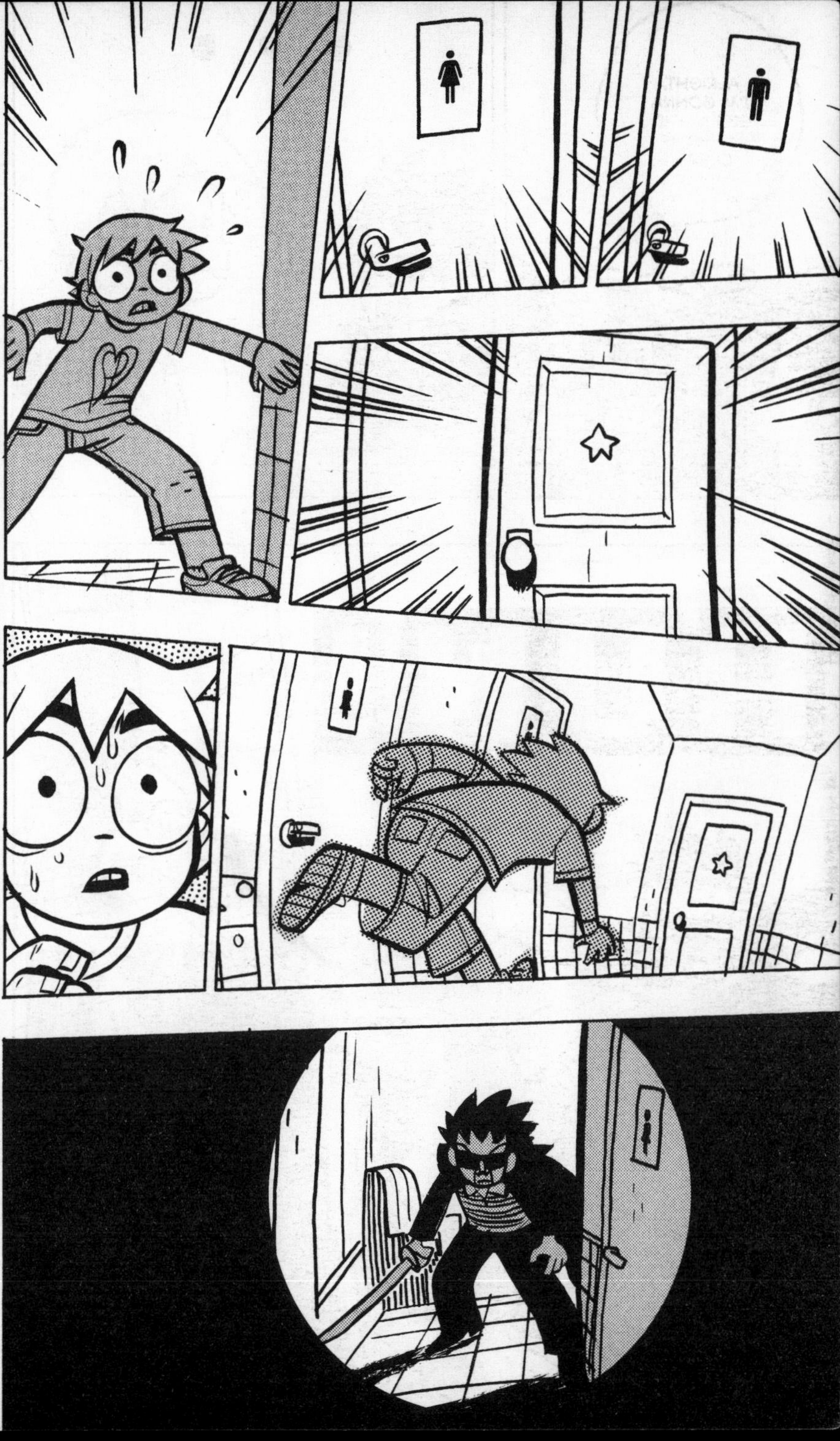

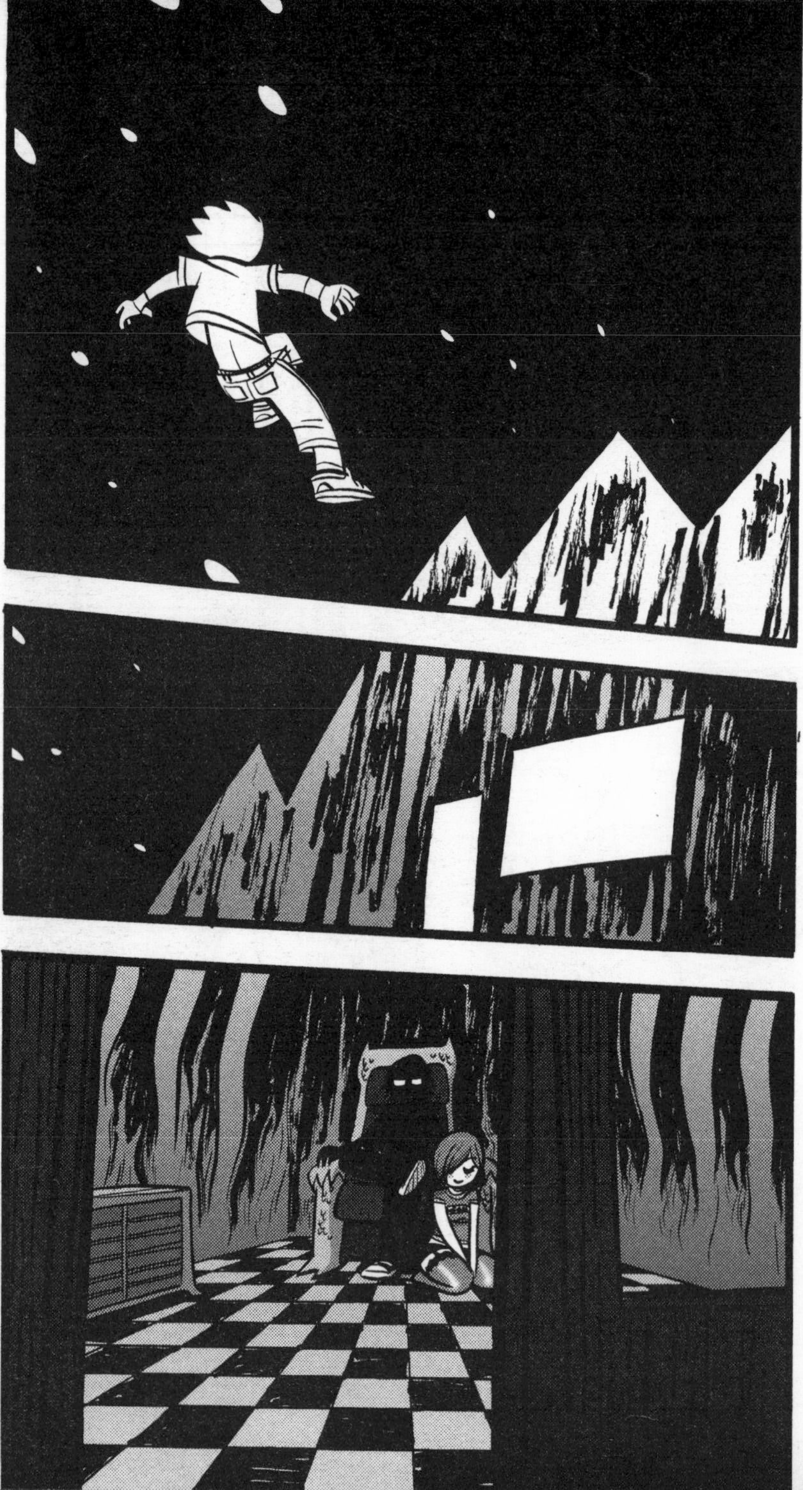

RAMONA? IS... IS THIS YOUR HEAD?

AM I IN YOUR HEAD?

WHAT ARE YOU DOING HERE? GET OUT!

WHAT IS THIS?

STOP LOOKING AT ME!!

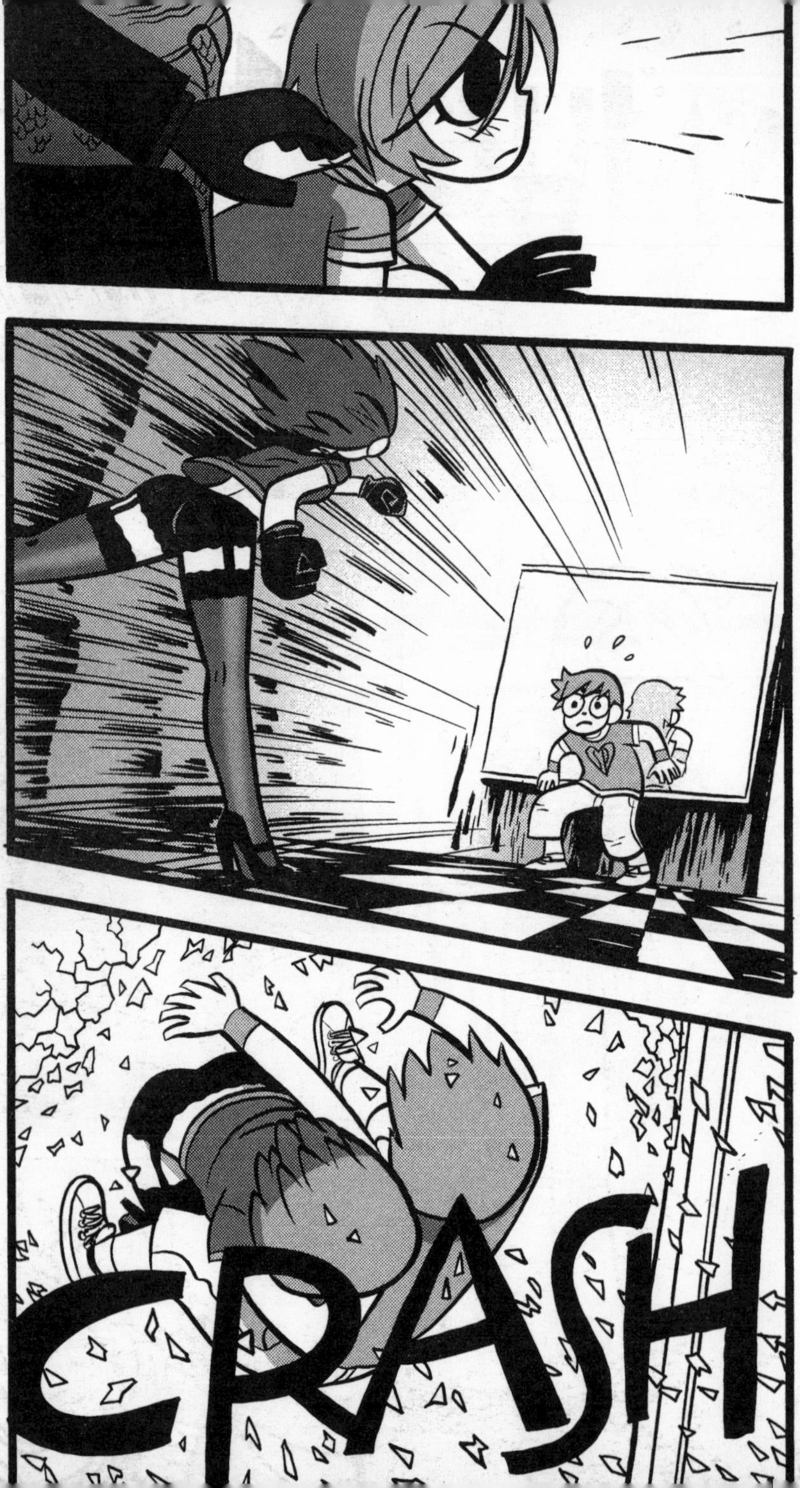
CRASH

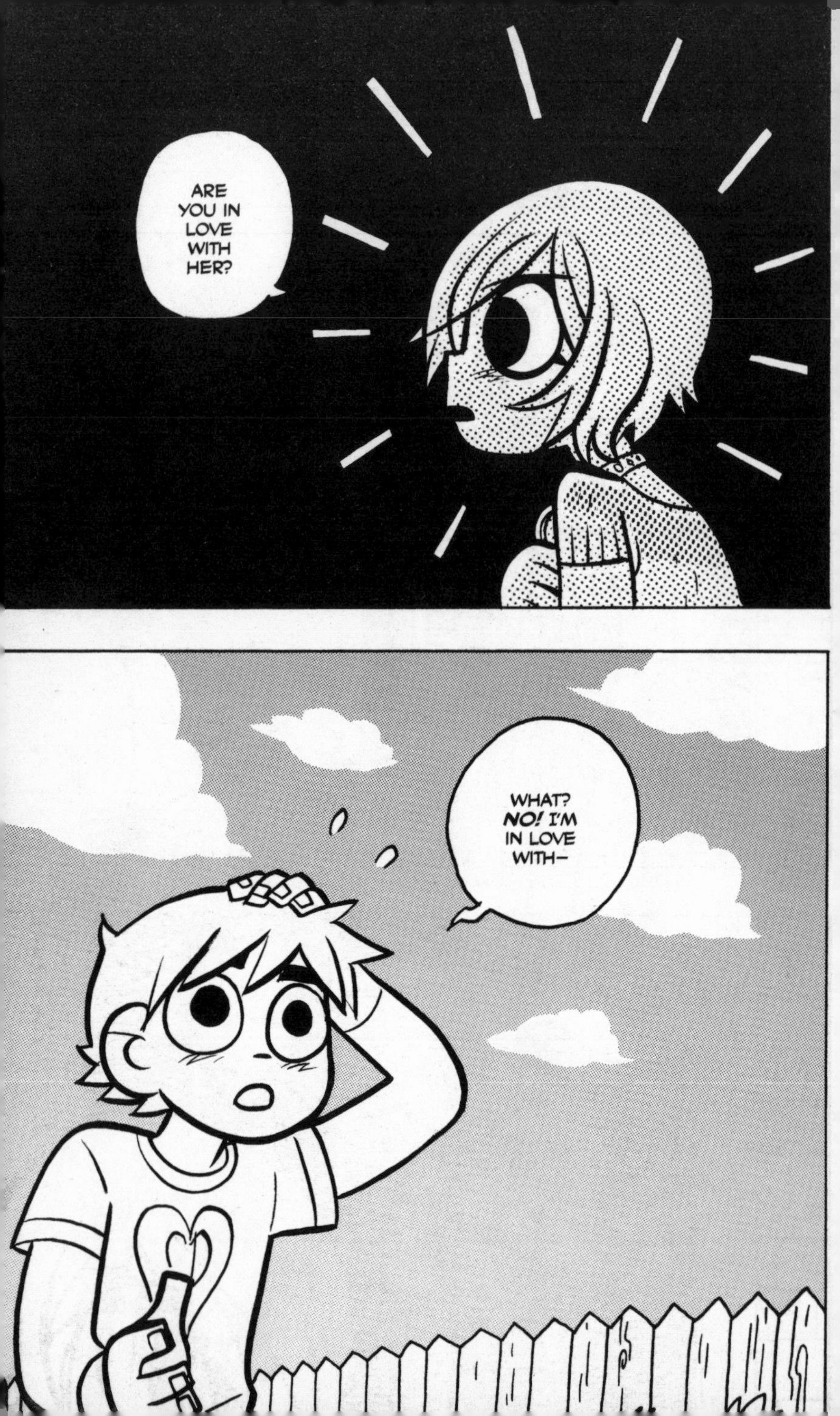
ARE YOU IN LOVE WITH HER?
WHAT? NO! I'M IN LOVE WITH–

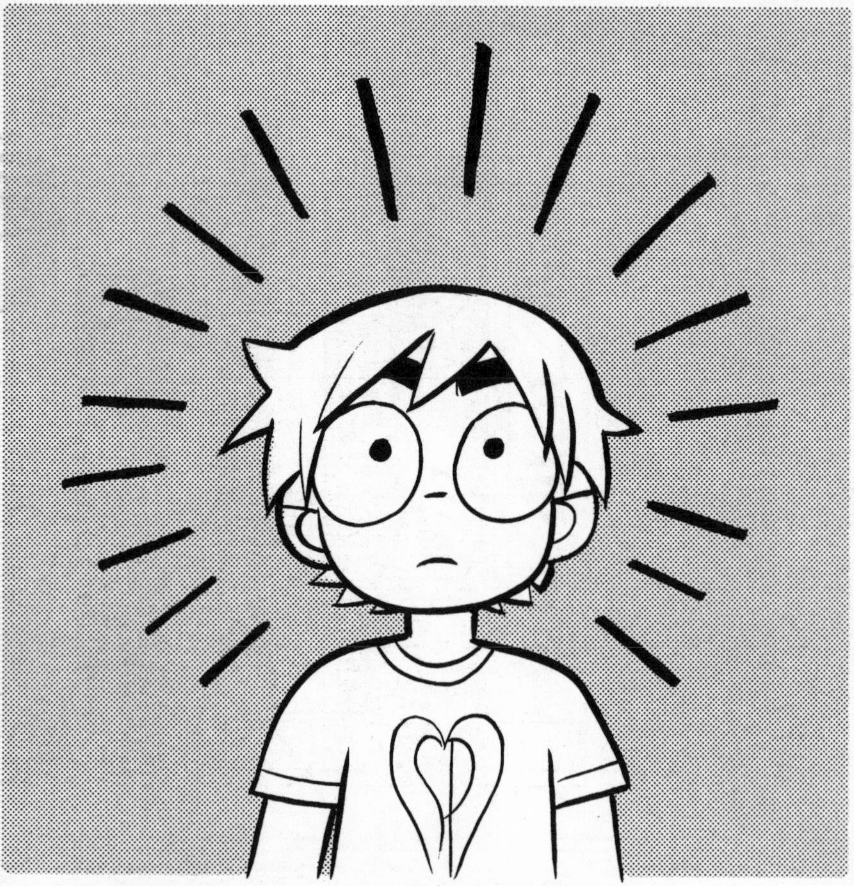

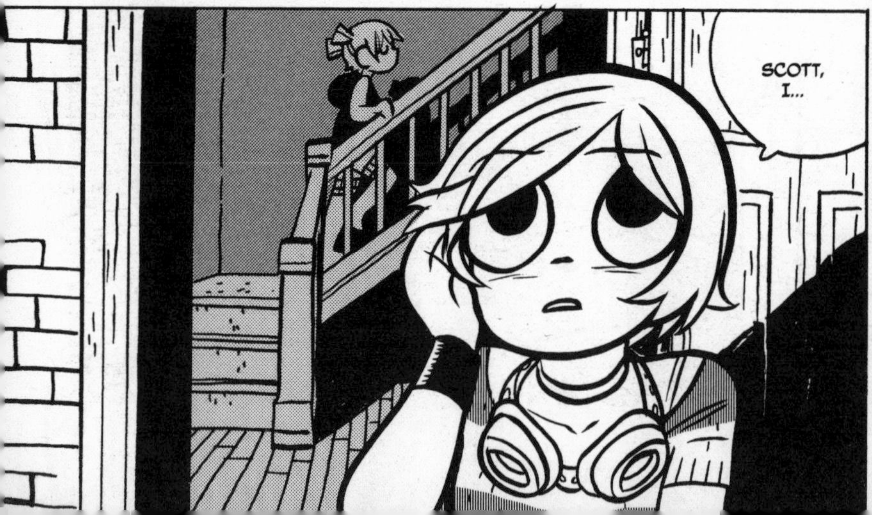
SCOTT,
I...

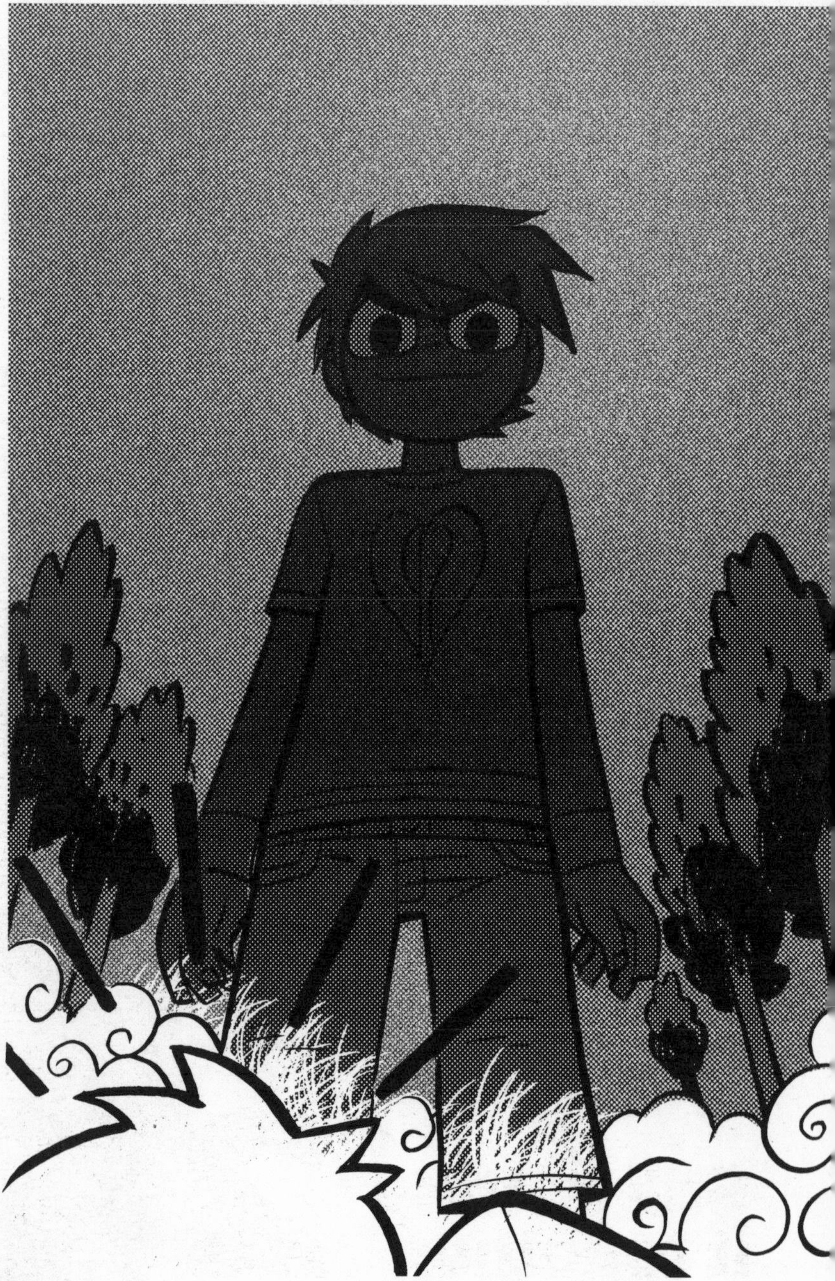

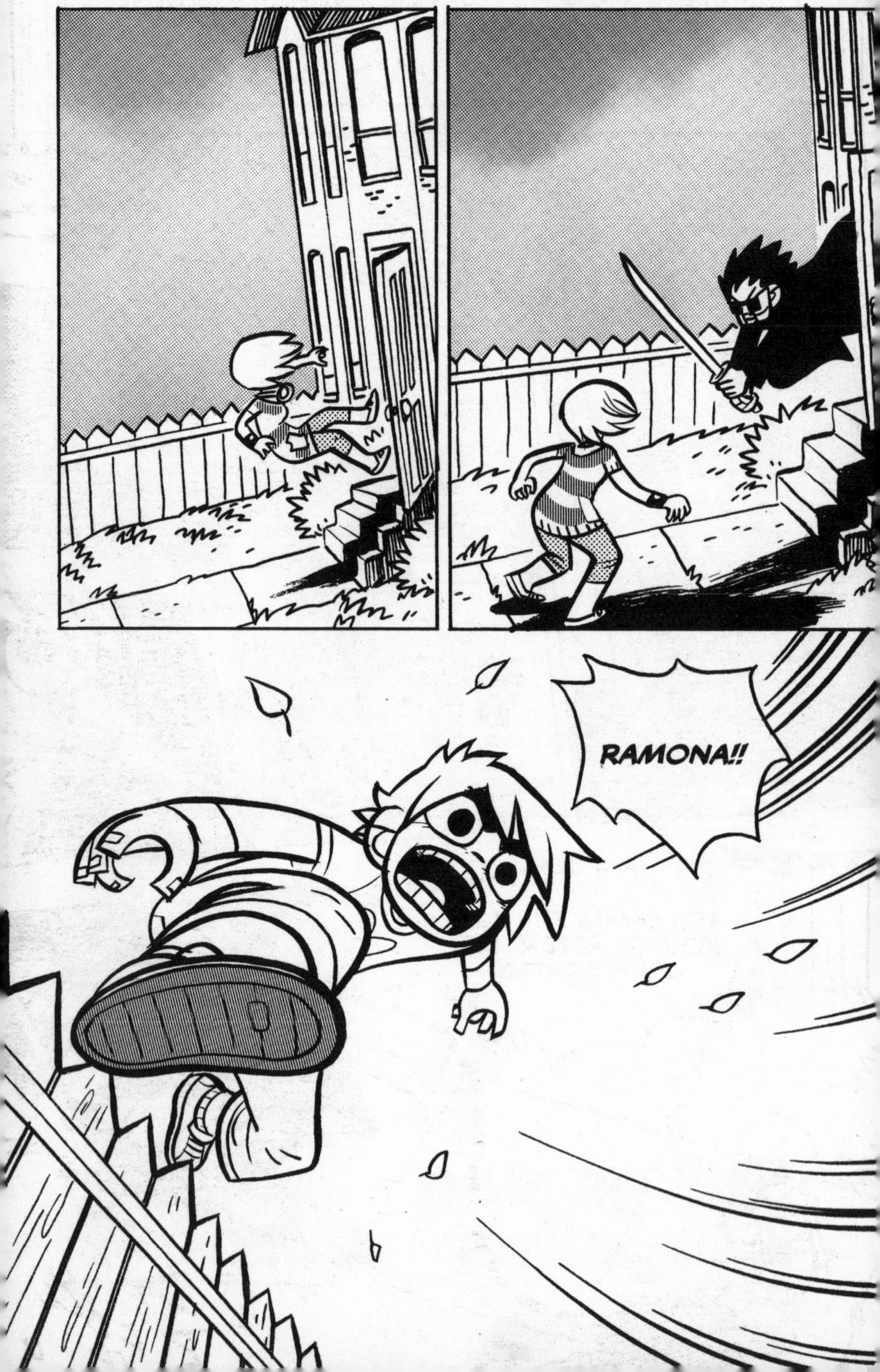
RAMONA!!

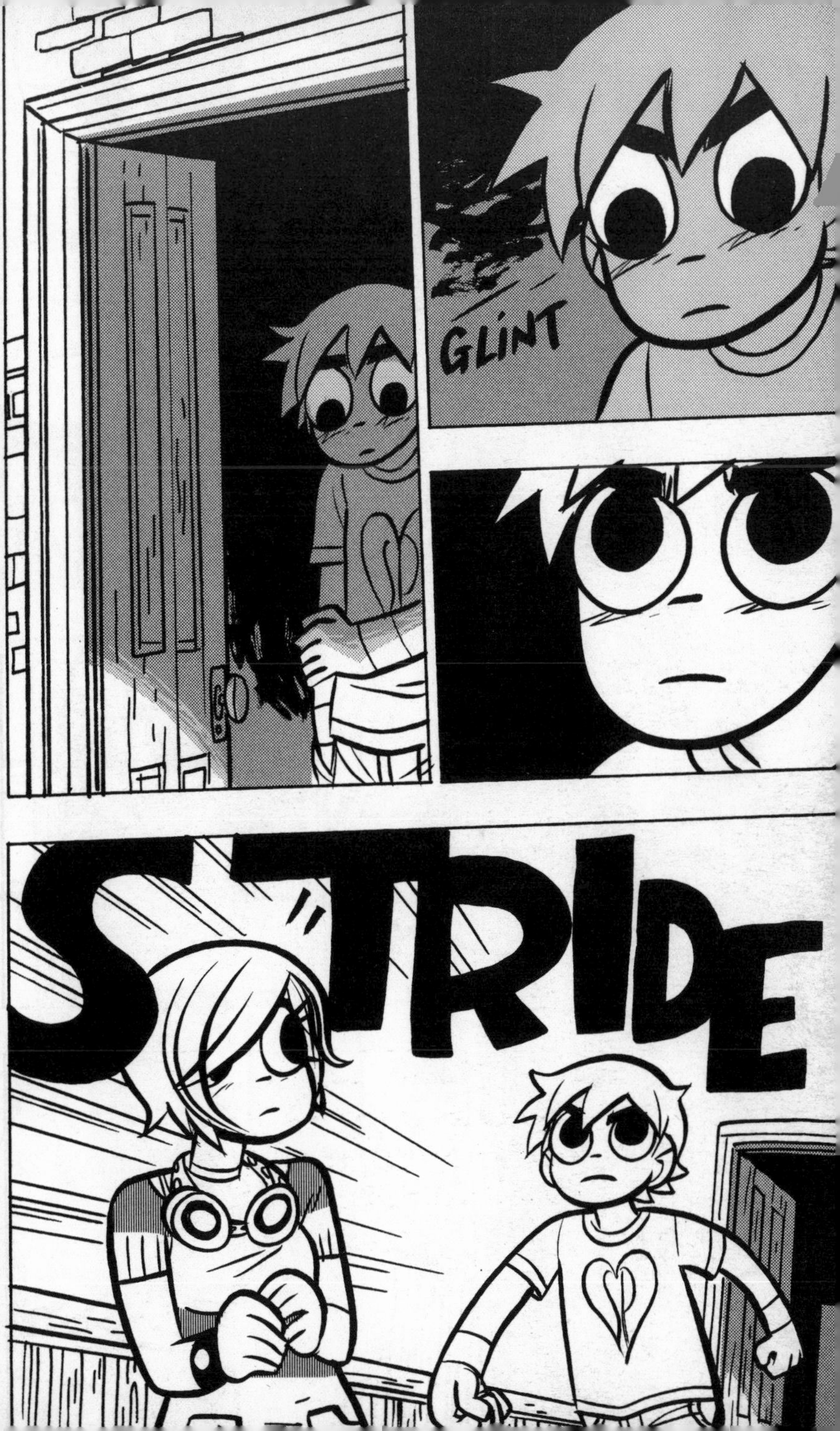
GLINT
STRIDE

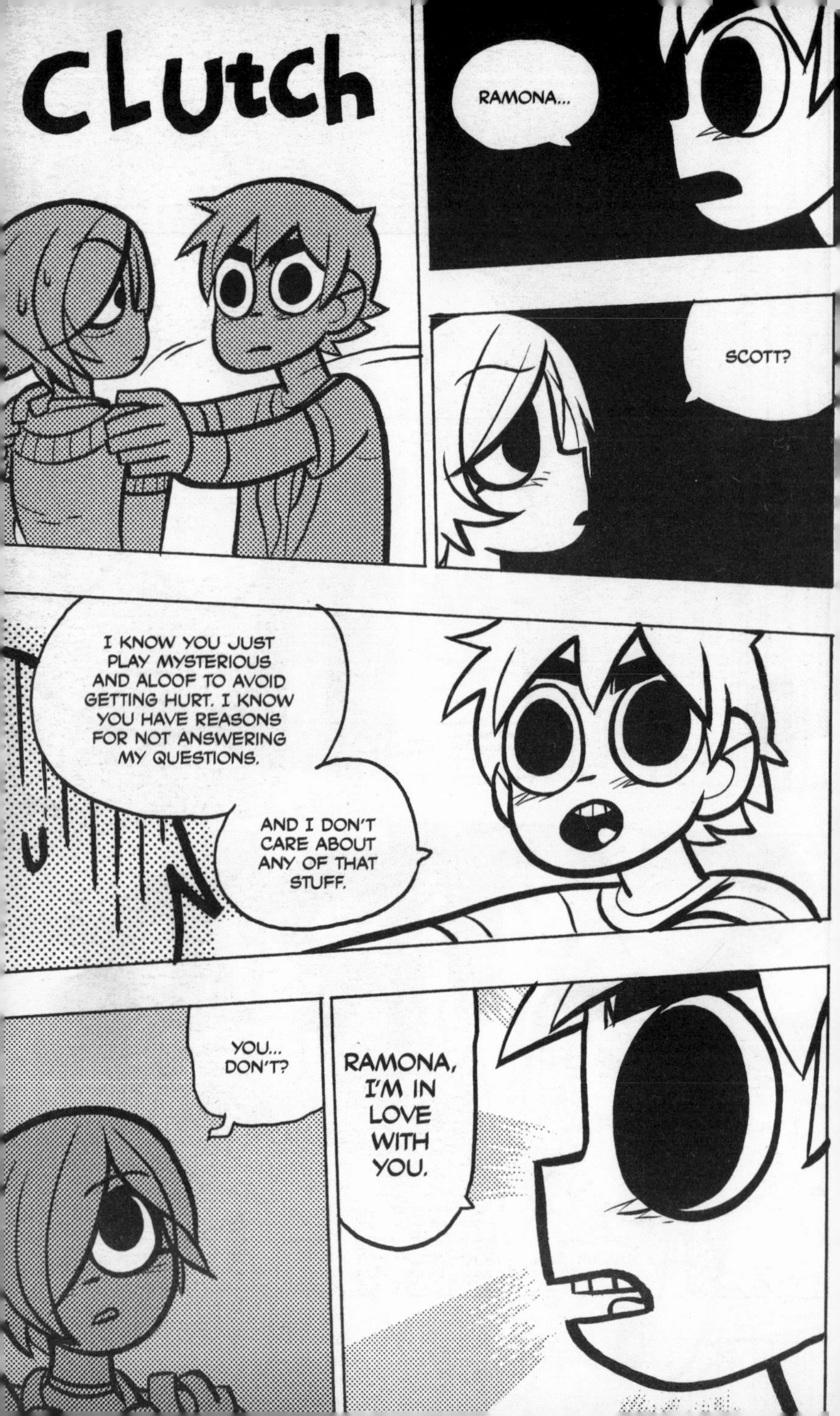
CLUTCH
RAMONA...
SCOTT?
I KNOW YOU JUST PLAY MYSTERIOUS AND ALOOF TO AVOID GETTING HURT. I KNOW YOU HAVE REASONS FOR NOT ANSWERING MY QUESTIONS.
AND I DON'T CARE ABOUT ANY OF THAT STUFF.
YOU... DON'T?
RAMONA, I'M IN LOVE WITH YOU.

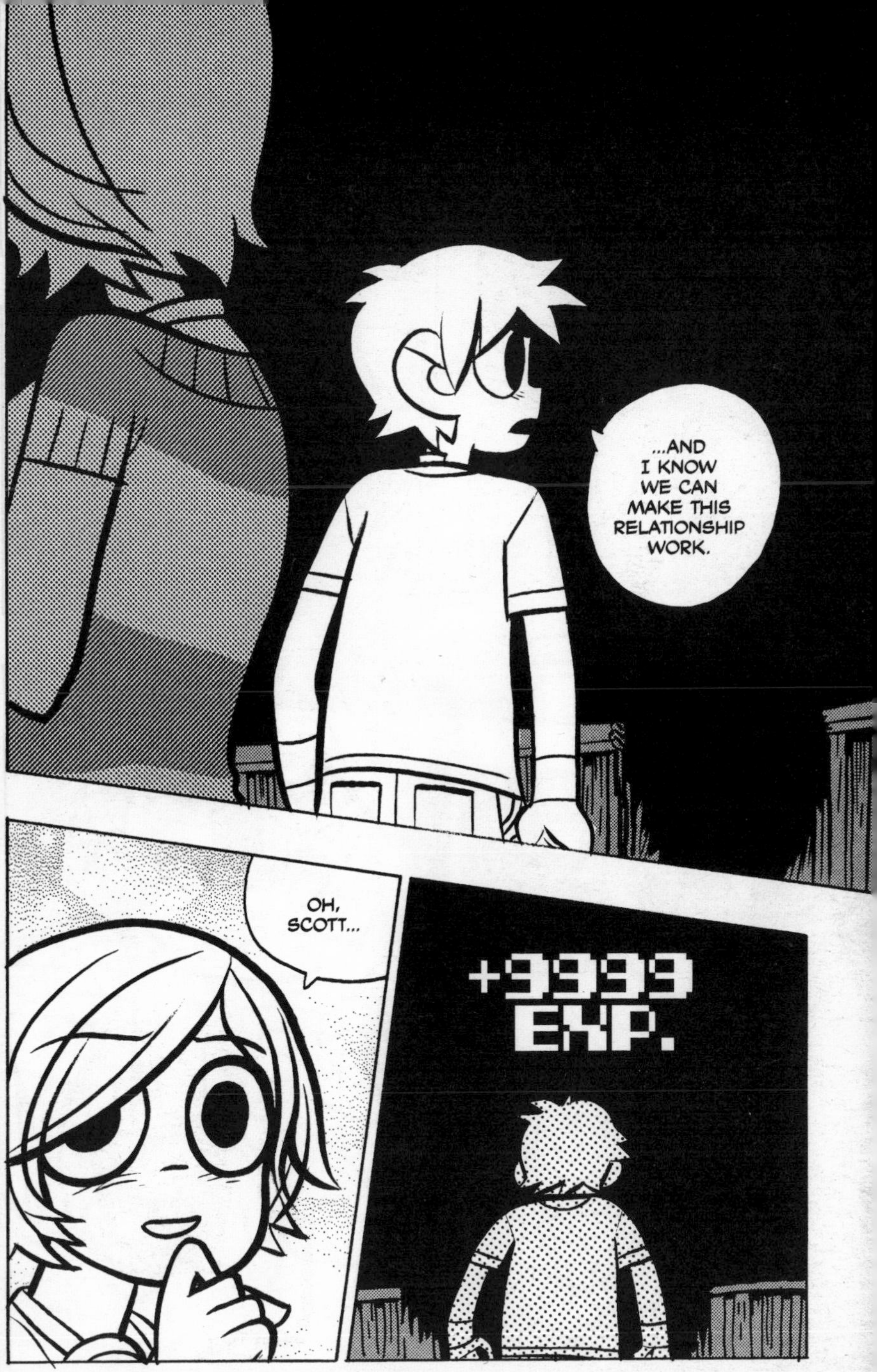
...AND I KNOW WE CAN MAKE THIS RELATIONSHIP WORK.
OH, SCOTT...
+9999 EXP.

LEVEL UP!

GRIP

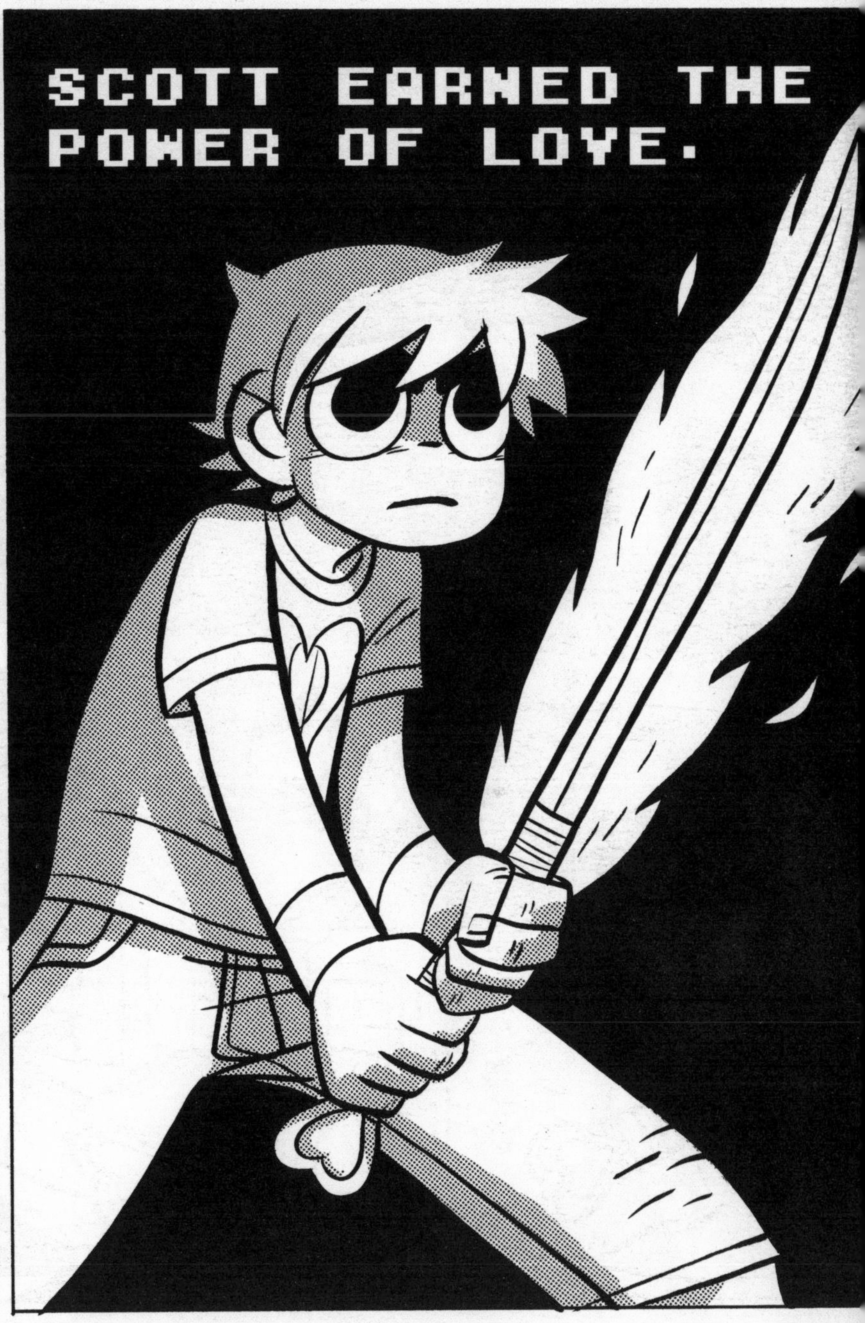
SCOTT EARNED THE POWER OF LOVE.

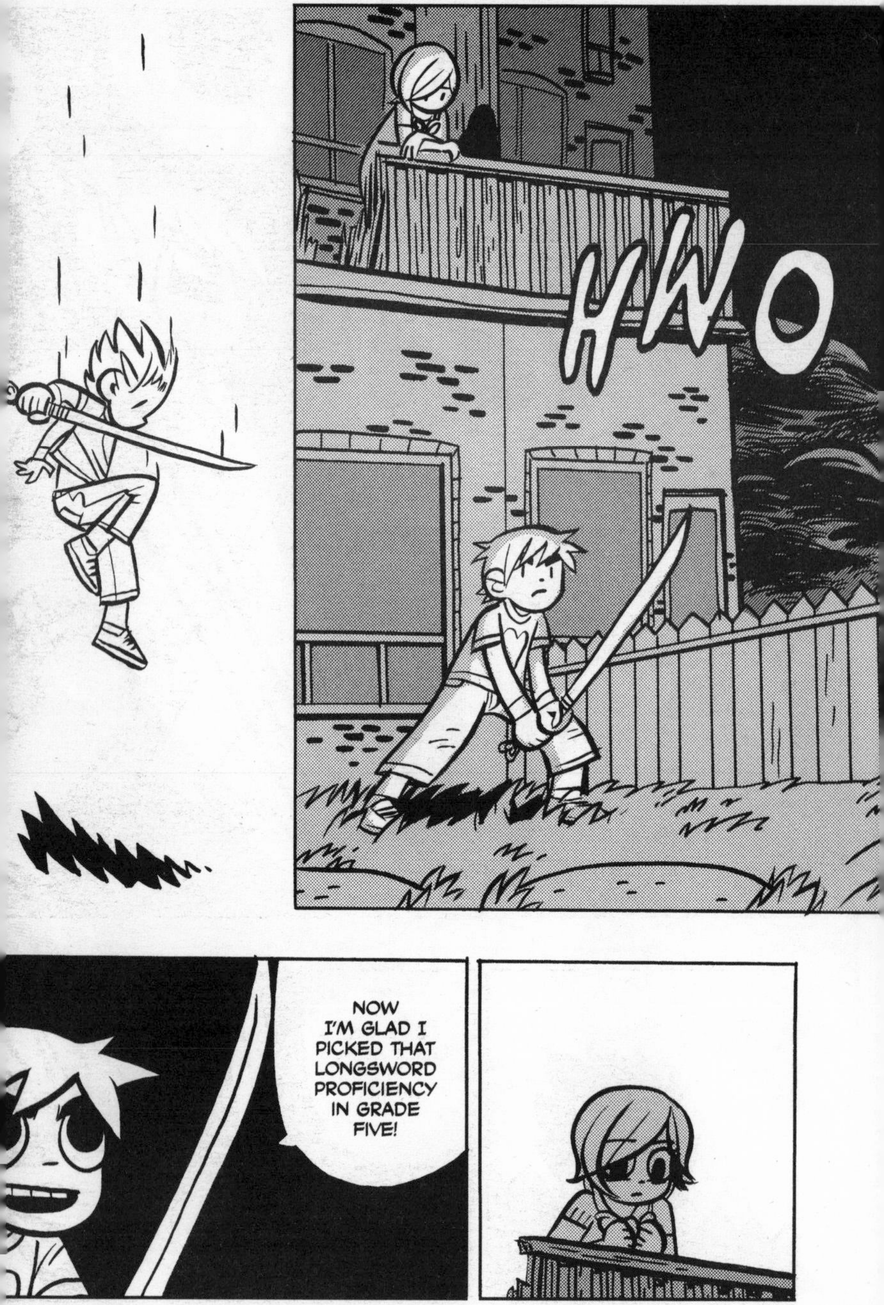
HWO
NOW I'M GLAD I PICKED THAT LONGSWORD PROFICIENCY IN GRADE FIVE!

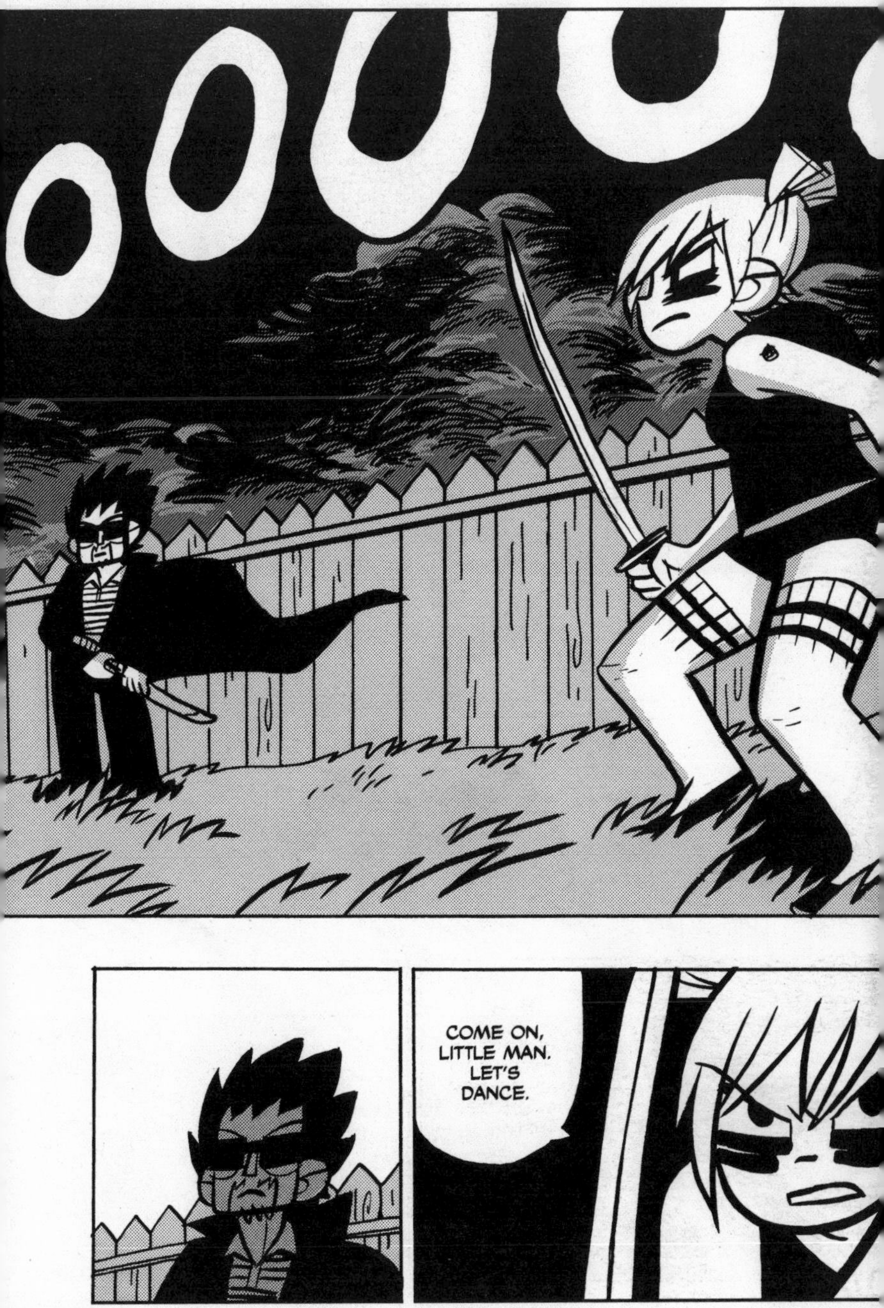
COME ON, LITTLE MAN. LET'S DANCE.

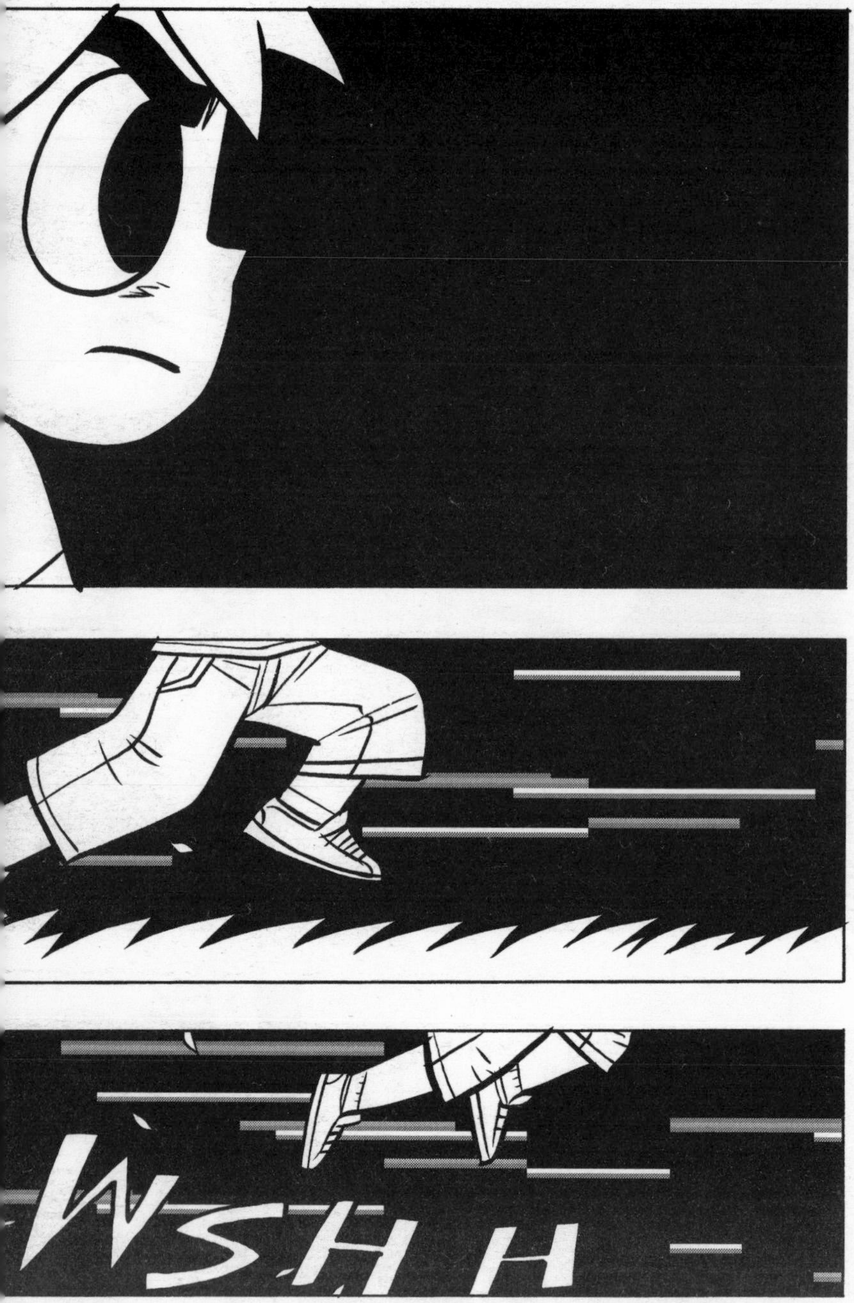
WSHH

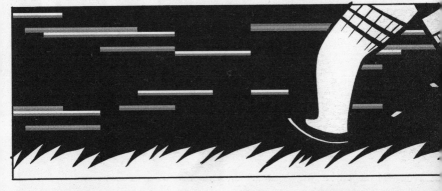

SHFF

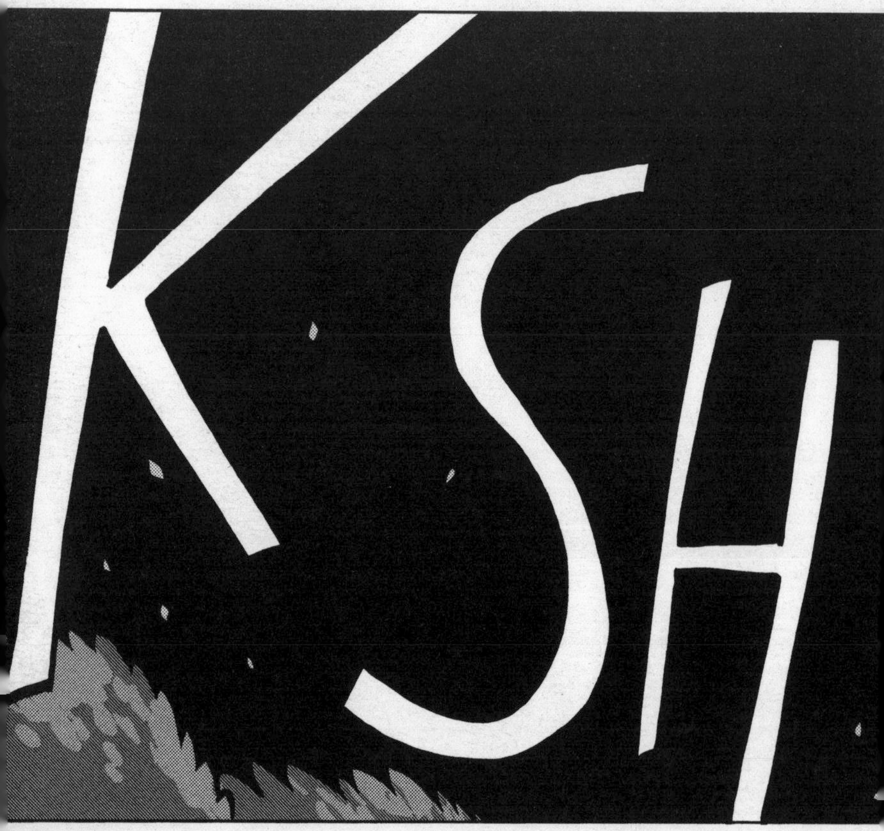
KSH
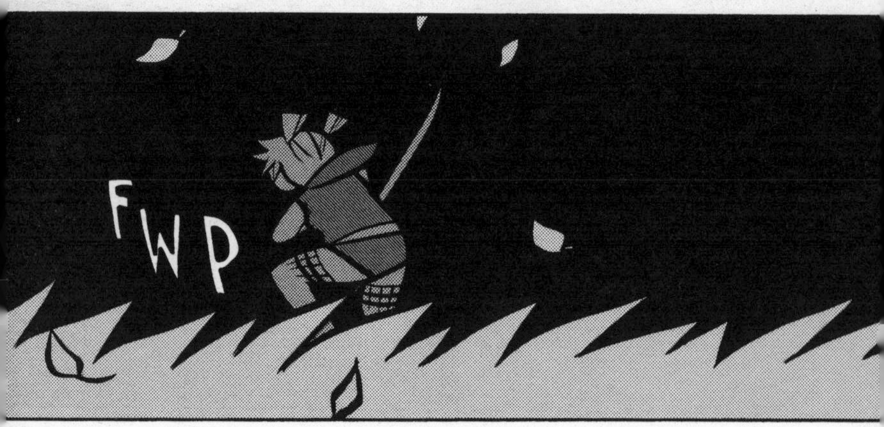
FWP

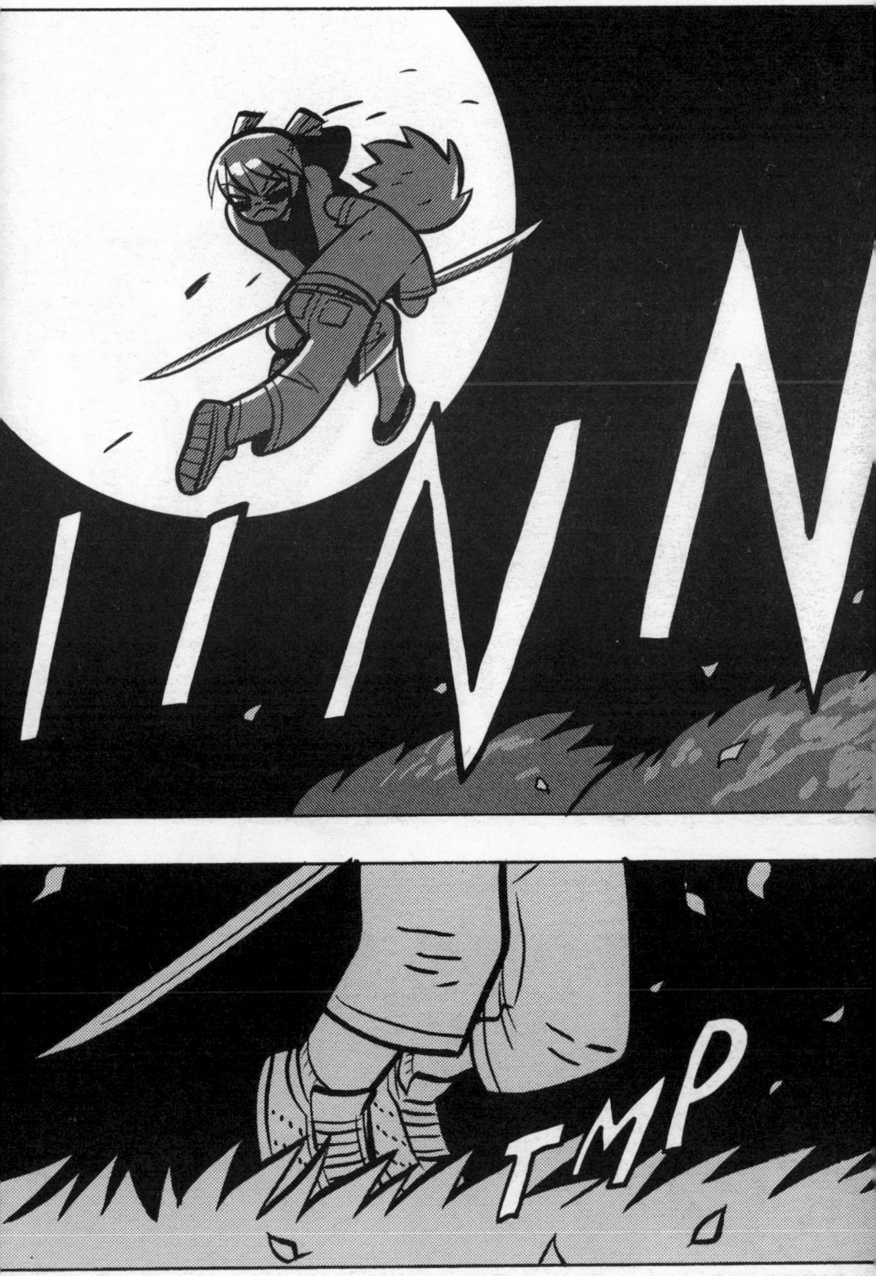
IINN
TMP

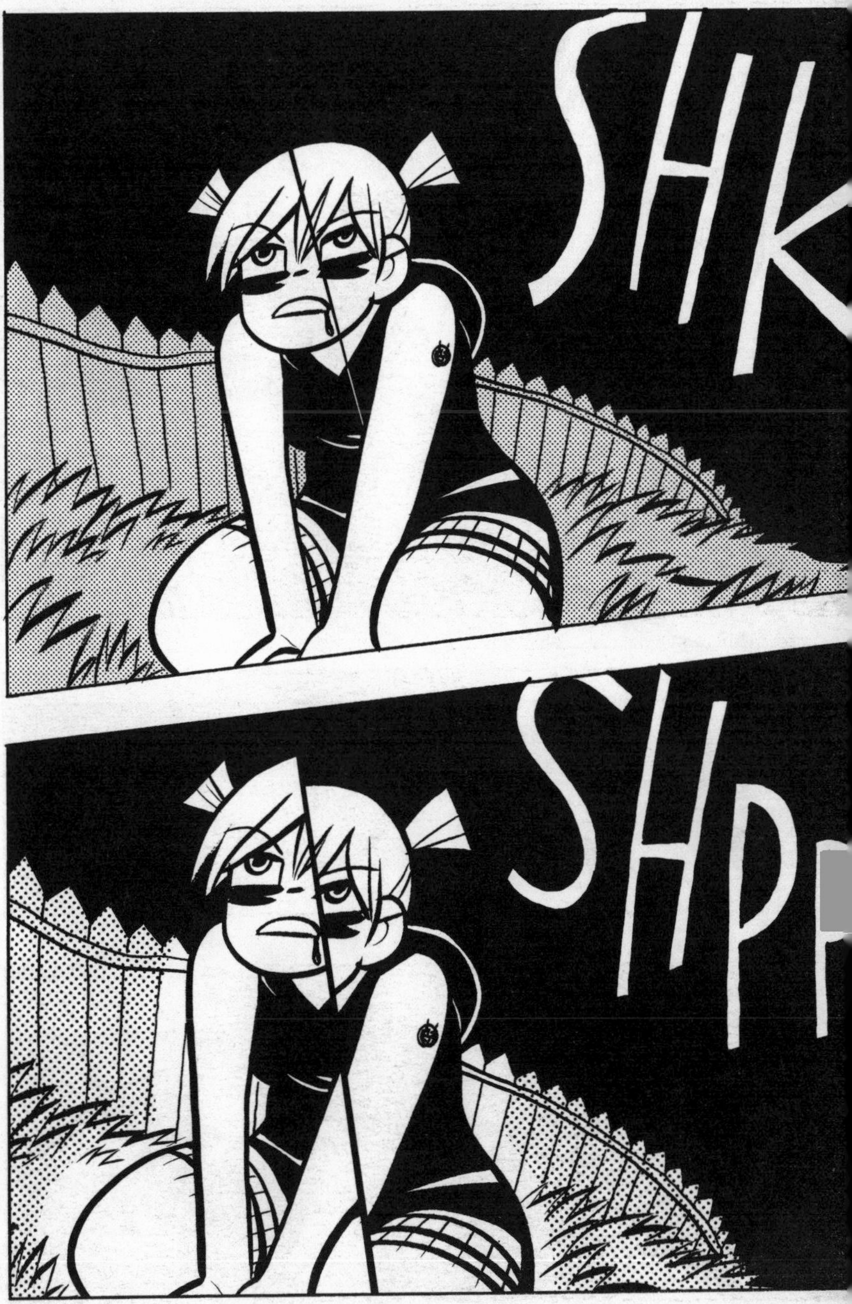
SHK
SHP

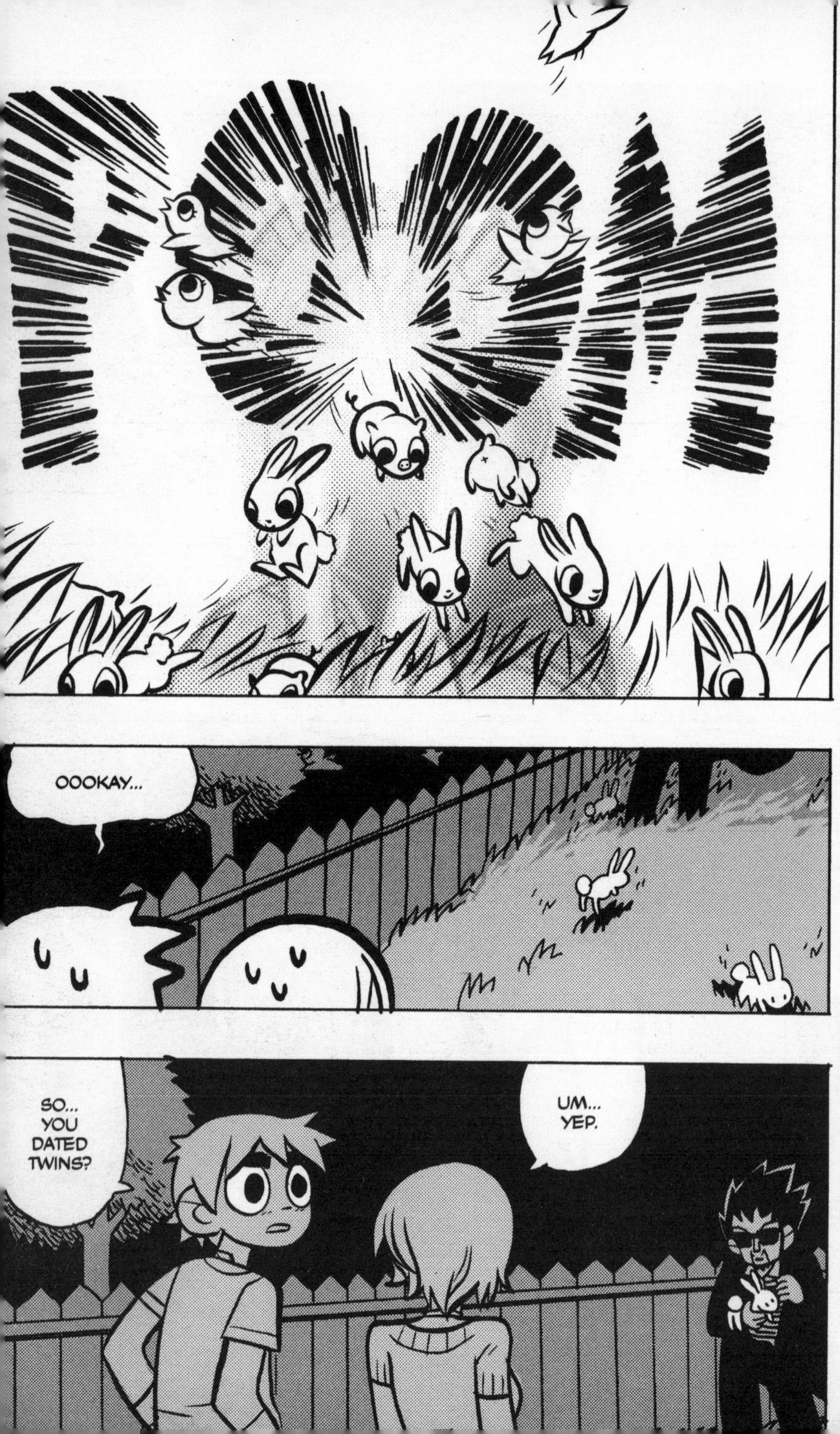
OOOKAY...
SO... YOU DATED TWINS?
UM... YEP.

Ramona's apartment
(A few days later)

THANKS FOR HELPING ME MOVE IN, YOU GUYS!

YEAH, WHATEVER.

I CAN'T BELIEVE YOU HAD THE *AUDACITY* TO CALL US OVER FOR *THIS*.

IS THIS SERIOUSLY YOUR ONLY BOX OF STUFF ASIDE FROM THOSE TWO GARBAGE BAGS? THAT'S KIND OF PATHETIC, MAN.

SCOTT

THERE'S ALSO THIS POSTER, IF YOU ACTUALLY WANT TO KEEP IT.

WHAT POSTER?

UH... THE IDIOTIC ONE? IT'S GOT GIRLS KISSING.

GLARE

196

The old apartment

...BECAUSE I SIGNED A LEASE ON A PLACE WITH MOBILE LIKE A WEEK AND A HALF AGO AND YOU WOULD HAVE BEEN *SERIOUSLY* SCREWED OVER IF YOU WANTED TO STAY!

YOU BASTARD.

YEAH, SO, GIVE ME A CALL SOMETIME, BUDDY!

Chau residence

ARE YOU SURE?

I DON'T KNOW. I'M PRETTY SURE.

WELL... DO YOU LIKE HIM BACK?

I... I THINK SO. I MEAN—

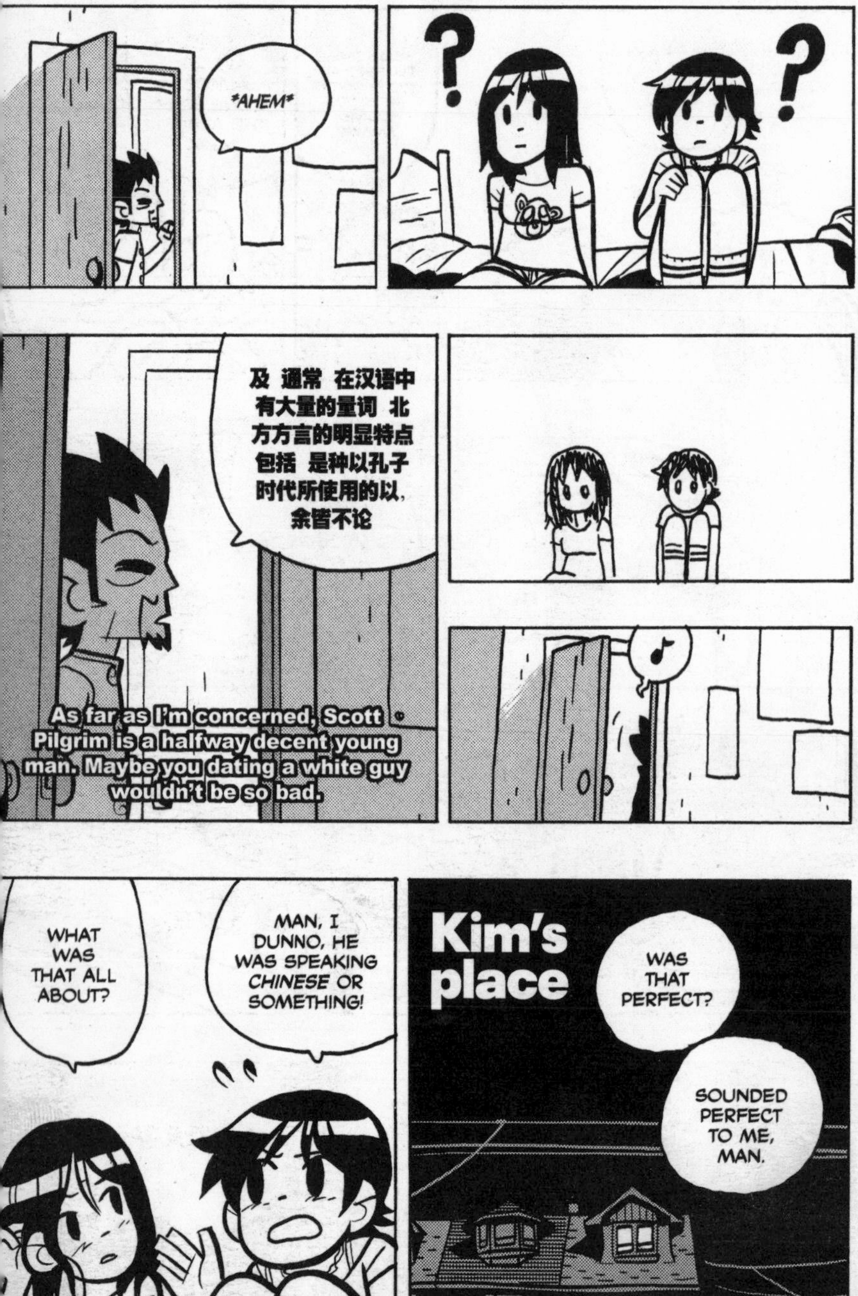
AHEM
?
?
及 通常 在汉语中
有大量的量词 北
方方言的明显特点
包括 是种以孔子
时代所使用的以,
余皆不论
As far as I'm concerned, Scott Pilgrim is a halfway decent young man. Maybe you dating a white guy wouldn't be so bad.
♪
WHAT WAS THAT ALL ABOUT?
MAN, I DUNNO, HE WAS SPEAKING *CHINESE* OR SOMETHING!
Kim's place
WAS THAT PERFECT?
SOUNDED PERFECT TO ME, MAN.

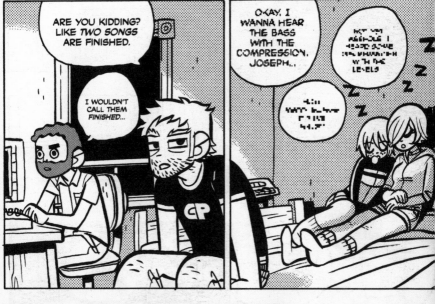

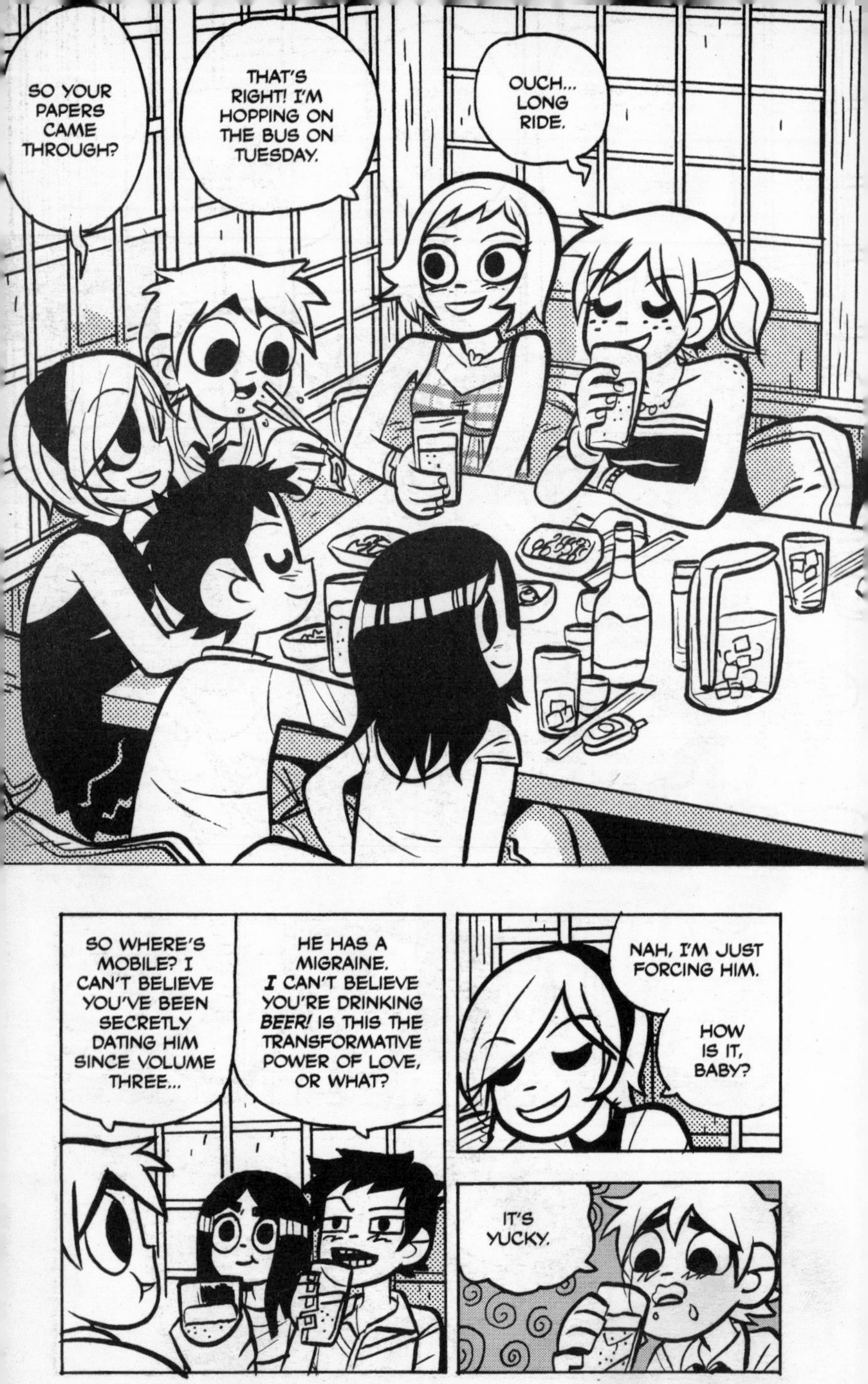
SO YOUR PAPERS CAME THROUGH?
THAT'S RIGHT! I'M HOPPING ON THE BUS ON TUESDAY.
OUCH... LONG RIDE.
SO WHERE'S MOBILE? I CAN'T BELIEVE YOU'VE BEEN SECRETLY DATING HIM SINCE VOLUME THREE...
HE HAS A MIGRAINE. *I* CAN'T BELIEVE YOU'RE DRINKING *BEER!* IS THIS THE TRANSFORMATIVE POWER OF LOVE, OR WHAT?
NAH, I'M JUST FORCING HIM.
HOW IS IT, BABY?
IT'S YUCKY.

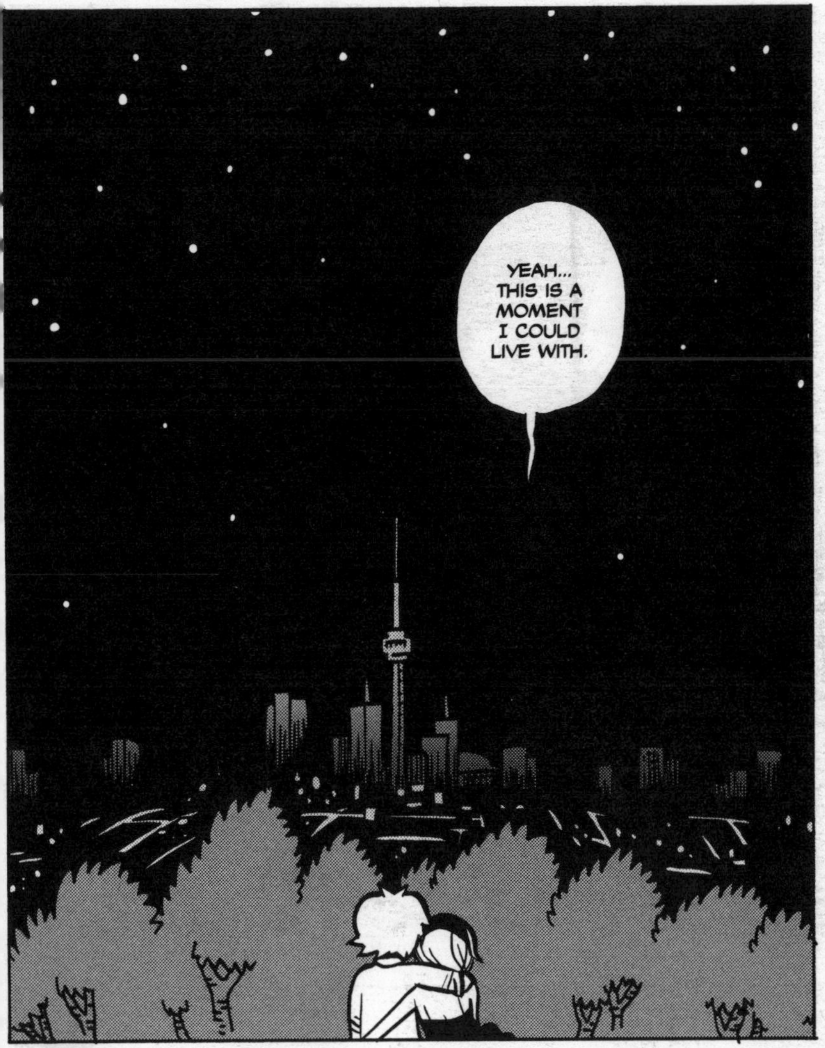
YEAH... THIS IS A MOMENT I COULD LIVE WITH.

NEXT: Twins!

Bryan Lee O'Malley has been alive since he
was born and will live until he dies, which will
probably be pretty soon. His dying wish will
be the wish that he hadn't wasted his best
years drawing this book.

His epitaph will be
whiny and narcissistic.

author portrait by **Hope Larson**

STOP
ARRÊT

This is the **back** of the book.
What do you think you're doing?
Who do you think you are?

Go to the other end of the book and start at page 1.
Your mother and I are very disappointed in you.

READING YOUR NEW GRAPHIC NOVEL: SOME OPTIONS

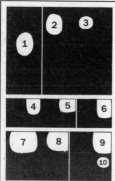

OPTION 1:
Follow the balloons from **left to right** and **top to bottom**, then move on to the next panel, the way you learned it at that sissy school of yours.

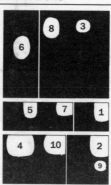

OPTION 2:
Read each balloon in whatever order appeals to you most. **Freestyle!** It's **your** book now! Don't let the **man** tell you which direction to read!

WARNING: For entertainment use only. Do not attempt to learn anything from this page.